Following a first-class degree from Cambridge, Sandi Toksvig went into the theatre as a writer and performer before becoming a founder member of the Comedy Store Players. She is well known for her television and radio work as a presenter, writer and actor. She has written six books for children and two highly acclaimed novels, *Whistling for the Elephants* and *Flying Under Bridges*, both available in Time Warner Paperbacks.

D0176415

*Also by Sandi Toksvig*

Whistling for the Elephants

Flying Under Bridges

The Travels of Lady "Bulldog" Burton
(illustrated by Sandy Nightingale)

# Gladys Reunited

*A Personal American Journey*

## SANDI TOKSVIG

A *Time Warner* Paperback

First published in Great Britain in 2002 by Little, Brown
under the title *The Gladys Society*
This edition published in Great Britain in 2003
by Time Warner Paperbacks

Copyright © Sandi Toksvig 2002

The moral right of the author has been asserted.

The author gratefully acknowledges permission to quote from
the following: p. 39. Excerpt from 'Hip-Hop Harvard' by Bruce
Kluger © 2002 by permission of Bruce Kluger. p. 159. Line from
*The Waste Land* from *Collected Poems 1909–1962* by T. S. Eliot
reproduced by permission of Faber & Faber Ltd. p. 243. Lines from
'The Past' by Stevie Smith, by permission of the Estate of
James MacGibbon. p. 269. Lines from 'It is Always Later than You
Think' Copyright © Estate of Robert Service from *Ballads of a
Bohemian*. p. 302. Lines from *The Search for Signs of Intelligent Life in
the Universe* by Jane Wagner © 1986. Reprinted by permission of
HarperCollins Publishers Inc.

Every effort has been made to trace holders of copyright. Any
inadvertent omissions of acknowledgements or permissions can
be rectified in future editions.

All rights reserved.
No part of this publication may be reproduced,
stored in a retrieval system, or transmitted, in any form
or by any means, without the prior permission in writing
of the publisher, nor be otherwise circulated in any form
of binding or cover other than that in which it is published
and without a similar condition including this condition
being imposed on the subsequent purchaser.

A CIP catalogue record for this book
is available from the British Library.

ISBN 0 7515 3328 9

Typeset in Palatino by M Rules
Printed and bound in Great Britain
by Clays Ltd, St Ives plc

Time Warner Paperbacks
An imprint of
Time Warner Books UK
Brettenham House
Lancaster Place
London WC2E 7EN

www.TimeWarnerBooks.co.uk

To Jesse, Meg and Ted

# Contents

# Acknowledgements

My father once wrote a book called *Edited Reality*. It dealt with the difficulties of covering the American presidential elections as a foreign journalist. He wrote about how tough it is ever to present an objective and factual account of a real event. Different people at the same occasion will perceive it differently. This is my edited reality of the journey I have taken. I hope that the women of the Gladys Society who took me into their homes and lives will accept that I have done my best to present a truth of what happened. Thank you to them and their families for making me so welcome.

Once again I find I couldn't have written a word without my mentor and friend Ursula MacKenzie, the splendid Viv Redman, who keeps me going with her eye for detail, and my agent Pat Kavanagh. Thank you as well to my travel companions Richard and Paul, my kids for letting me go, Alice for her support, the extraordinary kindness of my friends Carol and Sue and to Helena Taylor for needing something to read on her holidays.

# A Preface on a Horse

Can I just say right at the beginning that I like America? It's a country I feel comfortable in. I grew up in New York. I spent my formative time there: those growing years, which an advertising slogan for pap white bread in the late sixties/early seventies called 'The Wonderbread Years'. It is the place of my childhood. I know all about 'America the Beautiful'. I have seen its 'purple mountains majesty'; its 'amber fields of grain' and travelled from 'sea to shining sea'. This is the story of a journey to a country I know, to seek a group of women I used to be friends with. It's a trip that should have been a doddle, but it wasn't. It was endlessly surprising and, at one point, very nearly fatal. I suppose journeys ought to be related in the chronology in which they occurred, but indulge me while I take one incident out of sequence. I think it reveals a lot about the English woman travelling in the colonies across the water.

There is a quote attributed to George Bernard Shaw that says something along the lines of America and England being two nations divided by a common language. I always thought it was nonsense till I met a horse called Shirley and fell face-first into the Arizona desert.

It was like this. I had arranged to go to an all women's rodeo in Phoenix, Arizona, to meet up with two members of the Gladys Society. You don't need to know who they are yet because, suffice to say, neither of them showed up. Without the women I had come to meet, I found myself wasted on the sweet desert air and on something of a fruitless mission. Ever one to turn disaster to an advantage, my business partner, Richard, with whom I make television documentaries, decided the non-appearances were a good thing. We were in the Wild West and we should make the most of it. Without strange women to clutter up our day we could concentrate on making a very fine little film about the curious world of the rodeo. I like to think I am highly professional and so I agreed. I justified travelling five thousand miles to meet two women who never came by telling Richard that he was right; that I was keen to make a defining piece of film about the American addiction to the iconography of the cowboy and how that image had impacted on societies around the world. Richard nodded and said that sounded good but actually he just wanted to meet cowboys in tight jeans and have me do something amusing with a horse. It is my own fault for choosing a gay boy as a cohort.

We went to watch rodeo. We watched professional rodeo, where many people did quite dangerous things with huge animals; and then we watched amateur gay and lesbian rodeo, where many people did quite dangerous things with huge animals accompanied by a Barbra Streisand soundtrack. It was all looking rather jolly until the night Richard frankly had a Bloody Mary too far.

'I think what we need to make this documentary really special,' he slurred at me, 'is to have you actually take part.'

Now it is possible that I too had ingested a spirit or two. A tabloid paper would no doubt have said that I was 'pissed', but I prefer to use the show-business expression that I was somewhat 'tired and emotional'. Anyway, I agreed and forgot about it. The next day Richard asked the organiser of the Professional Women's

Rodeo Association, 'What would Sandi have to do in order to take part in a professional rodeo?'

The organiser, a charming woman in surprisingly well-fitting leather, tipped back her hat and drawled, 'Wheeell, she'd haaave to join the Prowfessional Women's Rodeo Association.'

One hundred and twelve dollars later and I was a member. I felt some pride at this and indeed, even now, as I venture down my local high street in England, I swagger slightly knowing I am probably the only paid-up member of the PWRA hitting that particular town. It was when the organiser passed me my membership card that I had my first misgivings.

'Do you not want to know if I can ride at all?' I asked nervously.

'No, ma'am,' she said. 'If you caaan't riyde then basically you just gaaave a donation.' She smiled at me and sauntered off to subdue a reasonably enraged bull.

Card in hand, I watched the many events with renewed interest. I was absolutely clear that I did not wish to get on anything bucking and I wasn't mad keen on any activity which involved roping together the four legs of a creature who was trying simultaneously to run away. In the end Richard and I settled on the least scary-looking event – The Barrel Race.

Basically it works like this: the rodeo arena is about the size of half an English football pitch. It is covered in brown, dusty dirt with a large entrance gate at one end for horses and riders and chutes along one side for the less tame entrants. Three barrels (in fact old oil drums) are placed at some distance apart in a triangle. Horse and rider then compete against the clock to enter the arena, ride a cloverleaf pattern around the drums and out again. A professional barrel racer makes this look like a very straightforward procedure. The fact that they seem to be able to take a huge thoroughbred animal almost sideways round an obstacle impressed rather than deterred me. I knew that the champions could do the whole thing in about thirteen seconds but I wasn't aiming to win, just take part. I decided my approach would be the same one I had had as a child to any running race – no point in rushing things.

Despite the fact that I have done many curious things in the course of my career (canoed across Africa – not to be recommended. You end up with something not dissimilar to trench bottom; sailed an ancient yacht around the whole of the UK and once, bizarrely, been blown up in the waters off the Isle of Wight while trying to manoeuvre a wardrobe which had been converted into a miniature hovercraft – it's a long story and we haven't the time), despite my many adventures in life, I am by nature a somewhat cautious person.

'I think,' I said to Richard, 'perhaps I ought to have, you know, at least the one riding lesson.'

'I thought you could ride,' he said.

There was a slight pause. 'Not as such,' I confessed.

Richard and I were on a very limited budget and this fact was reflected in our hotel. Les Jardins is a strange, deserted motel in downtown Phoenix. It is built round an open-air pool with much pale pink decor. I don't think you'll find it in any guidebook and there are reasons for this. The only pretension it has to being an upmarket hostelry is the name. Clearly the owners don't speak French for there are no gardens of any kind for several miles around. The hotel provides few amenities but in the lobby there is a rather shabby stand made of chipped Formica which holds the ubiquitous tourist leaflets you find all over the world. Richard leafed through them.

'I bet there are some riding lessons here,' he said. 'It's the Wild West; people must be gagging to get on a horse.'

'Are you?' I asked. He looked at me as though I had suggested he might also take up manual labour and produced a glossy slip with a flourish.

'Here we are! The very thing. MacDonald's Farm.'

'MacDonald's Farm?' I repeated. 'Do you think that bodes well? I mean it doesn't sound very . . . western.'

'Darling, it will be a triumph,' he declared and swept off to be charming on the phone to, presumably, Old Macdonald himself.

I was beginning to have rather serious misgivings. I like animals. I like them a lot but not so as I need to come into physical contact with them. I spend a good deal of time working for animals with the Born Free Foundation and I think animals should be free. They should be free and not made to walk under my not inconsiderable arse. The other thing that has happened as I get older is that I am much less bold than I used to be. I don't want to risk my life any more. I am acutely aware of my own mortality and I figure the grim reaper will come calling soon enough without me sending him a route map. I phoned home.

'I'm scared,' I blubbed to my nearest and dearest. 'I don't want to get on a horse and now it's all organised and I think something terrible is going to happen.' I received many long-distance strokings and soothings but it didn't help. I was still scared as we pulled into MacDonald's Farm.

The farm lay some distance from Phoenix, to the north, in a large area of desert. There is an expression in America used when someone has died. People often say 'He bought the farm'. I don't know where the saying originates from but MacDonald's looked like the sort of farm you might buy if your death was to be followed by mild punishment. Attempts had been made to turn the place into some kind of tourist Mecca. A row of sheds had been given false fronts to recreate the look of a Wild West town. They were rather small and lacked only Munchkins to complete the surreal picture. I was introduced to a cowboy called Bill. Bill certainly looked the part. He wore the pointy boots, the jangling spurs, the leather chaps and a long leather trail coat. He had a fine black hat and a splendid moustache. Sadly, he was also myopic. Bill wore the thickest spectacles I have ever seen. He appeared to view the world through the base of twin whisky tumblers and I found it unnerving.

'He can't see,' I whispered to Richard.

'So what?' he hissed. 'What's there to see? It's the desert. All there is out here are cactuses and you can feel those.'

Bill sized me up and went to select my horse. It was a girl horse. Bill led her towards me in the corral.

'Here you go, Sandi. This is Shirley.'

'Shirley?'

'Yup.'

'The horse is called Shirley?'

'Uh huh.' Bill wandered off leaving me with Shirl. It wasn't what I had expected. I looked at my steed. This was it. This was me about to enter the world of the cowboy. It was a world that I had spent some time trying to prepare for.

I live much of my life in the mistaken belief that you can ready yourself for anything if you have enough knowledge. I tend to seek my armour for daily battles in books. I had scoured bookshops in Phoenix for cowboy lore and I thought I was ready. In one of my many tomes it said, 'All you need to be a cowboy is guts and a horse, and if you've got the guts you can steal the horse.'

Well, I'd got Shirley with my Visa card and somehow it didn't feel quite right. Bill helped me heave on to the horse and we set off. Him in his great Western garb and me in an ill-fitting pair of jeans from The Gap. I was further from ready than I have ever been in my life. We wandered out into the desert amongst the feelable cactuses and, in a clearing of sand, began the lesson. Bill laid out the basic barrel pattern on the ground and Shirley and I began to master the cloverleaf ride. Richard filmed and everything proceeded quite sedately under the magnificent blue of the Arizona sky. I can't say I was at one with my mount but the trembling fear began to ebb away slightly. In fact, I thought it was all going rather well, which only goes to show how out of touch a human being can be with the equine mind. On reflection I realise, of course, that we had upset Shirley's entire world. She was not a creature destined for glory in the rodeo ring. This was an animal on a tourist ranch. An animal whose daily life consisted entirely of plodding along the same track, day after day, with her nose firmly up the bottom of the horse in front. We were making Shirley very unhappy indeed.

After about half an hour Bill declared, 'I think we should lope one.'

I shrugged my shoulders nonchalantly as if I even knew what that meant.

'Okay but not too fast.'

Basically what happened is simple:

Bill and his steed set off very fast.

I set off very fast and . . .

Shirley didn't.

Among the many experiences I have had in my life, being bucked off a horse had, until then, not been on the list. All I can tell you about it is that it is a surprisingly long way up before the inevitable drop down. Shirley kicked both back legs high in the air, I tipped forward, managed to stay on and then she did it again and I was gone. Up, up and away and then down, down, down into the desert. I landed with a rather satisfactory thud and lay moaning in the sand. Everything that I had feared had happened. I was in that instant consumed with terror. I thought I had broken my neck. I thought that I was paralysed and I also thought that it was terribly embarrassing. If I blame my English boarding-school education for anything (and, believe me, I have a very long list) then it is a burdensome sense of manners, which was so forcibly instilled that I cannot shake it off. I felt somehow that it must be my fault and that I had behaved badly. Bill had leapt off his horse and was by my side.

'Don't move, don't move,' he ordered. It was an unnecessary instruction. I couldn't move but I was desperate to get up and show that everything was fine. He tried to roll me over and sit me up. The pain and fear were overwhelming.

'I'm fine,' I said. 'I'm so sorry.'

Richard, finally taking the matter seriously, abandoned the

camera and ran towards me. However injured I was this was too much.

'Keep filming, you bastard!' I shouted through gritted teeth. I blamed Richard for the entire event but thought we should at least get it on tape.

Shirley snorted and went home. She knew when her day was satisfactorily done. She too was a bastard. Bill produced a brand-new sling from his inside pocket. If I had known it was something he habitually carried with him I would never have got on the horse in the first place. As I was completely unable to move my right arm, he fixed the sling around my neck and strapped my arm to my chest. Between them, he and Richard got me to my feet.

'I'm fine,' I kept repeating. 'I'm so sorry.' I wasn't fine. I was terrified and in agony but I was also still sorry. We limped back to Munchkinland. The owner gave us directions to the nearest 'medical facility' and bizarrely we all smiled and said goodbye. I was desperate to get away from the place so I got in the car and drove us off. Richard won't drive abroad and I steered our open Mustang up the road with one arm. I think he attempted conversation but I couldn't hear him. I was beside myself with distress.

The Desert Hills Medical Facility was quite some way further north. By the time we got there I could no longer do anything. I sat in the waiting room and began to sob and sob. The doctor and nurses were charming but I could no longer communicate. I was in what they charmingly described as 'exquisite pain' and beside myself with the fear born of an anticipated horror actually coming true. The decision was taken, not by me, to airlift me out of the desert to a larger hospital. Paramedics arrived and I was strapped to a rock-solid plastic stretcher, a neck collar was placed on me and my head was then velcroed to the board with immense severity. I could no longer move and was no longer in charge. The first I knew that the transfer was to take place by helicopter was the moment I was actually under the rotor blades of the thing.

Now the important point in this whole story is that at no time did the paramedics, or anyone else for that matter, take on board the fact that I was actually an English tourist. The noise from the helicopter was astonishing but the medical team were keen to assess me for the flight.

'Sandi!' yelled the young man in a white uniform, 'what day of the week is it?'

Well, now. Perfectly reasonable question but the fact was I had been travelling for some time and was still extremely jet-lagged. Nevertheless, Mrs Manners leapt to the fore and I wanted to be helpful.

'Just a minute,' I replied. 'Let me think.'

'Patient confused,' he yelled to the other paramedic and they rushed my stretcher into the craft. We took off at some speed while the young man at my side fitted me with a drip of unknown liquid and an oxygen mask. After a few moments in the air he tried again.

'Sandi, what is your date of birth?'

This seemed like a good question and I rather perked up because I thought, I know this. But then I remembered that the Americans do it the other way round. In Britain the date is given as day/month/year, while the Americans do month/day/year. So, ever helpful, I said, 'I know this, but you have to give me a moment.'

'Patient slow to respond,' he yelled to the pilot, who seemed to speed up even further.

After some considerable time we landed at the larger hospital. Immediately many people in ill-fitting green pyjamas arrived to haul me out on to a gurney. The young man removed my oxygen mask. I took the opportunity to say, I felt quite reasonably, 'Where am I?' meaning, Where have you taken me to?

'Patient disorientated,' he informed the many medical attendants and we all set off at a lick. Now they were running with me but with my head superglued to the board all I could see were fluorescent lights flashing above me as we made the dash to the ER. No one was speaking to me, what with me being confused, slow to respond and disorientated and I was by now convinced of the severity of my injuries.

The voice of a nurse rang out in the emergency room, 'Forty-two-year-old woman, level one trauma!'

Oh dear, I thought, there's some poor old cow ahead of me. She must be in a terrible state. Of course, it was me. I forget how old I am. It's the age I've reached. It's not like when you are young and people ask you every five minutes. The ER team hauled me on to some kind of operating table. The pain was indeed exquisite and I cried out. I was ignored and without so much as a by your leave people began to cut off all my clothes. They started at my feet, slicing through my jeans and working their way up to my good bra (you know how you have one really good one that you travel in). I tried to focus and remember what underpants I was wearing. I do have a couple of pairs of those big girls' pants and I thought if it was the ones with the double gusset they were going to need a knife. A young nurse tried to remove my signet ring and couldn't.

'Shall I cut it off?' she asked her superior.

'I'll sue,' I said, deliberately using the one word that makes Americans listen. They left my ring alone and carried on with their work. By now my head was clearing a little and I had time to think. I still didn't know if my life was about to go the way of Christopher Reeve's. Was I destined to be wheeled about for ever more and take my sustenance through a tube? What I did know with a fair degree of certainty was that the one thing I had failed to do on leaving England was to take out any travel insurance. Suddenly the mass medical attention seemed less welcome. It was all very well having the might of American know-how focused on my broken body but how the hell was I going to pay for it? The US of A is not a place to be poor and poorly at the same time. Naked and covered only by the merest hint of a sheet, I was wheeled off for a CAT scan.

I lay in the large white tube while the technician searched about with rays to see if I still had a functioning brain. White lights

· passed intermittently over my eyes and I found myself counting them in one hundred dollar increments. It all took a very long time. After five hours and many tests they were finally able to tell me that I had sprained my shoulder and I wasn't pregnant. I don't know which piece of information was the more surprising.

I think there is something to be said for the ages you have to wait to be seen in a British National Health hospital. After you've sat there for about three hours you think to yourself, Actually, I'm not as bad as I thought I was.

What happened to me is that I completely panicked. I was so prepared for disaster that the instant I fell I believed my fears were realised. I did hurt my shoulder quite badly and had some rather nasty bruises (mainly sustained, I think, during the helicopter transfer) but what I suffered from mostly were deep and profound shock and uncontrollable fear. Maybe it is an age thing. Here I was on a journey to retrace my youth and yet made to come face to face with my advancing middle years. The only good thing about the whole story is that when I got home I made a very pleasant discovery. A year before, I had taken out an annual travel insurance policy to cover a skiing holiday and it still had a week to run. The bills kept coming (a helicopter is a surprisingly extravagant expense) and I simply sent them on to be paid. An angel must have been sitting on my shoulder after all. I just wish she had been paying closer attention to Shirley.

I tell the story now as though it were a funny thing to have happened. It has become a set piece joke in my life and each time I tell it I get the same reaction. I lie dying in the desert and the Americans say:

'Gee, Sandi, weren't you scared?'

And the English say:

'What happened to the horse?'

# CHAPTER 1

# The Gladys Society is Born

*'Do you come to the play without knowing what it is?'*
*'O yes, Sir, very frequently; I have no time to read play-bills; one merely comes to meet one's friends and show that one's alive.'*

Fanny Burney

It was a German humanist called Martin Waldseemüller who named America. I don't know if it was what his parents had hoped for but in 1507 Martin was rummaging around for a name for the New World. He was writing up a trip that the Italian navigator Amerigo Vespucci had made five years previously. I know, he thought, *Ab Americo inventore . . . quasi Americi terram sive Americam* (from Amerigo the discoverer . . . as if it were the land of Americus or America).

Thus America, first South and then later the North, became America. I am sure it has occurred to other people that had Martin gone with Amerigo's surname instead, today the world would have 280 million Vespuccians.

The discovery of America is shrouded in confusion. Columbus, who I thought took the credit, actually only ever found the Bahamas; the Irish sent a monk called Brendan; and the Vikings got lost going to Greenland. The latest theory is that the Chinese got there first but they didn't stay. Presumably half an hour after they arrived they were hungry to discover something else. The only certain thing in all this is that no one was looking for what they actually found. Throughout the fifteenth and sixteenth centuries endless explorers prowled up and down the eastern seaboard of America seeking a passage to the sea, which they believed lay on the other side. The vast landmass that is America frankly got in the way of what was wanted. Who found it first is a matter of conjecture but discovered it was and in 1966 my family was delighted because that is where we were heading.

That summer, my father, mother, brother and I steamed in on the SS *United States*, past the symbolic welcome of the Statue of Liberty.

'*Bring me your tired, your poor . . .*'

And indeed you people in first class on that ocean liner.

I think it would be fair to say that my family, the Toksvigs, has always had a slightly strange history and connection with the United States. We come originally from Denmark. The name Toksvig literally means 'burial ground by the small river' and indeed there is a farm in Jutland still called Toksvig Farm (*Toksvig gård*) where you can go and see a small tor or burial ground, next to the advertised river. (I recommend this, as there is little else to do in the area.) Not, I think, genetically predisposed to working with soil, the family drifted away from farming after some generations and moved to the big smoke of Copenhagen. It was a time when the young United States was calling across the waters for the energy of Europe to come and make its mark.

Great-grandpa packed his family on to a vast steamer and headed west across the waters. They passed through the immigration controls at Ellis Island and on to the glories of Albany, the capital of New York State. Here my wise relative did what anyone fresh off the boat would do – he started a Danish language newspaper and worked as a spectacle lens grinder. These were, sadly, not happy business choices. Either there were not enough Danes to buy their own paper or their eyes were so poor even glasses couldn't help them read. Within a very short time both enterprises foundered and Great-grandpa Toksvig lost every krone he had arrived with. The whole clan returned to the fatherland entirely penniless. The folklore of America is packed with tales of peasants who arrived poor and became rich. My family went poor and came back poor. The American Dream but not as we know it.

My more immediate family and myself landed at Pier 92 on the island of Manhattan. We had travelled across the waters from Denmark to England and then journeyed for five days over the Atlantic from Southampton. 'Strangers In The Night' was a huge hit, skirts were mini, deaths in Vietnam were escalating and Lyndon Johnson was in the White House. Coming from a tiny suburb of Copenhagen, the city of New York seemed unbelievably fast and noisy to us. Manhattan, once sold to the Dutch for $24, was impossibly modern.

I arrived, aged eight, knowing my family followed not just our own tribe west but also a swathe of immigrants from across the world. I came with an English mother, who felt comfortable in a foreign land where she could speak the language; a Danish father, who loved an adventure; and a ten-year-old brother who had watched too many movies and thought we were sure to be gunned down in the street.

From the late 1960s, my dad, Claus Toksvig, was the most famous man on Danish television. He was Foreign Correspondent for Danish television. I say this as though Danish television had many men in the field but in fact Dad was *the* Foreign Correspondent for Danish television. When he was first appointed in 1966 TV was still in its infancy in Denmark. There wasn't much to it. Nothing happened until about 7 p.m. Then Dad would come on and read the news. This might be followed by an hour-long programme on the Queen's silver spoon collection, then some rather thrilling indoor circuit racing for bicycles with close-down coming around 9 p.m.

My father was excessively handsome. There was much of the Paul Newman about him and he was the first TV star Denmark had ever known. Sending him out to cover the whole world seemed very glamorous and daunting. The naive TV company (still known to this day as Danish Radio) sent him to New York to view the world via the offices of the United Nations.

We moved into the Hotel Concord in downtown Manhattan and spent our days marvelling at the fact that television was available whenever you wanted, that there was such a thing as 'fast food' and that people in the street thought yelling was a reasonable form of communication. Dad treated all life as an endless education but as autumn approached, the notion of formal schooling for me and Nick occurred to him. With this in mind we moved out to the small town of Mamaroneck in 'the burbs'.

Westchester is a wealthy suburban county just north of New York City with many large, detached houses. Here rolling lawns run one from the other under a barrage of sprinkler heads. The town of Mamaroneck is not large. It has one main street of shops, which runs up from the small harbour. The name is of Native American derivation. Originally it was 'Merrinack' meaning 'the place where the fresh water falls into the salt'.

By the time my family arrived the Native Americans were long gone, bought out for a few dollars, some beads and a final case of smallpox. Now the harbour that had once cradled the swift and silent canoe was filled with endless ranks of expensive sailing boats. On summer evenings all you could hear was the clang of halyards against the aluminum (not aluminium) masts as even larger, sleeker, more expensive yachts sailed in to Robert's Boatyard for a tweak before some challenge on Long Island Sound. We settled in. We wore sneakers, ate peanut butter and rode chopper bikes. We were American kids. Summers were endless as we ran from sea to shore and back or played 'spies' in the early twilight with the neighbourhood kids. Then things changed. When I was twelve my sister Jeni was born and by high school, aged thirteen, I had fallen hopelessly in love. Not with any one person, I wasn't that precocious, no: I was in love with The Theatre.

I had always been interested in writing and performing. From my earliest days I had crafted small plays to perform in the garden with reluctant friends in unsuitable garments from my mother's wardrobe. By the age of twelve, I had spent some time in the American public school system. I had learned the rules of baseball, become a fan of the New York Mets, was accustomed to thundering out the Pledge of Allegiance every morning and knew how to save myself from Russian nuclear attack by standing facing my metal locker in the corridor. To my father's horror, my accent changed and soon I was suffering some kind of irritable vowel syndrome where 'school' became 'skul' and I wasn't 'sure' about things, I was 'chure'. I don't know that I learned much but I was happy.

Then, inexplicably, my parents decided to send me to one of the most exclusive, most expensive girls' schools in the state. It involved a car journey from home of just under an hour. Every morning a black station wagon would tour the neighbourhood collecting other offspring of the faintly wealthy and transport us to the girls' or boys' school.

My brother Nick and I travelled with Homer, a bespectacled and spotty young man. None of the other kids liked him. The car was quite elderly and everyone always made Homer sit by the dodgy door. Then we would lean on him as we went round corners. We were supposed to be heading for an expensive education but no one said you had to be a good citizen on the way.

I don't know why, but the school and I didn't get on. There was Miss Coe, the English teacher, who I felt could take the heart out of a book with a single breath. Miss Coe's great skill was to take a sentence and 'deconstruct' it. This was done with a diagram of many branches upon which you placed the noun, the verb, the adverbs, adjectives and so on in their correct relation to each other. I would sit and look at a rather fine piece of J. D. Salinger reduced to a small, spiky diagram of the Hudson River Railway and want to weep. I couldn't see the point. It just looked ruined to me. To this day, although words form a huge part of my life, I cannot spot the parts of any sentence. I wouldn't know an adverb if it wanted to marry my daughter. I have Coe dyslexia.

Then there was the social studies teacher. She was getting divorced and as that was a social issue, she decided to involve the whole class in it. We learned nothing about society or the ills of the world but I became quite adept at 'therapeutic listening'. This was, after all, the sixties, when love was free and therapy was about to heal the world. I remember a small group of us going to her apartment to help her pack up. She sat on the floor and wept a great deal. Some of the girls hugged her. I've never been good at that kind of emoting so I stolidly packed things in newspaper and wondered why grown-ups needed so many different kinds of glasses to drink out of.

I quite liked the art teacher. He had only four fingers on his right hand and would insist on pointing things out using just the stub. We did very little art and mostly sat watching black and white French films in the dark. He was particularly fond of one called *Jeux Interdits* (Forbidden Games) about a group of children who took to torturing and killing small animals during the Second World War. I used to go home feeling quite disturbed and utterly unable to play with the dog.

In the yearbook photo, I look quite the individual in my peaked captain's hat and rather firmly tied boy's tie. I don't know why I wore a tie. I had never been to an English school in my life but I thought it marked me out as a European. I didn't know then that I was gay but I already felt different from everyone else and it was important to me to stand apart from the crowd. To stand up for myself. Although I had never lived in England, in that American school I inexplicably decided to be rather English. In the end the school decided that I didn't belong. The headmistress called me and my parents into her office at the end of the year.

'I'm afraid, Mr and Mrs Toksvig, this is just not working out. Regrettably we have come to the conclusion that Sandra is not academic. We think you might find somewhere else more suitable.'

She paused and looked at me with utter bewilderment. Clearly nothing more suitable occurred to her. 'Maybe agricultural college,' she finally managed.

I think about that now. That crossroads in life where I might have been taken from the halls of academia and made to plunge my hands into large piles of animal manure instead. Perhaps it was the ancient Toksvig rebellion against the soil but my father exploded.

'It is, madam, not my child who is inappropriate for your school but you who are inappropriate to judge anyone. You have failed her and it is a disgrace.'

I loved my dad. He was great. I left and, after a summer by the sea, was sent to the local education establishment up the road, Mamaroneck High School.

## Oscar was Wilde but Thornton was Wilder

I joined Mamaroneck High as a freshman, the first year of senior high school, a ninth-grader. In my high school yearbook picture, I have abandoned the tie and the hat but now look like a small boy with a haircut from a well-meaning charity. The plaid workshirt suggests I had given up trying to be English and was now going for something a little more native. I had braces on my teeth (well, this was America) so I kept my lips firmly clamped shut even when smiling. I don't feel too bad about the picture. There are a couple of old friends in the book who look like serial killers.

The school was daunting. One thousand five hundred students, a mile sometimes between classrooms in the labyrinthine building and endless choices of classes. From the outside it was the classic American high school building of the movies. A gigantic red-brick construction with towering white pillars over an entrance into which streamed clean-cut youth awash with orthodontic work. The long corridors smelled of disinfectant. They were lined with grey steel lockers and ceramic tiles, presumably because tiles are easy to disinfect. A few teachers had made a stab at displaying art-work but the corridors were not places to linger in and admire. The only corridor-dwelling was done outside the gymnasium where the 'jocks' posed for the cheerleaders and the cheerleaders pretended not to notice.

I don't think I had cheerleading in me and I certainly wasn't going to run for anybody. I wanted to 'do' theatre. I knew no one and yet I had the gall to audition for the autumn play. It was partly because I had already fallen head-first for the drama teacher.

Regina must have been in her late twenties when I met her. Even in America there was still a modicum of respect for teachers and I didn't know then that her first name was Regina. I don't think I even knew she had a first name. Regina had long brown hair, wide eyes and a rather freckled face. From my first day in her English class I felt she smiled only at me. Choosing classes at all had been something of a lottery. On arrival at the high school I had been introduced to my 'Guidance Counselor'.

The school buildings ran for several blocks between Palmer Avenue and the Boston Post Road. The guidance counselor's small office was on the Palmer Avenue side. It took me some time and a small compass in the heel of my shoe, to find the place. I had never come across the concept of the guidance counselor before and I sat in his untidy booth of an office with no clear idea of what to expect. The office had all the charm and creative stimulus of a tax inspector's in a deep recession. On the wall, a careers poster advised me that 'You can always teach.'

This notion of the teaching profession as a bit of a fallback position didn't inspire me with confidence. My counselor wore a dark, faded jacket which didn't match his trousers and an open-neck white shirt with no tie. Coloured shirts for men had not yet really come into fashion. My own father had only recently begun to accept that wearing a blue shirt to work didn't make him a faggot. The no tie thing was to show that the counselor was on the side of the students. The high school had eight full-time guidance counselors. Their job was to keep an eye on the students. In all the schools I had been to previously the teachers had done this. At Mamaroneck, however, every student had an individual timetable. Classes were selected from a long list and juggled to fit into some kind of coherent day. It was the counselor's job to assist me with this but he had many people to get through and a limited amount of time.

He put his feet on the desk and rubbed his hand over what was left of his hair, while I sat the other side of his small and worn wooden desk.

'So, Sandra, what are you interested in?'

Apart from the theatre, I had no idea. I was thirteen. I was probably interested in being fourteen. He handed me a thick sheaf of papers stapled together in one corner. They had that smell of the old Roneo duplicating machines and the bluish type was smudged in places. Each available class, of which there seemed to be hundreds, was numbered, titled and accompanied by the name of a member of staff. The counselor told me to make my selections and return the form to him. This was not as easy as you might think. I had no idea who anyone or anything was. I had no notion of what might be required. Before this I had just turned up at school and been told what to do and when to do it.

I sat outside in the corridor examining my pieces of paper like a city dweller looking for edible mushrooms on a forest floor. Some of the class titles were so badly smudged that I couldn't even tell the general area they might be dealing with, so I didn't choose them. One of the classes which had been printed clearly was 'drama'. How odd to think the direction of my life might have been determined by a faulty copying machine. Had the words 'physics', 'chemistry' and 'biology' been legible I might today be removing someone's spleen for a living.

I seem to recall the final timetable included French, maths, social studies, English and drama. I think games was thrown in for good measure but it was never my strong suit and I have no recollection of it whatsoever – I suspect that I have blocked it from my mind. Even now, when I look through the yearbook at the pictures of all the staff, not one of the 'Phys. Ed.' department looks familiar. Actually, one member of staff looks so old and unfit that I can only presume she was included in error. Looking back, it seems a curious system of education.

Regina encouraged me to audition for the school play. Drama in the school, particularly under her fragrant direction, was a very big deal. The auditorium was massive with a large balcony and seated several hundred people. With its wide wooden stage, red velvet curtains and rows of tip-up seats it looked like a proper theatre. Each fall a straight play was produced and then in the spring, a full-scale musical that was always recorded and turned into an album. Joining MHS Drama was no mean feat.

It must have been late September when I turned up for the open auditions. I wore trousers, a big bulky sweater and carried quite the strangest book bag you can imagine. The physical size of the school meant everyone humped their things around in something, but the world of the rucksack had not yet come of age. Most people had a sort of satchel and a few still transported their stuff with a book strap, a piece of leather like a belt which you cinched around your volumes to keep them together. My father had brought me back a satchel from Greenland. It was made of sealskin and was entirely covered in seal fur. It was quite possibly the single most politically incorrect piece of luggage ever created. It was also enormous and I was not. I must have looked as though I had a terrible hump that required both lancing and shaving.

If that wasn't enough there were two other counts against me. First of all my haircut. I said it looked as though it had been done by a charity and that may be unkind. Perhaps it was just a barber rushing towards closing time. Perhaps I had worn a hat for so many years of my childhood that when I finally took it off it didn't occur to my mother to take me to a proper hairdresser's. I had very blonde hair, cut short and swept across the top of my head with a low side parting. The second was the complete set of railway tracks on top and bottom teeth, which I've explained kept my mouth shut but I forgot to mention also preserved pieces of old food.

All the kids who were already confident of jobs backstage were lounging about in the auditorium seats when I arrived. They could relax as they didn't have to audition. Even I could hear the whispers.

'It's a boy.'

'It is not. It's a girl.'

'What's the name?' Someone looked at the list where I had signed myself confidently as 'Sandra'.

'Sandra! Sounds like a girl but . . .' said another.

A handsome boy of about sixteen, called Ray, was clearly what everyone called 'a shoe-in' for an acting part. He was obviously well established and was merely attending auditions for form's sake. From the stage, he announced in a booming actor's voice heard by everyone, 'She's a girl. She's in my English class – she wore a dress on the first day of school.'

Cathy arrived late. She waltzed in with the confidence of the beautiful and the thin. She shook out her long hair and said, 'Sandra's in my social studies class. Hey, Sandra, what's with the book bag? How weird is that?'

I smiled. I still thought the book bag was cool but I tucked it under a seat. Ginger arrived, carrying a large number of books in her arms. Ginger was a senior and a Grade A student. How she managed to fit in the acting with all her work no one knew. What they did know was that, like Ray, for her auditioning was a mere formality. She was already a leading light in the drama department. Ray wandered over to flirt with her, confident of his place. Then Regina stood up to announce the play for the season. A petite and attractive woman, as she spoke everyone male and female hushed and became a bit reverent.

'We're going to be doing *The Skin of Our Teeth* by Thornton Wilder.'

There was some general murmuring especially from the 'techies' about what this implied. To me it implied nothing. I had never heard of either the man or the play. The auditions began.

'Okay.' Regina clapped her hands. 'Let's get you into groups and up on the stage. First, we're going to imagine you're in the Arctic, okay? It is very cold. Let's go.'

I froze in the Arctic, I suffered in the Sahara, I went on to pretend I was a tree, that I was unexpectedly growing or dying or a cat . . . The kind of thing that is supposed to express the very heart of make-believe. The auditions lasted a couple of days. I didn't bother to read the play. I just wanted in, so when I found I had got the role of Gladys Antrobus I had no idea what that meant. I particularly didn't understand that I seemed to be sharing the part with Rita and Cathy from my social studies class.

Regina explained. 'Now this is a complicated play. *The Skin of Our Teeth* is the story of the Antrobus family. It is set both in prehistoric times and in a modern-day New Jersey suburb. It's about family life but it is also about the vast dimensions of time and place. So, what we are going to do is have the kids in the play, Gladys and Henry Antrobus, played by six different people. In the first act, Sandra and Billy will be Gladys and Henry when they are small children. In the second act, Rita and Ray will play them as teenagers and in the third act we have our older Gladys and Henry with Cathy and Mike.'

Fran, the stage manager, pushed her glasses back on to her nose and began giving the call times for rehearsals.

'So, Monday afternoon – the whole Antrobus family, all the Gladyses and Henrys plus Mr and Mrs and Sabrina.'

Six of us became the Gladyses and the Henrys. Everything took place out of school hours and had nothing to do with what year we were in. Consequently we were a mixed-age bunch. I was easily the youngest, while Ginger, who played Gladys and Henry's mother Mrs Antrobus, at seventeen, nearly eighteen, was one of the oldest.

I think it was Lori or maybe Sue, at any rate it was one of the backstage crew who saw Rita, Cathy and myself arrive one day for rehearsal and called out, 'Here comes the Gladys Society!'

Everyone loved Ginger who played our mom. Then someone noticed her initials, GS, were the same as the Gladys Society so we decided she could join. We took to socialising at Sue's house because it was big and her parents never seemed to be around. Her initials, SG, were nearly the same so she joined. I had always been Gladys One because of being the first on in the play, Rita was Two, Cathy Three and as each new person joined the fold they received the next available number. Soon, almost every female in the company was part and parcel of the Gladys Society. Ten high school girls, aged thirteen to eighteen, and of course, Regina. Eventually we would be twelve, as I will explain, but that year there were eleven Gladyses. The women of the play formed a group of friends that was to sustain many of us for years to come. I wonder if there is a tiny sociological study to be drawn from this? I don't believe there ever was a Henry Society.

It should all have been splendid and, in fact, I thought it was. But after that one year I was packed off to English boarding school. With my departure abroad, the Gladys Society transmogrified into People from the *International* Gladys Society or PIGS. That was thirty years ago. I didn't know then that that year at Mamaroneck High School was to be one of the happiest times of my life.

# CHAPTER 2

# Going Back

*There is one kind of extravagance rapidly increasing in this country,
which, in its effects on our purses and our habits, is one of the worst
kinds of extravagance; I mean the rage for travelling . . .*

Mrs Lydia Maria Child, *The American Frugal Housewife*, 1883

I have been blessed all my life with being a person who has never
once knowingly had their finger on the pulse. If there is a zeitgeist
floating in the air then I will almost certainly find some kind of
spray to get rid of it. However, there does seem to be something of
a vogue for seeking out old friends. Hardly a week goes past without some well-meaning shop assistant or chiropodist asking me,
'Have you logged on to the Friends Reunited website yet?'

The answer is I haven't. I was rather put off by a chum who
declared she was getting nowhere with her social life and wanted
to seek out some friends from the past. She logged on, and a week
later the only person who had contacted her was her sister who
lived round the corner. But there is a fascination with tracking
down the significant fellows of one's past life, of trying to put a bit
of personal history in perspective. I think there is also a soap-
opera element to it. It's very satisfying to find out what has
happened to so and so, rather like catching up with lost episodes
of a drama in which you once took an active interest.

It was my friend Richard who suggested I track down the
Gladys Society. I don't think I would have done it on my own.

Despite having first circumnavigated the globe at the age of six weeks, I am not crazy about travelling by myself and I can be quite hopeless at arrangements. Richard was not to be deterred. He arrived at my house in the country.

'How many Gladyses are there?' he said, taking out a large notepad which I knew meant business.

'Twelve. Including me, except one joined late and—'

'And how many are you still in touch with?'

'Uh, Rita, she was Gladys Two, and Lori and Sue occasionally. I've seen a couple of the others but the rest . . . well, it's been thirty years.'

'So they could be anywhere?'

'Uhm, yes.'

Richard and I looked at a map of the States. It's a big place and I realised this was not going to be a weekend jaunt. Indeed, the trip was clearly not one trip but several. Even to me the place to begin was obvious. The Gladys Society had been formed in New York and I knew at least two of the women had not drifted all that far from their childhood haunts. Richard adores New York almost as much as he adores the internet. Before I knew I had agreed, he was on-line, booking us on the cheapest flight possible stateside. Richard didn't have to come but I needed him to. Without him, I would never have gone. The whole idea seemed mad. I had always recalled that year of high school as incredibly golden but it was more than possible that it wouldn't stand investigation.

## The Bowery, New York City

*An autumnal Wednesday, 2000*

I am back in the USA in search of Gladyses and, I suspect, in search of myself. I am not here, however, for a long counselling session. I have had enough experience of psychoanalysis to realise that therapy is a great way to ruin your self-esteem. But I do have some big decisions to make. My foray into the world of theatre at

Mamaroneck High School left a lasting impression. I have just concluded my twenty-first year in professional show business and I am beginning to have the doubts I think I should have had twenty-one years ago. I am not at all sure the life is for me. A fellow treader of the boards once said to me, 'Being an actor is like being a grown-up but still playing at shops.'

And then, I have been thinking about my passport. Forgive me while I segue into my rather complex national identity. I come from a Danish-English alliance that produced three children. Each of us holds the passport of the place where we happened to be born. My sister Jeni was born in America and thus holds American citizenship. I arrived in Copenhagen so I am Danish and my brother is a Londoner with the appropriate documentation.

My dad always used to say, 'Good job I only had three children because you know, one in four children in the world is Chinese and that would have been too confusing.'

It's an old line but it's always appealed to me as a delightfully unjingoistic position. It is difficult, however, to remain an ardent internationalist. We are all affected and infected by the culture in which we live. When I left the United States, aged fourteen, I had become very American indeed. I had lived there for six years, had adopted a thick New York accent and was American through and through. I arrived at a very small, very provincial, girls' boarding school in the Home Counties. I had visited relatives in the UK often but I had never lived there. I knew none of the cultural references that natives take for granted and was now three thousand miles from what I regarded as home.

The woman the school had deemed fit to employ as matron was a mean-spirited, great Bismarck of a woman. Being a girls' boarding-school matron is a job no sensible person would undertake and, not having a jot of sense in her entire body, she fitted the role perfectly. I arrived with some vague notions of Enid Blyton pranks in the dorm, jolly japes and lashings of ginger beer. Instead the matron introduced me to a new world of utter isolation. If I feel sorry for myself at all, it is for the moment my father departed and left me in that woman's care. She huffed and puffed her way down the dark corridors ahead of me and threw open the dorm door.

'This is Sandra. She is, I'm afraid, an *American*.'

She managed to convey more disdain in that one word than I have ever heard again in any given circumstance. The girls, who were all old hands, couldn't have been more charming. For the next six weeks they sent me to another new destination – the silent hell of non-communication known as 'Coventry'. They wanted me to be less foreign. I determined then that nothing would stop me making a life stateside as soon as I was able. Ever ornery but now deeply unhappy as well, I did the opposite of what I had done when I arrived in America: I did not pretend to be English at all. If they wished to exclude me for being American then I would be very American indeed. I told everyone my name was Sandi not Sandra and that I would not kow-tow. Eventually I won them round. It is the classic comic's tale. I got them to speak to me by being funny. They spoke and they called me Sandi. I had given myself an American name but I replied in the crustiest of English accents.

I think it would be fair to say that I suffered some crisis of national identity: I did not feel English, I wanted to be American but I was actually Danish. Over the years, particularly since my dad died young, I have taken great pride in being Danish, in flying the rather attractive Danish flag, but the fact is I don't live there. I haven't lived there since I was eight. I have, however, been in the UK for nearly thirty years now and I have begun to wonder about national identity and what it really means. I am toying with greater political involvement in Britain, yet it is a country in which I have never been able to vote. Does the passport you hold determine who you are? I guess I am going back to find out who I was then and who I am now, which I think sounds pleasingly like an American statement. Who knows, I may even have 'identity issues'.

I am travelling with Richard. Indeed, I would not be travelling without Richard. He is very English, quite big and borderline camp. He has convinced me that this journey is a good idea. I love Richard. He is one of my best friends. As well as coming to New York to track down people who never bothered to look me up, Richard has also convinced me that it would be fun to rent an apartment in the Bowery. We now have an apartment in the Bowery and Richard is not here. He has gone out, leaving me to have the fun on my own. It is early evening and I realise that I am jet-lagged and horribly nervous. What if no one else remembers? What if the other Gladyses never liked me? Maybe the year meant nothing to them and everything to me? The whole search for these eleven women could all turn into an expensive and embarrassing mistake.

It isn't a bad apartment. Quite clean and free of the notorious NYC cockroaches that can crunch in the night as you try to make your way to the loo, sorry, bathroom in the dark. There is a large sitting room with a single bed in it, a half-dividing wall to form a double bedroom, a breakfast bar with a pretend kitchenette and a small bathroom. It is all rather modern. A bicycle stands upside down on top of the wardrobe. I cannot tell if it is art or a useful piece of transport. Everything seems strange and unreal.

Unsure of what to do with myself I sit and watch some television on the oldest set I have seen in a long while. It reminds me of the great wooden cabinets which served as TVs in my youth. Then we had never seen a colour television. We arrived to the entirely new notion of daytime programmes and colour. The colour was poor and mainly green. It was achieved by means of a panel of three large lights in front of the box – one red, one green and one blue. I suspect there was a poor scientific rationale behind the concept and for some time we thought everyone in American show business had some mild form of gangrene.

The set in this otherwise trendy apartment has not moved on much from the 1966 effort and certainly the coverage has not improved. I feel assaulted by the TV. I remember when the thing about American television was that programmes were regularly interrupted by television ads. Now it seems to be the other way round and the tiny programme sections are merely an irritant to the main function of selling. Ads pound at me every few minutes to buy shares, lose weight, get a new mattress or have the experience of a lifetime, all with the same urgency.

Some American woman athlete has lost in the first round of something and she is being interviewed. She smiles, with teeth so glitteringly filled that they rather make up for the lack of gold round her neck, and declares, 'I don't mind losing because, you see, it is God's will for me.' I think about that. In the UK it is not God's will but a lack of lottery funding.

My sister, who is living in New York, has sent over a video of a very bad B-movie, *Reptilicus*, made in the 1950s by a director called Sidney Pink. It's a rather gripping story about a monster that tries to eat Copenhagen. It's all in English and includes a thirty-second sequence with our dad playing a journalist telling the people that 'There is no reason to be afraid. The military has everything in hand.'

Fantastic. Like father, like daughter. Another Toksvig brush with the fringes of fame.

I move back to 'live' television. Martha Stewart is planting pansies and making 'tomato cobbler'. I don't know what tomato cobbler is – either a vegetarian main course or a rather unusual profession. I hit the sound and let Martha speak. She doesn't explain about the cobbler but she does tell me that 'Pansies are the thoughtful flower'.

Martha looks thoughtful. Not surprisingly. She has much money to be thoughtful of. She is a curious American phenomenon. She is the ultimate homemaker. Her television series and vast website encompass the whole American Dream of home life. She serves up an endless diet of the myth of home-grown vegetables, hand-made quilts and pets that don't shed hair. It is, of course, the

American dream existence shot through twenty-eight layers of gauze. I think the director intended to make Martha even more ethereal than she actually is, but it is like watching TV through a tube of KY jelly. Martha, in a thick gelatinous fog, wanders round a farm with a tray of lettuces while young men let soil run through their fingers and talk about organics. She never actually touches the soil but everything is clearly fresh and beautiful. Martha is my friend. If I went to her house she would make me soup and we could decorate the tomato cobbler or play with him or whatever. Then she smiles and spends some time telling me what I can buy on-line. The Pumpkin Carving Kit!, all wrapped up in a beautiful cloth roll, is certainly a must have. Perhaps I could just hole up in the Bowery and order things. Perhaps I need never meet anyone or have any kind of reunion with people who think they know me . . .

The final shots of tomato cobbler make me hungry so I look in the fridge for something to eat. In the freezer compartment there is an empty ice tray and a solitary frozen TV dinner. I check out the dinner. On the side of the roast beef plate it says:

'Serving Suggestion – Defrost'

I like the fact that it is only a suggestion and that some people might decide to suck the thing frozen, but it is still too much cooking for me so I put it back. What would Martha have said?

Although the apartment is small I check it again for anything untoward. This is unnecessary as I have already looked in every cupboard, under the beds and indeed down the loo. The loo thing is important and I'm not sure everyone would think of it. When I was a kid it was a well-known urban myth that many, many people brought baby alligators back to New York from Florida holidays as souvenirs. Of course the creatures grew and no one knew what to do with them so the general solution was to flush them down the toilet. There the reptiles refused to die and thrived in the excrement of the NYC sewage system. Every now and then one of them would seek freedom back the way they had come. The toilet bowl was not a dumping ground but an escape hatch. How the thing was supposed to get round the U-bend I have no idea but, even aged forty-two, I did just look. Really, I shouldn't be left alone.

The phone rings at 9.30 and reckless as to whether a serial killer is calling for an appointment I answer. I think I would have spoken to anyone. It is Rita. Gladys Two. Of all the Gladyses, Rita is the one I have kept in closest touch with. We talk for about an hour. It is easy and fun. I find my accent slipping into the New York of my childhood. She says that the one year at high school, the year of the Gladyses, *was* high school for her. Then we cover the fact that we are both worried that each of us will think the other is fat and hang up full of promises to meet the next day. I turn away from the telephone and see myself reflected in the television screen. I am fat. I am a fat forty-two-year-old woman. I can't think how I got that old or that fat but at least I have started my journey. At least it had been important to Rita too.

Now there is a talk show hosted by a man called Maury. Maury is an older man. He has a thin handsome face and looks very fit. I am sure Maury works out. He also must be exhausted at the end of the day because all his guests scream at each other. The theme of this programme is women who are controlled by their men. The men on the show happily admit to beating their wives.

'I am the man,' one fellow called James keeps repeating. 'I am the man. You women want to talk to me, you get down on your knees and then I might listen. I am the man. I am A-class and women are B-class and I think you know what the B stands for.'

James is a big man with a vast stomach yearning to be released from the confines of his clothing. I am surprised that James can spell anything. Indeed, getting as far as B in the alphabet must have been a challenge for his local education authority.

There is a shot of a woman listening to James. Her mouth is wide open in horror. She is wearing headphones and carrying a clipboard so we know she is a professional. This one shot tells us a lot. Clearly this woman works for *The Maury Show*, clearly she has heard a great deal in her time but today takes the biscuit. This show, that one shot tells us, is unique. James wants to marry his girlfriend but James is clearly not the bridegroom every girl dreams of.

Maury is fantastic. Maury is a real man. He stands between James and his woman when James wants to ask her to marry him.

'In all my years as a talk-show host I have never stood between a man and his girlfriend if he wanted to marry her.'

It is noble. It gets cheers, but you have to ask yourself how many times Maury has had to deal with on-air marriage proposals.

There is a constant trail, teasing us that James has asked his girlfriend to marry him backstage. The cameras were there. Did she say yes? I have no idea. I go and have the swiftest of baths. Swifter than I intended, actually. The plug system for the bath is operated by a three-foot silver lever at the side. The plughole shows no sign as to how it might actually seal. The workings are concealed by a silver plate with holes in it. I cannot figure out if the lever should go up or down. I try both but the water escapes in a rush either way. This is shower country and I am a fool to want to sit down at all. Only English people want to lie full length in their own soiled water, but I am nothing if not determined. In the end, I opt for wedging my arse over the hole and there is sufficient suction from the escaping water to make this a rather successful plug. With one cheek between me and the New York sewer system I now realise that I have placed the soap too far away on the ledge for me to reach without moving my plug. And anyway suction has been greater than I thought and there is some doubt as to whether I shall ever be able to move again. I envisage Richard eventually returning to find me naked, wrinkled, still filthy with a mark round my derrière like a love bite from a Koi carp. Then, I remember the baby alligators and imagine that one of them is even now eyeing up the new moon I am presenting via the plughole. I am out of there pretty quick.

By the time I return, the woman-beater seems to be confessing that his mother is a prostitute. I decide I must revise my initial opinion of the man and realise with some humanity that he has had a difficult life. In fact, during my short absence Maury has disappeared and Jerry Springer is talking to an entirely different young man whose mother has just become a prostitute. She is an enormous woman wearing a yellow brassière and Lycra cycling shorts. It is not at all attractive and as I haven't eaten I turn it off. I have every confidence that should I find another moment of leisure later in the day someone else will be talking to Siamese twins who were seduced by their uncle just before he became archbishop.

I don't know what all this means. I don't know why people would want to come on a television programme and expose their lives in this way. Is it for fame? Is it actually seen as helpful? As some kind of therapy? I once read that the American people are by nature pioneering spirits, who moved restlessly across this great continent from the East coast to the West until they hit the Pacific. After that there was nowhere left to go so they began to explore inside themselves. I don't know if it's true. Therapy is big here. Clearly the people on the *Maury* and the *Springer* shows come from the poorer section of the population. Perhaps they can't afford to go and see someone to pour their hearts out to; so they go on television. It is a horrible gladiatorial display, which is somehow compelling. It has the same balance of fascination and repulsion as watching surgery on TV. These people's lives are dreadful and exposing the minutiae of them to the world is not going to help. Maury promises the line of beaten and bruised women that therapy and assistance will be found for them, 'And if it takes money then you come to me.'

St Maury. Everyone cheers and then watches a product endorsement for a spray furniture polish. It gets rid of scratches in fine wood. It makes things whole again, just like Maury.

I wonder if anyone has ever done a study of the actual impact on people post-talk-show appearance. Perhaps they all just go home, have a beer and contemplate their brief flirtation with fame.

Anyway, now it's 4 a.m. and I can't sleep. I blame the mattress. There's nothing wrong with it but I have watched four hundred mattress ads and have been bludgeoned into thinking that there might be. The CBS news people are up as well, which is nice. There is a very plastic woman and a man with quite grey hair being very cheery about stocks, weather and the price of internal airline tickets. The neighbourhood is not slumbering either. Someone appears to be washing out the *West Side Story* look-alike backyard with its Tate Modern collection of metal fire escapes. Richard is still out because he is a gay boy and knows how to party.

The sounds outside are building into endless, relentless noise. People are washing streets, backing up trucks, dumping giant pallets of stuff on the road just in case things quieten down. Directly across the street is Bowery Building Supplies, where sheet metal is apparently only ever delivered at four in the morning and no worker has ever been employed who didn't have butterfingers. My ears are assaulted by the city. The Bowery still has many timber yards, service stations and small industrial units that all take deliveries. It could correctly be described as a 'colourful neighbourhood'. All the trucks have beepers to act as a warning when reversing. I'm sure they have them in England but not so loud. I think the idea is that blind people won't get hit by an un- expected high-volume delivery of broccoli, but the noise is unbelievable. On our street (I am beginning to feel proprietorial), no truck seems to want to approach a delivery going forwards. Every blind person in the neighbourhood is safe from unexpected death by tyre but only deaf people can get any sleep.

The news people move on to Barbra Streisand. She is giving a farewell concert at Madison Square Garden in NYC that night and I feel depressed. I will never see her sing. How awful. It reminds me of being a kid in New York. Of hearing that Judy Garland had died and feeling bereft. I do so love the divas of show business and it is a peculiarly American love. The news reporter, wearing a staggering amount of make-up for the time of morning, is managing to be very earnest about la Streisand.

'A woman picking up her $2,500 ticket before the show told a friend, "It was either another face-lift or Barbra. I chose Barbra."'

I hope Barbra feels bad. Standing on stage looking out at all those saggy-faced punters.

As soon as it was light I headed out for coffee. On the way I passed a huge 24-hour shop promisingly called Tower Books and went in. There were only ten books in the apartment. Nine of them were self-help programmes for co-dependency and the last was Volume I of *Contract Bridge*. I did read that and now know more about bold bidding than might be useful. Inside Tower Books there were acres of racks holding magazines on every subject imaginable and one or two that I had never even heard of. There was a substantial amount of very tacky gay stuff and, bizarrely, a thing called *Scandinavian Press* with news from Denmark.

I wandered around but really I wanted something more substantial than a magazine, so I went over to the counter. Here a very smiley young man was keen to help me.

'What can I do for you today?' I liked the question. It suggested he was going to come to my aid on a regular and future basis.

'Yes, hello. I was wondering where the books are?'

He smiled again. 'Right. We don't sell books . . . as such.' This caused us both to pause for a moment.

'But there is a huge sign outside that says Tower Books,' I said, feeling like a pedant.

'Yes.' He nodded in agreement. 'We've been thinking about taking that part of the sign down. If you want books you really need to go to a bookstore.'

'Right.' I couldn't let it go. 'How will I tell it's a bookstore? It could say Bookstore and sell something else.'

By now the young man was confused but still smiling.

'Barnes and Noble sell books,' he finally managed. We both smiled. 'But they're closed,' he added.

I bought the *New Yorker*, *MS* magazine and the *Gay and Lesbian Review*. Then, as a kind of homage to my great-grandfather and his failed Danish newspaper in Albany, the *Scandinavian Press*. The latter was a cracking read. It appeared to have been printed on paper so recently recycled as to contain living memories of a former existence. Small pieces of Scandinavian log floated through all the articles. Apart from an 'In-depth guide to rune reading', the big news of the week was an interview with Helge Ingstad, the hundred-year-old Norwegian who had definitively proved that the Vikings discovered America. Old Helge was clearly full of beans and was quoted as saying, 'Now, even UNESCO accepts it. So now it is no question at all.'

Bless. How my old English teacher would have hated him. Great explorer, lousy grammarian. Still, one in the eye for old Columbus. Despite my Scandiwegian leanings it was, however, the *New Yorker* that hit home. Inside was a cartoon of a woman being served by a clerk in a large shop. The young man was clearly trying to be helpful. 'The guy who knows about the books isn't here today. I'd be more than happy to suggest a bookmark.'

On the way back I did a very New York thing and hailed a yellow cab to take me home. There was a strange pot-pourri of street life out and about at this early hour and I tried to get the cab driver to wait till I got in my front door. I think he probably would have, except he didn't really speak English or even seem all that aware of which city he was in. He dropped me half a block from where I needed to be. A rat scuttled across the sidewalk from a pile of rubbish towards the Cocteau Theater on the corner of Bond Street and Bowery. A man was sleeping in the doorway of the theatre. Homelessness or true desperation to get first-night tickets? The rat stopped to look at me so I spoke clearly to it, 'There is no reason to be afraid. The military has everything in hand.'

I missed my dad.

# CHAPTER 3

# Rita – Gladys Two

*Susan B. Anthony*
*knew to rock the boat.*
*Carrie Chapman Catt told the la-*
*Dies they could vote.*
*Stanton was relentless,*
*and Steinem unforgiving.*
*So how did we end up with 'Mar-*
*tha Stewart Living?'*

Bruce Kluger, *Los Angeles Times*, 13 Jan 2002

I've been in touch with Rita on and off over the years since I left high school. Indeed, she was one of the first Gladyses that I met back in the autumn of 1971. After we had all auditioned, the results were processed and posted on the door of the music room later in the week. I remember the excitement when they went up. There was a great crush of would-be Gielguds and Redgraves in the narrow corridor trying to get a look. I was small and managed to squeeze in ahead of the throng. It was a tense moment but there I was on the list. It read:

'Sandra Toksvig . . . Gladys 1.'

I was thrilled. I had no idea what it meant but I was thrilled. I recognised a girl behind me, Rita, from the auditions. She had lustrous dark hair cut into a shoulder-length bob and a wide Italian-looking face with slightly olive skin. She was well groomed and wore a polo neck decorated with a single pearl on a gold chain. There was nothing ill-thought-out or ungroomed about Rita. She was sixteen and not that much taller than me. She was craning to see what the notice said.

'You're Gladys Two,' I informed her. 'Whatever that is.'

'Don't do that!' she said, clearly annoyed with me. 'I wanted to look for myself.'

'I'm sorry, I didn't know.' And I didn't. I thought she would be just like me, pleased to be in it at all. It was the sort of mistake that I was to make with Rita all my life. Rita and I get along but sometimes it is despite ourselves.

Much of it has been my fault. In 1975, when I had been living in England for three years, Rita came over to visit. For my first two years at boarding school I had seen my parents only during the long holidays when there had been time to fly back home to New York. It had taken me almost exactly six weeks of silent isolation by my dorm at school to develop the most perfect of English accents. I had survived in an alien place by fitting in, by becoming the most appalling chameleon. I had unexpectedly turned into a model student. Well, there was nothing else to occupy the hours of tedium. The common room had an old record player with three singles, no radio and a TV which we watched for half an hour on Thursdays and an hour and a half on Saturdays. The TV was colour but it had been retuned to black and white after an appearance by Gary Glitter on *Top of the Pops* had been deemed too exciting for us girls. The rest of the week I worked hard, tied my tie with great care and wore the Englishness of it all with a necessary enthusiasm.

By the third year my parents had abandoned America and had moved back to Europe. There was no longer any need for me to live at school but I think they had got used to my being there so I stayed. I didn't want to but I stayed. Then Rita came over to Britain for a holiday. My mother picked her up from the airport and brought her to school. We hugged when she arrived and then I whispered, 'What are you wearing?'

Rita looked down at her plain black trousers. 'Pants, why?'

'You can't wear trousers at the school.'

'I'm not at the school,' she said reasonably.

I was appalled. She did not fit in. I did not fit with her. Everything I had built up could be destroyed. I had, in a remarkably short time, turned into a prig. A prig with received pronunciation. She and I went off to Paris. She wanted American food and I wanted her to hold her knife and fork properly. I behaved badly. I thought she was ill-mannered and gauche.

'She is, I'm afraid, an American' echoed in my head. It was I who had lost my manners and certainly any ability to just relax, live and let live.

Four years later it was my turn to visit America. The Gladys Society had been formed through a mutual love of theatre but of us all Rita was the one who seemed to hunger for theatrical success. The only daughter of doting Catholic Italian-Americans, she had had a suburban upbringing as far from the bright lights as it was possible to get. Her parents, Rosemary and Angelo, were practical, good people. I don't know what her father did but I am pretty sure her mother was one of the first to teach computer skills. They were kind sorts but not live-wires. These were not people who listened to show tunes and had an opinion on the impact of Bob Fosse on Broadway. They liked to keep the yard nice and make decent cabbage and beans. Rita, however, was determined to follow a more glittering path.

The last time I stayed with her was in 1979, when she was living in a tiny apartment in the shadow of the 59th Street Bridge in New York City. That year, Rita had graduated in journalism from a university in Binghamton, New York, a place upstate that I had never heard of before and couldn't think of any reason to visit. Now she had a Jewish boyfriend called Ron and was busy trying to break into show business. Rita had decided to become a stand-up comic. I was twenty and had just completed my first year at Cambridge. I wasn't really sure what a 'stand-up' was. Britain always lagged some way behind the States in terms of development and the great 'comedy as the new rock and roll' boom had yet to arrive. It would be another year before I first appeared on the opening night of the fledgling Comedy Store in London. Rita and Ron's apartment was small and my then partner and I slept on a pull-out bed in a sort of corridor between their bedroom and the kitchen. Through the dusty windows you could see the bright lights of the bridge. It seemed a very daring place to live. Down the hall an unbalanced tenant had lined her entire front door with aluminium foil. She lived in fear of a UFO invasion and did what she could to protect herself.

'Aliens up your asshole!' she could be heard to shout as you tried to pass silently. It was a world away from the quiet halls of Cambridge academia where returning library books late caused shock.

Rita wasn't actually working as a stand-up at the time but wanted us to see her act. She stood in the tiny sitting room of the fourth-floor apartment doing her routine.

'Welcome to the Smegma department store where we . . .' she started doing a comedy voice. I tried to laugh but it wasn't going all that well because I didn't understand all the references and, being a nice gay girl, I certainly didn't know what smegma was.

As well as the stand-up, Rita was also co-writing with two others, trying to break into the situation comedy writing field.

'Do you think you'll make it?' I asked her.

'Making it' was a big subject for discussion.

'Success is out there,' she assured me. 'You just have to want it enough.'

Meanwhile, Ron was earning a living as a lighting designer at the Manhattan Light Opera Company. My partner and I went to see one of his shows. It was very light and very pink. Ron and Rita were in the thrust of New York theatre. Their apartment was decorated with posters from shows, they had every musical album ever recorded and there wasn't anything going on in 'the business' that they didn't know about. Theatre was everything.

Ron and Rita are now married. I went to the wedding many years ago. It was a sweet affair, the highlight being Rita's mother reading a poem she had found on a Hallmark card in the local newsagent's. Sixteen years later and Ron has turned into a 'good husband', 'a marvellous father' and a man who runs a human resources company. Rita is a mother of three and earns her living teaching computer skills. She lives in the suburbs, about a mile from her childhood home. We are all grown-up.

After my night of therapeutic television, Richard returned to the flat full of good spirits and bearing morning coffee. He was excited. He was about to meet his first Gladys. Not a concept I had ever thought to hear him utter. We grabbed a cab on Bowery and spent the next ten minutes trying to explain to the driver where the Empire State Building was. We would have been quicker but my Somali is not really up to scratch. New York is a city where cab drivers make a living by simply driving but having no idea where anything is. If the metropolis wasn't laid out on a grid system, God knows how anyone would get anywhere. We drove on through the bright morning. Richard was busy trying to take home movies out of the window but I just couldn't stop looking. It is an incredible place.

The assault on all my senses, which had started so early, went into a higher gear. Fires and police emergencies erupted around us like small volcanic bursts, steam hissed up from the subway rumbling under the street, while everywhere people seemed to be yelling. On a street corner, a man dressed as a pharaoh in purple and gold silk proclaimed his religion of choice while a soberly suited businessman took time out to shout his disagreement. We passed homeless people wailing in madness, as music poured from shops and passing cars. Scooters and skateboards scratched across the pavements all carrying adults in neat suits wearing trainers. Smart executives roller-bladed to work. I saw hardly any children. It is a place of grown-ups, restless, noisy grown-ups.

I think life on Manhattan is like that because of four things:

1. Everyone drinks too much coffee.
2. It's an island.
3. Everyone wears comfortable shoes. Even for the business person, the trainer is king.
4. Getting a cab is a nightmare.

So if you put all that together – they are pumped up with coffee, living in a confined space, no one can get a cab and everyone is pounding around in comfortable shoes – you get a hive of bursting activity. If I could think of eight more things I could turn the whole lot into a twelve-step programme.

I was expounding my theory to Richard when he pointed out a street sign – Broadway! Just seeing the name again, I could hear Gene Kelly singing. I have a mock Broadway street sign in my office in London, which Rita gave me years ago, but here I was back at the real thing. This was where my ambitions had started. This was showbiz. I felt odd. There was a time when I knew every show in the city and what every critic had said about it. Now all I knew was that *Cats* had closed – a victim of its own success. No one had known it would run as long as it did and there had been actors in it with 'run of the show' contracts. Some had stuck it out for twenty years. The producers couldn't refresh the show so they closed it. Fair enough. Even cats don't live that long.

We stopped abruptly at a traffic light and all around us every piece of street furniture carried some sign, some essential instruction. Americans are sign mad. There are instructions for everything. Even the inside of the cab was littered with notices. Not to mention the hideous recording which goes off every time you get in the back of a yellow cab – 'This is Judge Judy telling you to be safe. Put your seat belt on.'

I didn't know who Judge Judy was but I didn't do it just to

spite her. At this particular light on my right a notice read: 'Don't Honk! $220 fine.'

On the opposite street corner was the identical instruction except this one said: 'Don't Honk! $350 fine.'

Extraordinary. It was $130 cheaper to honk on the left side of the street. I didn't have time to analyse why. The driver behind us honked to get the cab going. Our driver was being lethargic. The light had turned green at least half a second ago. No one fined anyone on either corner and we moved on.

In the shadow of the Empire State Building, I carefully watched the office doors where we were to meet Rita – and there she was. Only a little taller than me, and slightly less round, she walked towards me with her arms spread wide and we hugged and hugged. The streams of New Yorkers slipped past, ignoring us. Two mad ladies crying in the street. For that moment at least I was glad to have come, glad to have started my search.

While Richard carried on filming, we headed off for Central Park. On the way, Rita and I took stock. Thirty years of friendship, thirty years of change. Rita smiled as if she would burst. Her dark hair and olive skin bespoke the thousands of Italians who had passed through Ellis Island to make a life in America. We looked out at the city where she was once going to be a great comic and where I . . . I didn't know what I was going to do.

We wandered to the boating lake and I found myself slipping into our old relationship. I had always been the kid of the group and now I was the one to rent a toy boat to sail, while Rita sat and watched.

I bought us a bottle of water each and sat down to take great gulps. My boat had drifted off to the far side of the lake and the wind had all but died. I put the remote down and enjoyed just sitting.

'Did you check the seal on your bottle?' asked Rita.

'Sorry?' I gulped some more water.

'You have to check the bottle is sealed before you drink it. Otherwise they could put anything in there.'

'Like what?' asked Richard.

'It was in the papers. People putting stuff in water bottles.'

The city was awash with unknown dangers. I could have been drinking anything. All around there were signs telling me how to behave, how to 'protect this lawn', 'leash' my dog, 'say no to sports' and so on.

'Why do you have so many signs?' I asked Rita as my boat crashed once more into the stone retaining wall of the lake.

'You crashed your boat,' she pointed out.

'I didn't, I . . . docked it.' We were teenagers again. Rita looked at the signs.

'In England you seem to know when something is "not done". Here, everything is done, so we have very clear signs about what you can and can't do to keep society civilised.'

Richard didn't want water. He was 'good'. He had already picked up the lingo. It is very important in New York at any given moment to be 'good'. You can't walk two yards in the city without someone asking:

'Are you good?' The answer to which is, 'I'm good.'

We'd been in the city a day and a half and already Richard had started saying terrible, ungrammatical things.

Me: 'Would you like some water?'

Richard: 'No, I'm good.'

Not even, 'No *thank you*, I'm good'. Just being good is enough. There is no need to be grateful as well.

The wind was poor and I was not Stuart Little so I gave the boat back.

Later in the day we headed off for dinner. I had taken some trouble to select a restaurant for the evening. Rita and I had emailed back and forth about what kind of place she wanted to eat in. New York is full of fine dining and I wanted to give her a real treat.

Perhaps I even wanted to show off a little. She had emailed back that, by and large, she was now vegetarian so I had commissioned my sister to seek out something veggie but with class. Personally I think the two ideas are mutually exclusive. I don't think it matters how smart a restaurant it is – all vegetarian food looks like it's been eaten once before. But Jeni had come up with something that sounded promising – a vegetarian restaurant with a Buddhist theme not far from the theatre where I got tickets for us to see *Kiss Me, Kate*, a musical revival that had recently stormed Broadway. The perfect night out for my old theatre buddy and me.

Okay, the restaurant was a disaster. However desperate you are for some vegetables, I wouldn't recommend it. It all looked very zen when we arrived and met up with Jeni and Richard. All very calm and oriental fusion but the muzak was disturbing. It was very un-zen.

'What the hell is that music?' I asked Jeni, who is younger and knows about these things.

'It's the soundtrack from *Titanic*,' she whispered.

'Why?' I managed before noticing that there was nothing on the menu any of us wanted to eat. I don't have anything against vegetables as such – it's all that horrible pulse business served with it. Fundamentally I disapprove of any food which has to be soaked overnight before you can eat it. None of the descriptions shouted 'eat me'.

There were dishes like:

Basiled Vegetarian Ham – Vegi-Ham (Soy Protein) Low-Cal Conjex, Fresh Soy Bean, Black Mushrooms in a Basil Sauce with Brown Rice.

Low-cal conjex? What the hell was conjex when it was fattening? Whatever it was, it was popular. I narrowed down my choices to anything without conjex in it but it was hard.

Moo Shu Mexican Style – Kidney Beans, Soy Gluten Served in Spinach Crepes with a Guacamole Sauce, Carrot Coleslaw and Cous-Cous.

Apart from an intense desire to achieve regular bowel movements I could not imagine why any chef would put that list of ingredients into one dish.

'How long have you been vegetarian?' Richard asked Rita. I think she detected a hint of blame in his voice.

'Actually, I eat fish and chicken,' she replied.

While the music assured us that 'life will go on' the waiter came to see if we wanted a drink.

'Yes,' I said emphatically.

'What would you like?' he enquired.

'Why don't you just show me the wine list,' I said.

'No,' he replied.

He wasn't being difficult. They didn't have a wine list. In fact they had no alcohol at all. Visions of missed chicken and fish mixed with an evening of iced tea swam before my eyes. Jeni and Richard went outside for a very zen cigarette. Rita and I were laughing by now.

'This is awful and it is all your fault,' I told her.

'Absolutely,' she agreed. 'I tell you what, you come out to Westchester and I'll take you to Walter's for a hot dog.'

Walter's Hot Dog Stand is famous throughout the county. I was aghast. 'Don't tell me you eat hot dogs as well?'

'Sometimes, but only at Walter's.'

That kind of vegetarian I can understand. I asked her if I had changed and she said 'No!' and then laughed. I find it hard to believe. I feel like an entirely different species from that child in the yearbook picture.

Jeni and Richard came back in, grinning. Jeni slipped two small vodka miniatures into my iced tea and the whole evening progressed rather pleasantly. Oh, one more thing: never allow anyone to serve you pickled aubergine. Even the aubergine would sit up and tell you it's a mistake.

We went on to the theatre. Richard was relentlessly filming and I had the strange sensation of actually being in a film of my life. I

passed under the great lights of the marquee at the Martin Beck
Theater where the stars' names, Brian Stokes Mitchell and Marin
Mazzie, were emblazoned in lights. I used to wonder if my name
might ever be up there. Now it never crosses my mind. I didn't
know yet if Rita was disappointed with her lot.

After the show we dropped her at Grand Central Station.
There was a little time before her train so we had a drink on the
wide stone terrace that overlooks the main concourse. The station has been completely renovated and it is a fantastic building.
A marble hall of marvel with its vast green ceiling decorated
with golden stars showing astrological signs. Large boards indicated the general direction of Trains to Poughkeepsie while
people came and went to points north, south and west. No
wonder so many movies have scenes set there. It is a wildly
romantic place.

The drinks terrace was advertised as part of the Michael Jordan
Steakhouse. A curious establishment that includes a gift shop selling,
among other things, dog bones signed by celebrated basketball
players. Everything, I was discovering, is a consumer opportunity.
The waiter was relentlessly cheerful and chatty. It is the New York
trademark of those who serve.

'Those gifts for the dog,' I said, 'tell me, does Michael come in
often to sign bones?'

The waiter paused in his service and took my question very
seriously. 'Michael's not the actual owner here. He's a franchise.'

I doubted that Michael himself was actually a franchise but we
let it slide.

While we're on the subject, there are quite a lot of words in
American advertising whose meaning eludes me. Richard
showed Rita a doll he had bought. It was battery-operated and
danced the hula-hula while holding a microphone. If that were
not enough it was also proud to boast that it had Non Fallaction.
Everyone we encountered had a different pronunciation for this
word, some being more sexual than others. It was only when we

allowed the doll, Gigi, to hula that we discovered what it means. As she glides across a table top she reaches the edge of the surface and turns away. She does not fall off. She has, as advertised, Non *Fall*action.

I am fascinated by the difference between American and English humour. On his show, Michael Parkinson once asked the American comic Steve Martin what the difference was. Martin took a pair of scissors out of his pocket and said, 'Well, Americans would find this funny,' and cut Parkinson's tie off. The English studio audience fell about with laughter and Martin looked at them quizzically.

'Gee,' he said. 'They find that funny too. Well, I don't know what the difference is.'

Richard and I both thought the Non Fallaction doll was funny and I was pleased that Rita did too. Feeling emboldened that we were on the same comedy wavelength, I went on to show her a device that I had found promoted in the Delta Airlines Sky Mall Catalog. It was an invaluable item which tests the 'doneness' of your cooking. The word made me laugh. Rita wrinkled her brow at me as if I were foolish.

'Why is that funny?' she demanded.

'I don't think there is such a word,' I said rather feebly. 'Doneness.'

'Doneness,' she explained patiently, 'means whether something is done or not.'

That's right and it's not funny.

Rita's train was due and Richard was off out again. I realised I faced more time alone in the apartment. I pursued my friendship with the waiter.

'Do you know where the nearest bookshop is?'

The question clearly introduced a new concept. He looked blank.

'A bookstore,' prompted Rita helpfully. 'A store that sells books.'

There was a long pause.

'Right,' he said finally. 'I think there is a newsstand downstairs that might have a book.'

*We set out for New Rochelle where being come we had good Entertainment and Recruited ourselves very well. This is a very pretty place well compact and good handsome houses, clean, good passable roads, and situated on a Navigable River, abundance of land well fined and cleared all along we passed, which caused me a Love of the place, which I could have been content to live in it.*

Madam Sarah Kimble Knight's Journal – travelling by horse from Boston to New York, 1704

Rita and her family live in New Rochelle, a small town neighbour to my old home town of Mamaroneck in the county of Westchester. What can I tell you about it? It has a little fame – the first US Post Office was established here, George Washington stopped by on his way to assume command of the army and the cartoon *Mighty Mouse* came to life here. It's not much but then it's not an earth-shattering kind of place. It is one of the archetypal suburbs of America, the place where all English people believe all Americans dwell.

Rita's family live in what her husband Ron calls a 'homogenous community'. That means mostly families and mostly white. It could be the neighbourhood of my childhood. The kids play ball outside in the street while the American flag flutters over many a doorway. They have a neat timber-frame house standing on a corner plot on a quiet street. Rita and Ron have two sons, David who is fifteen and Paul who is thirteen, and a daughter Julie, who is nine. Julie lives in a very girly bedroom and the boys share a room with bunk beds. Everything looks about as 'normal' as you could expect from American married life.

It was Thanksgiving and Rita had invited Richard and me to join the family for the traditional dinner. Despite the joys of Grand Central with its great trains and fabulous dog bones, Richard and

I decided to drive out in 'the rental'. That's what you say in New York. You 'take a drive in the rental'.

You don't need to say the word car at all.

Richard won't drive abroad (see story with horse and have sympathy) so I piloted. Out through the Bronx, across the Triborough Bridge following the signs for New England Upstate. A place as far from anything to do with England as one can possibly imagine. We did buy a map but there was no need. The forty-minute trip out to the suburbs was etched in some forgotten part of my brain.

The dinner we were heading for is one of the biggest events in the American calendar. When you list American things Thanksgiving and apple pie are right up there with the Rocky Mountains and the Mississippi. In the scheme of American history the event is ancient as it goes back some 480 years. This makes it a few years younger than my sitting room at home in England.

Samoset, the Native American credited with getting the pilgrims through the winter so that they could invent Thanksgiving and give the card industry a boost before Christmas, is said to have greeted the settlers by crying in English, 'Much welcome, Englishmen! Much welcome, Englishmen!'

There are none left now of course, the tribal peoples having made the mistake of settling on such prime stockbroker belt real estate in the first place. I don't think anyone remembers Samoset these days. Now Thanksgiving is a time of gigantic football games, family get-togethers and turkey. Probably even more than Christmas it is a time when Americans travel long distances to be together. There are cardboard and real pumpkins everywhere, greeting the nearest and dearest. It is an honour to be included. Richard and I drove past endless place names which in America, in particular, hold some kind of key to its quilted history. Places like the Bronx, named after the first recorded white settler in the region who just happened to be a Dane like me.

We took some wine with us. It was, after all, the first gift of the

Europeans. That, and things which needed to wait for penicillin to provide a cure. The Native American languages, which were rich and expressive, had no word for drunkenness. I don't know if I would have liked the early meals. One settler writes of going to visit a chief where supper was prepared by 'killing a fat dog and skinning it with great haste, with shells which they had got out of the water'.

Clearly, boy scout badges all round for ingenuity if not pet care. Richard and I were hoping for something a little more civilised. Every Friday night the Gladyses used to get together for spaghetti and coffee ice-cream. I expected Thanksgiving would be a touch more elaborate.

Rita's husband, Ron, is a fairly big man with a full salt and pepper beard. He is also funny. He started telling jokes as soon as we got there. Some of them were good: they were even funny the second time around.

Ron was, as he says, 'raised Jewish', while Rita was brought up Catholic. When they fell in love not everyone was delighted although Rita's parents coped.

'My mother would have preferred an Italian Catholic but she was happy with Ron as long as we got married. Now it's great. My mother thinks he's wonderful and his mother thinks I'm wonderful.'

'She calls me John or Don a lot,' muttered Ron and then smiled. 'Hey, Richard, did I tell you the one about . . .'

The boys wandered off to be funny while Rita got me a drink in her kitchen with its over-large American appliances. She was sixteen when we first met. Now she has a son nearly that age and my oldest daughter has just become a teenager.

'Is this what you imagined?' I asked her.

'Not at all.' Rita shook her head and looked straight at me. 'I am so glad no one told me when I was sixteen that this is where I was going to be.'

She spoke of wanting to be an actress, of leading a glamorous life and of her determination never to marry and have children. We would have talked more but the children wanted drinks, sustenance, help with maths homework and all the other essentials of juvenile life. Julie asked me if I would like to learn some 'New York things'. I thought I probably would.

'The New York State beverage is milk, the New York State fruit is apple, the New York State flower is the rose . . .'

She has clearly not been wasting her time at school. Julie took me through all the many New York State official things. I stopped listening after learning that the New York State animal is the beaver. There are certain things in life that hit my Achilles' heel of comedy and for no reason at all the beaver is one of them. She continued as I drifted off, wondering who makes these decisions about official matters of state and how you get to do that for a living. Julie is in the fourth grade, which is what I joined when I first came to the United States. I asked her if she knew what she wanted to be when she grew up. All right, it was a dull adult question but I had gone into something of a state coma.

'I really want to help endangered animals, ' she said. I know that I had no such global ambitions at nine.

'I don't think we had those in my day,' I said, rather lamely, and left to get another drink.

When I went back into the kitchen I realised that we had been there for some time and there seemed to be no cooking preparations whatsoever going on. Thanksgiving dinner is the full roast turkey affair served up by a devoted mother, so this was a little strange. Certainly it was very un-Martha Stewart. Where was the bird, where were the potatoes and yams, where, at the very least, was the tomato cobbler?

'My mom's bringing dinner,' Rita explained.

'Your mom is coming for dinner?' I asked.

Rita shook her head. 'No. She's just bringing it. I was busy so she made dinner.'

Ron slapped the counter. 'Nature abhors a vacuum, well,

nature, get in line. Rita does not want to do housework. I tell you, what we both need is . . .'

'. . . a wife!' they concluded together as Rita's father Angelo appeared in the driveway with a complete roast turkey and all the trimmings. He had driven from his house which is practically round the corner. A sprightly older man with a lived-in face and a bulbous nose he might have borrowed from a retired boxer. At least, I thought, Rita and Ron have *his* wife. Everything went in the oven to stay warm. I couldn't understand Rita's mother cooking and not eating so I asked if we could at least go over and say thank you.

Rita drove Richard and me over. The house was just as neat as I remembered. We entered the trim cul-de-sac and I saw that in thirty years very little had changed. I was fairly sure if we went into Rita's bedroom it would still have a single bed with a lace canopy. I asked her what her parents had thought back in the days when their daughter wanted to be a stand-up in Manhattan.

'It wasn't what my mom had envisioned for me – the bartending really got to her.'

'You loved stand-up. How come you didn't stick with it?'

Rita thought for a minute. She thinks carefully about everything she says. Gives it all weight.

'I had some . . . psychological difficulties . . . sometimes just getting through the day was the biggest challenge. For a long time I was deathly afraid to go in front of an audience. I had my mid-life crisis very early. The whole thing overwhelmed me very much. Joyce (Gladys Nine) asked me to do a reading at her wedding and I couldn't do it.'

This seemed extraordinary. This was a woman I remembered as desperate to read at anybody's wedding.

'What the hell was it?'

'I don't know. Fear of success? Maybe.'

And I liked that answer. It was an answer strangely packed with confidence while also accepting defeat. Just as no English person will ever tell you whether they are actually good at something or not, so no English person would ever give such a reply.

'I perform now,' she continued. 'I teach computer software and that is a kind of performing. It doesn't have to be but that is the way I do it.'

Her mother opened the screen door to her house. I remembered her as a petite Italian woman with glasses and hair set once a week by someone else. Now I saw a slightly older, petite Italian woman with glasses and hair set once a week by someone else.

'Sandra, how nice to see you.' Sandra? I was tempted to look over my shoulder and see if someone else had turned up.

'Enter ye who have faith!' called Rita's father, from the comfort of his armchair. We went into the sitting room. It was rather plain and dominated by a television in an elaborate wooden cabinet. It had looked like this thirty years ago except for two things. The large framed portrait of Rita, which had always been the only decoration, had been replaced by a large framed portrait of Julie, Rita's daughter. And the room was now cerise. Deep cerise. A cerise which I was unaware you could buy as wall paint. Her dad never got up but held court from his chair. It reminded me of so many sitting rooms when I was a kid and the father of the household held power, for he and he alone had the remote control to the television.

Rita's mother is now seventy-seven. She told me she was seventy-seven. She told me a great deal for she is happy to talk. She too seemed to remember all about the Gladyses.

'They used to rehearse right here, in this room.'

'They practically got started in this house,' said her father.

'Why the Gladyses, they were practically invented in here,' agreed his wife. She looked at me. 'I can still see you at the table eating – cabbage and beans. That's what Angelo said it was, cabbage and beans.'

'It was,' said Angelo, so we all agreed.

This put Rita's mom in mind of food and she whisked Richard

off to the kitchen. Here she had large containers of cabbage and beans to show him.

'I made it yesterday. I hope it's okay. Cabbage can be funny.' She poked at the funny cabbage and said, 'She's just the same . . . a little heavier, but don't tell her I said that. Rita adores her. You should eat this with Arthur Avenue bread from the Bronx. You heard of Arthur Avenue?'

Richard shook his head. Clearly he was at fault.

'It's famous,' admonished the chef. 'The next time you come we'll have Arthur Avenue.'

Mother and Richard returned to the sitting room. He was carrying a giant Tupperware container of cabbage and beans for us to take home.

'We love your sitcoms,' said Father, making conversation. '*Keeping Up Appearances* and *As Time Goes By*.'

Mother nodded enthusiastically. 'It's wonderful. Our sitcoms are nothing like yours. Yours are much better.' This was clearly a pet subject for the couple.

'The turns are so great. The comebacks from one person to another.'

It was not an opinion I think I had ever heard expressed before. Generally the British world of comedy is made to feel deeply inferior to the land of *Friends*, *Cheers* and *Frasier*. We all agreed that if Judi Dench or Patricia Routledge ever wanted cabbage and beans I would tell them where to call.

'Patricia Routledge – she is very talented.'

Mother headed back for the memory trail. 'I can remember the day Sandra left New York – everyone was teary eyed. That's the last time I saw her. The day before she left for England . . . twenty-nine, nearly thirty years . . . it's almost a lifetime. Rita, you remember, Aunt Caroline's twenty-fifth wedding anniversary? Even Aunt La La remembered her.'

I looked at Richard and had a strong feeling that I was going to hate this story.

'Aunt La La was supposed to be watching you and you got drunk. Aunt La La said so the other day.'

Drunk? I recall one glass of wine only but we all laughed anyway. Rita's parents had many videos of Rita's brood performing. We all sat and watched the kids on video. I found myself saying, 'The kids are so cute.' It's an expression I never use.

'Aren't they?' agreed Rita's mum.

Then we watched Rita and Ron performing for their church at some event singing Cole Porter's 'You're the Top'.

'They've been good friends.'

I didn't know if her mother meant Rita and Ron or Rita and me. As we drove away Rita was reflective.

'It was a different time when we were growing up. No one ate out on the spur of the moment. Even going for pizza had to be planned. Everything is faster now, everyone has other people doing things for them. Lot of things which would have been unthinkable when I was growing up. We now have someone to cut the lawn.'

Having someone to cut your lawn. I suppose that is a sign of growing up.

Back at home the kids were setting the table for the big meal. Richard was obsessed with the cranberry jelly which sat on a glass plate still carrying the shape and indentations of the tin can it had come out of. He kept poking it as if it might come back to life. Everyone was given a formal place with Richard and Ron, as the grown males, each taking one end of the table. It is well known that women lack the testosterone to survive eating without physical support on either side.

The meal warmed in the oven while we ate our starter. Everything looked like a Norman Rockwell painting. Rockwell was the quintessential American artist who, in the first half of the twentieth century, captured many a scene of Americana. He made all American life look like a James Stewart movie. I had told Richard about him. What I hadn't told Richard was that Rita and

Ron are not without their religious side. I think I particularly enjoyed watching my friend nearly sink under the table when asked to hold hands with everyone and take turns to say what he was grateful for. Richard is English and does not want to be grateful to anyone.

Rita and Ron's kids are as chatty as every American child is born to be and I think the conversation would have made Mr Rockwell's hand freeze over his palette. Perhaps they were trying to put Richard back at ease but they talked about high school where they have both a 'Tolerance' club and an 'Aids Awareness' club. This seemed extraordinary to me when the raciest thing I could recall was a French conversation club. I tried to imagine who would spend their teenage years being an active member of Aids awareness. What would you do each week? How would you have outings? Actually even the word 'outings' would take on a different meaning. I thought it was commendable but very forward indeed.

Julie talked about how much she liked going to church, so I asked her what kind of morals the church taught. She didn't understand the question so I tried again.

'What is it right in life to do?' I said, the boring adult with too much wine in her.

'Don't run in school,' she answered firmly.

Finally the moment arrived for the grand entrance of the turkey. It was trumpeted by an advance party of potatoes and vegetables and then Ron, the man of the family, went to collect the bird. There was silence at the table as we waited in anticipation for the symbolic bird to appear. When it did, it came flying through the doorway in a manner that suggested Ron had taken up levitating the dead with a remarkable degree of success. The bird, fed up with its confinement in the oven, had made one last flight of freedom off the plate and on to the floor. It wasn't quite Rockwell, but we ate it anyway.

*

The next morning, riding on the crest of a wave of gratitude, we all packed into the family people mover to head off for church. I think it would be fair to say that everyone had slightly forgotten the spirit of the season. Richard was irritable because he hates religion. Rita was irritable because we were waiting for Ron. Ron was irritable because he couldn't find what he was looking for. He called from the house.

'Rita, do we have a Bible?'

'I don't think so,' she yelled. He disappeared for a moment and then returned.

'Can you get the Bible on line?'

'Try King plus James,' shouted Richard.

'Does he have to have a Bible?' I asked.

'He's teaching Bible study today,' replied Rita.

This struck me as a stretch for a man who doesn't even own a Bible but I had not yet been to the church. Their church, it turned out, was rather a relaxed place. The sort of place where owning a Bible wasn't at all necessary for joining the club. The first thing I saw when I entered the Universalist Unitarian Church of Westchester was a large diagram pinned to a board. Here each member of the congregation had been asked to place an arrow to indicate the extent to which they did or did not believe in God. I was heartened to see that the minister himself, a youngish fellow with a grey moustache and dog collar, had firmly plumped for the No category. I asked Rita's younger son, Paul, what it meant.

'If you don't believe in God then you don't believe in God. That's fine.'

I'm not religious but I liked this church. Everyone was very cheerful and huggy and wore a name tag with a pink triangle on it. This was something of a surprise. The pink triangle was the symbol gay people were made to wear by the Nazis in the concentration camps. It has become a badge of pride for the gay community. I didn't think it was possible that everyone in the congregation apart from Rita and Ron's family could be gay. Paul was a little shakier on this.

'The pink triangle is the symbol for patience and the rainbow . . .' He frowned. He knew it was important but couldn't think why. 'I think the rainbow is the symbol for love.'

Leaflets describing the church as 'A Religious Home for Bisexual, Gay, Lesbian and Transgender People' were everywhere. In fact, I think Richard and I caused a bit of a stir. I'm not at all sure we weren't the first actual gay people on the premises – even if Richard refused to do anything except stand in the car park and smoke. I headed off for Bible study class with Ron. There was a small group of kids all sitting in a circle.

'We need another chair,' said Ron. I stood, waiting to be seated. No child moved. Ron went and got another chair, placed it carefully and sat on it. I stood for a moment and then got my own chair. I decided it wasn't about manners. It was just a difference in formality. You may have to fend for yourself in America but you do also get the credit for your achievements. The English endlessly stand on ceremony, pretending to be self-effacing, and then are surprised when they are left behind in the dust. I just wish there was some compromise between the two extremes. I had manners drummed into me at my English school and I suspect they will be the death of me. I will be standing on the prow of a sinking ship saying to everyone else on board, 'No, please, after you.'

I was worried that I would know nothing in the Bible class but it turned out to be about Adam and Eve, which was good, I thought. Like starting right at the beginning of a soap opera and not having to catch up.

The kids told me that 'The story of Adam and Eve is about making choices and pressure.' It made the whole thing sound like a modern business allegory.

Rita and Ron are heavily involved in the church. They help with the classes and take an active part in 'structuring programs' for their kids.

'What do you do just for *you*?' I asked my old friend and she looked somewhat flummoxed.

'This is not the year just for me,' she replied but I wonder when that year will be. I also wondered what had happened in the last thirty years. The woman who had wanted to shake the stand-up world had been sucked back into the life her parents led. Perhaps there is such a pull from the collective vacuums employed by the suburban housewife that it is not possible to escape. Or perhaps it is simply that people are, in general, destined to follow in their family's footsteps: it is hard to break away. Rita has followed her parents' life and I, in pursuing a life of writing and travel, have followed mine.

Although I think they would hate the idea, I realised Rita and Ron represented a kind of Mr and Mrs America to me. Living the suburban dream in which adult life is put on hold until the children are on their way to adulthood. It is admirable and is how life has progressed for centuries. Each succeeding generation helping the next to do slightly better than themselves. Rita's father mowed his own lawn, now she has someone to do it for her. So what happens if your own kids grow up, have children, put life on hold and on and on . . . ?

When I was a kid growing up in the sixties, the women's movement was very much in its infancy. Certainly it had no impact in the quiet, safe streets of the small towns of Westchester. I watched my parents' friends interact and I saw the women doing the work at home and the men going off and having the fun. I may not have wanted to go off and save endangered wildlife but even then I knew I wanted to save myself. Of course, Rita also works but I suspect she does so because she has to.

'Don't you need something just for you?' I persisted.

She shrugged. 'I do need that but you can't ever have everything. You do get things back from the kids in ways you don't always expect.'

When the kids are grown up Ron and Rita plan to 'move back

to the city'. Ron is quite clear that he much prefers '... cement, none of this gardening stuff – the theatre, the energy, the museums ... this is great now, this is exactly what we want now ... once we get the kids established then our dream is to own a nicer apartment in the city.'

'We won't have cats though.' Rita recalled how much I hated their cats but the decision is not for my benefit. 'Ron was always having an allergy situation with them.'

An allergy situation? Is that a medical term?

Pay attention to the things that are critical in your life.
Play with your children.
Take time to get medical checkups.
Take your partner out dancing.
There will always be time to go to work, clean the house,
   give a dinner party and fix the disposal.

                                        Email from Julie

I'm not sure why Julie sent me this email. She sends me lots of things with little aphorisms and guidances in them. I don't send any back because I don't know where you get them and I couldn't possibly think of any. I am too busy wondering why I don't have a 'disposal' to fix in the first place. I also can't think why a nine-year-old girl would think taking time for medical checkups was an important message to pass on. I realise that the things Rita highlights for her kids as significant and the things I choose for mine are poles apart. My son, who is eight, has little sayings but they are almost all attributed to cute woodland creatures or Bart Simpson.

# CHAPTER 4

# Cathy – Gladys Three

Despite having grown up in the States, I had already come across things on this trip that I didn't understand. Richard and I went to a drive-in ATM bank machine in Westchester which had Braille on the numbers. How many blind people would use such a facility? Cathy was our next Gladys on the list, mainly because she lived practically round the corner from Rita. She lived round the corner but they didn't see each other. I thought there had to be something in that. Cathy had the distinction of being the only Gladys I ever attended a class with. Actually going to lessons was not my strong point in high school but Cathy and I did do social studies together. Cathy was two years older than me so I have no idea how that came about. Maybe they thought I would know more about life and society because I originally came from Europe. At any rate I think there was something about the topic which attracted a certain kind of teacher. I hadn't had much luck with social studies teachers. The first one had had a personal crisis and now I had to deal with what I felt were the poor communication skills of my new teacher. It is hard to imagine how she had ever come to the conclusion that teaching was a good idea. As far as I could see she had no skills of command whatsoever. What she did have were very wide glasses that flipped up into little wings at the side and an astonishing obsession with vowel sounds. Her accent was extreme New York.

'Seeeew, we aaare lookin' at Whirl Whor Won and Whirl Whor Two.'

Not only did she have a unique interpretation of historical facts but it was a skill to refer to the two world wars as if they contained no consonants whatsoever. No one was interested in either of the world wars, however badly they were pronounced. Most of the sophomore class were looking at what was going on outside the window. The teacher went on alone to expound her theories that America had saved the world on most occasions thanks to sheer will-power and the Hershey chocolate bar and how grateful the Europeans ought to be. I tried to be grateful but it was difficult to follow.

'Whirl Whor Won and Whirl Whor Too was in Yarrup and if duh Americans hadn't come duh Jurmans woulda won.'

It was like taking lessons from a John Wayne movie. Until recently I thought the notion of Europe as 'Yarrup' was unique to her, but it is now listed in the *Oxford English Dictionary* as the correct spelling for the American pronunciation of Europe. Perhaps she was just ahead of her time.

Despite my ancestors' own narrow escape from the German boot, my mind drifted off. Cathy would sit next to me and pass me notes. I remember there were a lot of notes in the spring of '72 because she was splitting up with her boyfriend Mike. I was sympathetic but hopeless. I knew nothing of dating, less about kissing and absolutely zero about sex. All the other Gladyses were older than me so almost everyone was dating. Everyone, I think, except Sue who liked to watch TV with me. Even her older sister, Anne (who would come to learn that boys were not her preferred option), had a boyfriend called Jimmy. Jimmy was kind of a geek and had very bad acne. I couldn't imagine wanting to get close to that at all. Rita talked about boys all the time, everyone wanted to go out with Ginger and certainly Cathy had no problem getting boyfriends. She was beautiful, with long, sleek golden brown hair, similar golden brown skin and a great waistline. She looked more like a Californian than a native New Yorker. She and Mike, who was very tall, had been going out for some time. Their breaking up was only important to me in that it might affect the casting for the musical. Both Mike and Cathy would audition and Regina would want them both to get in but if they broke up it might be tricky and . . .

Cathy and I would go to social studies, pay no attention at all and then rush from the room to be picked up by Anne (Gladys Six) in her Ford Pinto. By then the car would already be full of Gladyses and Cathy and I would have to ride in the hatch at the back. We were the youngest. It was what we deserved.

Richard and I had been invited to Cathy's for lunch at a quite specific hour so there was a bit of time to kill. I dragged Richard out to show him the haunts of my past. We drove along the shore to Mamaroneck, the town where I had once belonged. The south-easterly shore of Westchester County and the Bronx is indented with bays and estuaries of which Mamaroneck is one of the largest. It is an ancient place. As kids we used to catch horseshoe crabs in the harbour. Huge armour-plated black creatures with a spear a foot long sticking out of the front. One of the few species of animal and sea life that look exactly the same as they did in the period when dinosaurs lived. Still there, helping to clean the waters of Long Island Sound.

Thirty years later, everything was pretty much how I remembered it. Even all the old houses where I used to live. Six Wildwood Drive, where my sister had first come home as a baby. The Coulters' house opposite, where Mr Coulter, a local clothing store owner, had persuaded Dad in 1968 that coloured shirts were no longer effeminate. Ten Brookside Drive, where Lori (Gladys Ten) had once driven into the hedge while coming to collect me.

Five Seventy, Shore Acres Drive, where we had first settled in, pilgrim style, on the shores of the local waters. Here we had lived next to a retired couple known to everyone as Dearest and Uncle Frank. Next to them were Aunt Evie and Uncle Walt and their children Margie, Robin and Brucie. Everyone was your aunt and uncle. All the neighbourhood kids were awash with relations who kept an eye on you, yelled at you and bought ice-creams from the Good Humour Man who came round in his white truck wearing a peaked cap and black bow tie.

'This is the first house we lived in except it's brown now and it used to be green . . . and this is the house we lived in when my sister was born . . . my brother wanted Jeni to be a boy and when he was told about her he said, "Rats! I'm outnumbered."

'. . . and this is the harbour where I learned to swim and a boy died swimming under the docks and there used to be a great fourth of July party . . .' and on and on.

Historically, it was an interesting time. Vietnam was proving to be an American nightmare, civil rights protestors continually took to the streets and, even at the time, I had an opinion on all of it. In photographs taken then I am often captured reading the paper and I don't think it was just because my father was a journalist. The late sixties and early seventies was a period of political awareness the like of which we may never see again. Both the US and the UK have undergone massive political changes since then. I think the devastating legacy of both the Reagan and the Thatcher years was the destruction of a social conscience. They ushered in the era of the ego and the single-minded pursuit of self-achievement. We went from the ideals of John F. Kennedy, 'Ask not what your country can do for you. Ask what you can do for your country,' to Margaret Thatcher categorically stating, 'There is no such thing as society.'

Fitting in with American society back then seemed easy for the whole family. We moved often during our time in New York but the first property Dad rented was right on Mamaroneck Harbor. It

had a long gangway to a small dock. Those were long hot summers where we ran about in our swimsuits all day; where we lived
in and out of each other's houses and sat on the dock counting the
blasts from the volunteer fire department whistle to see if a fire
was close enough to take our bikes to. It seemed an innocent place
to me. Our neighbours were a mix of Red Cross helpers and volunteer firemen. Either blue-collar workers in boat salvage or
white-collar workers who went into the city every day. Everyone
had a family, a mom and a dad, and getting divorced was still a
rather shocking occurrence. Being foreign and from Europe, we
were far and away the most unusual people on the block. Now, in
the new millennium, there had been subtle changes.

Richard and I stopped at the main shopping street,
Mamaroneck Avenue. We parked for twenty-five cents, which is
what a slice of pizza at Sal's Pizzeria had cost when I lived there.
On this street my parents' friend Sid Albert had owned the coolest
shop in town. Sight and Sound sold melted coke bottles, posters of
The Desiderata and records. Sid had shocked the good burghers of
the Mamaroneck Chamber of Commerce by not only being a successful black man but by marrying a very white Danish woman
called Lisbet.

Sid liked to shock. He even managed it on my confirmation
day back in 1972. Lori, Gladys Ten, had made my dress for the
occasion. Lori was the daughter of a hairdresser and there was
nothing to do with scissors she wasn't adept at. She made me
dresses, trimmed my dad's beard and gave my baby sister her
first haircut. Although Lori was only sixteen the whole family
trusted her and Dad used to let her drink beer. The dress she made
me for the ceremony was traditional. Plain white with just a little
lace trim, long to the floor and with short sleeves. She had done a
great job and came with us in the car as we drove down to the
Danish Seamen's Church in Brooklyn.

The church was tiny and looked like an ordinary brownstone
house from the outside. Inside, it was small and plain with an

elaborate model sailing ship suspended from the ceiling as the only decoration. I don't know how many seamen from Denmark took regular refuge there but it was a small corner of New York that they could call home. Despite having no religion himself, Dad was pleased I was doing such a traditionally Danish thing. For weeks he had driven me up for my confirmation instruction at the church with Pastor Madsen. The day of the ceremony, the other Gladyses headed for the church along with Sid and Lisbet from the Sight and Sound store, the Danish ambassador and his wife and various other people who had been invited. The only other person taking a vow of adulthood was a young man, also thirteen. He wore a traditional dark suit and bow tie. When the moment came we walked up the aisle together as Pastor Madsen conducted the service in Danish.

The pastor wore Danish clerical robes that consisted of a long, black vestment and a fluted white collar which stuck out round his neck like a ruff to prevent injured dogs licking themselves. The boy and I knelt before him as more Danish was spoken.

'What the hell is this?' I could hear various Gladyses whispering. 'Are they getting married?'

Afterwards we drove back to Westchester and out to the very expensive yacht club on the Point. We weren't members but Dad had hired the place for lunch. In keeping with Danish tradition, it was very formal with many speeches and then comic songs written especially about me. Mum and Dad sat Sid next to the Danish ambassador. As he had a Danish wife I suppose they thought he and the ambassador would have some Danish things in common. The ambassador, however, had obviously never been near a black person who wasn't actually providing some service. It was not something he disguised well and Sid spotted it immediately. The Danish dignitary could clearly think of nothing to say and finally uttered the unlikely phrase, 'Have we met before?'

To which Sid smiled and replied, 'It's hard to say. We all look alike.'

I can't remember now why I got confirmed. Certainly it wasn't my parents' idea. In Denmark, all citizens are automatically a member of the church. I don't know if it's still the case but you used to have to apply to Parliament for leave to depart the fold. Dad was so anti-religion that he actually did this, which caused the devil's own trouble years later when we wanted to bury him in some corner that was for ever Denmark. I think I was already, at that age, battling between individuality and some terrible quest to 'belong'. To belong to almost anything.

Now, thirty years later, Sid's store was long gone. While Richard went to do some essential retail therapy, I sat in the sun outside Sid's old place and flicked through a copy of the local newspaper to try to reacquaint myself with the area. The *Westchester County Weekly* is a typical suburban broadsheet with huge savings on offer for sports recreation vehicles but it also had a worrying number of sex ads at the back. Were these around when I was a kid? Or had things changed that much? There was a whole section just for Threesomes.

'Attractive MWC, in their 30s and 40s seek attractive BIF for 1st experience, who is looking for friendship and who enjoys the finer things in life. Must be D/D free.'

I had no idea what any of that meant. I didn't even know if I qualified as a possible applicant. I didn't think so but it was hard to be sure. Richard turned up with a three-foot statue of Babe Ruth under his arm.

'Richard, do you think I'm a MWM or a BWM?'

'I don't know, darling, I expect you're entirely unique.'

As we drove up the Boston Post Road I saw Westchester in a slightly different light. As well as being awash with extremely appealing real estate it was clearly also packed with people seeking something new under the sheets. So much for the quiet calm of the suburbs.

Cathy was always the prettiest, the thinnest and, as far as any of us noticed these things, the richest. Today she is pretty, thin and rich.

So far, with the two women I had met, the notion of elastic social mobility in American life was not proving a strong point. Cathy lives less than a mile from the place where she grew up and no doubt belongs to the same tennis, yacht and golf clubs as her parents. The house could be a million miles from Rita and Ron. There is no antipathy but there is the chasm of a social divide. Where Rita's house would seem large to a European, Cathy's house would seem large to anyone. It stands on a wide street that would shriek affluence if anyone in the neighbourhood ever did anything so low as shrieking. The garden is vast enough to swallow up several more properties. Clearly they too have someone else to mow the lawn. The house next door was for sale for $700,000. It was much smaller and had infinitely less 'yard'. I tried to picture myself living there but failed.

Cathy had married a boy called Billy who had been at high school with us. Rita had been to the house before but it was a long time ago. At first she took us to the wrong place where we met a neighbour. Everyone was laughing as we finally trooped up Cathy's path. She emerged looking stunning in a stripy top and deep tan. Her husband Billy and two of her daughters were just leaving for the day with their dog.

'I thought I'd set the dog on you.' The first words Cathy had spoken to me in maybe twenty-five years. The dog was going mad at the possibility.

We were all amused. I shook hands with Billy and there was much chatter. I suspect everyone concerned was nervous. Cathy told us that one of her three daughters was at rehearsal and it occurred to me that that was the sentence our parents must have used a million times. I gave Cathy and Billy's youngest child a tin shaped like a London bus. I couldn't remember if it had toffee or tea in it or indeed why anyone would want such a tin, which I had bought at the airport.

'How long has it been?' asked Billy.

'Nearly thirty years,' said Rita.

'Well, for you all!' snorted Cathy. 'Because I am only twenty-nine.'

'You were a mere twinkle in our eye,' I assured her.

Cathy's house was gorgeous. Rooms spread from other huge rooms. There appeared to be a different sitting room for every mood or activity you might choose. Pensive in the sunroom, crossword-puzzle solving in the sitting room, musical appreciation in the den and on and on. In a large basement room of indefinable use there was a television, which was at least four foot square.

'It's great for Nintendo,' Cathy told me. We were all slightly hyped up to see each other.

'You look great,' I said to Cathy, because she always did and I suspect she always will. She looked down at her brown arms and shrugged.

'Tanning – it's the only thing I do well. If you do something well you should stick to it. Would you like a drink?'

Billy had also found something he did well at. The handsome young boy had grown up to be in charge of tax exempt securities for Morgan Stanley.

'Tax exempt securities?' I said. 'That must be fascinating. You must be desperate for him to get home and tell you all about his work.'

There was no pause as I made the glorious discovery that the concept of irony was not lost on Cathy. She nodded enthusiastically.

'Absolutely. He gets in the door and I say "Tell me every little thing about your day."' She looked around her huge kitchen in which we were sitting. 'It's been very, very good to us.'

Billy and Cathy had dated in high school and then for ten years didn't see each other until they met again at the tenth Gladys reunion. The Gladyses had met first followed by a high school party which I had missed due to working in pantomime that year.

'I owe my life to the Gladyses. No question,' said Cathy.

I asked Cathy for tea.

'Hot tea?' she asked as if I had suggested vodka stingers first thing in the morning. I watched her boil the water on the stove. It took for ever.

'I don't make tea – work with me here, people.'

Neither she nor Rita has an electric kettle. I decided that Americans are very advanced till it comes to the subject of boiling water. Maybe it's because they only ever need to use the coffee machine. It was when she made me a second cup by pouring some more from the pot and putting it in the microwave that I could sense Englishmen turning in their graves. I talked about going to England. About how strange it had been as I had never lived there before.

'Still,' I said, 'England is that bit smaller and that bit easier to excel in.'

Cathy dismissed this with a wave of her hand. 'In China you would have done well! Really, a little dark eye make-up and you would have done fine. There are a billion and a half of us – we love her. I saw you on TV one time and you're talking with a British accent and it seemed so weird to me. I'm yelling at the TV, "Sandra, are you unwell?"' She paused for breath. 'I love England. You know, British women have lovely skin because it is so wet and damp over there.'

So far I was batting two out of two for finding others who also thought the year of the Gladyses was important.

'It was good. We had a lifestyle, we had a menu.' She paused and then added, 'None of us named our children Gladys. I find that odd. I don't remember my junior or my senior year,' she said. 'High school was the year of the Gladyses.'

Of course, just like Rita's mother, Cathy had a story to embarrass me.

'Do you remember when you went up to Wing Foot to be a caddy?'

I am mortified even now. Wing Foot Golf Club was and still is one of the most exclusive clubs in the United States. It is, to paraphrase Mark Twain, where the rich go to have their good walks spoiled. That year my brother, Nick, then fifteen, was making good money working at the club as a caddy. He would go up there at weekends and come back with cash in his pocket. I thought it was a great idea, so I went. Cathy is still wide-eyed with the horror of it all.

'My brother John comes home and says "Sandi is trying to caddy". And you kept going up there, kept going up. I don't know if you could have carried the bag. What did you do?'

'I just sat on the bench all day. They kept saying no. And the caddy master was so horrible that it just made me more determined. He said to me, "You can't even come in this room," but I was very, you know, American rights. So I would go up and sit.'

Cathy was incandescent at my stupidity. 'Sandi, the only reason caddies are men is because it's a horrible job. Girls go babysitting because there is no heavy lifting. They should have said to you, only idiots caddy, and you'd have said, "You're right, I'm out of here."'

I was not the only one to be teased that afternoon. Rita had had a racy reputation with boys in high school which Cathy set about taking apart as fantasy. Her manners were impeccable. Just when the stories began to become uncomfortable she softened the moment by telling a story against herself.

After high school, like Rita, Cathy had been heading for a theatrical career. Then, while she was at college, out of the blue her father died. This unexpected event left her feeling responsible for her mother and three younger brothers. She had switched immediately from studying theatre to business administration and graduated on a fast track.

'I just knew I had to start bringing in the cream of wheat. I just felt this overwhelming obligation to help.'

'Are you sorry?' I asked.

'That my father died? Yeah, it bummed me out. It was a big bummer ... It sucked.' We both laughed at her deliberate misunderstanding of my question. She smiled and became serious again. Said she had no choice. That she had grown up 'in half a minute'. Sitting in her comfortable home she seemed philosophical. 'It all worked out.' She sees the horror of show business from her brother-in-law who is a well-known actor. I asked her if she had a job now and she was very clear.

'I don't work because I don't have to. My husband says I am on full scholarship.' So there she was, content with three kids, a husband and a dog.

She knew that she was not leading a typical American life, that she was fortunate. 'I am very happy. I have three wonderful children, a dog I can't stand, I love my husband . . . if it ended tomorrow, it's been a great ride.'

I looked at Gladyses Two and Three, the next in line after me. Both had made their children the focus of their lives. I wondered if this was what I was going to find with all the eleven middle-aged women who had once had different dreams and ambitions.

I asked Cathy about the future. About life after the kids had grown up. She talked vaguely about 'issues' and 'getting involved'. She was exercised about a homeless man who had taken to walking around the local area. He had a shopping cart piled high, which he trundled past, as she said, 'Two to three million dollar homes'. She had a good heart and it obviously bothered her but when I asked her what she intended to do about it, she shrugged.

'I don't know. I haven't gotten to that point yet.'

Cathy remembered everything about the year of the Gladys Society. That we took naps on the asbestos curtains lying around on the stage. It was, she said, 'The happiest time we ever had. Nothing went wrong for us. It was fun, no one got into any trouble, no one had really hit the real world yet. We always just had the best time. I never felt that connected again.'

The three of us planned a reunion. We said we would eat spaghetti, drink iced tea and play charades as we had done every

Friday night that high school year. It would be at Sue and Anne's old house, which their parents had sold years ago.

'It's going to be tough,' said Rita, who is practical.

'I'll rent it,' said Cathy, who is rich.

We laughed at the idea that it might still not be too late for me to graduate high school. 'Will you come if they let me?' I asked her.

'I'll laugh my head off,' she declared. 'I'll be in the front row throwing popcorn.'

'Come into the city and I'll take you out for dinner?' I suggested.

'Yes!' she said emphatically. 'Rita? Your mom still on Blossom Terrace?' It was all very familiar and jovial. 'Sandra,' she called as we began to drive away, 'get rid of that fake accent. It's not working for you.'

It had been a wonderful afternoon and we had promised much more but I am fairly certain that I will never see Cathy again. I discovered that she had been to Europe and had not looked me up. I think she was really just being polite to someone who had called. Cathy has made a tidy life for herself in which I do not belong.

That evening, quite late, Richard and I made our way to the Algonquin Hotel, one-time home to my comic muse. Richard headed off to make some calls and I was glad to be alone; I needed to think about my trip so far. It was in this legendary hotel that the American writer Dorothy Parker had often strutted her stuff in front of an admiring throng. Here my great-aunt Signe Toksvig had broken bread and martini glasses with Parker and the rest of the Round Table. I sat and thought about Cathy and Rita. I have three children, just like them, but the circumstances have been so different. I had mine after much thought and deliberation with my then partner, Peta. She bore the children and I earned the money. We went through much pain at the hands of the British tabloid press and we are both fiercely protective of our brood. Although we have separated, the children are still the single biggest focus of both our lives. I do not have a husband to put me on scholarship and I suddenly wondered if I minded very much. I miss the kids terribly when I travel. Indeed, it is because of them that more and more I try to find work that allows me to stay at home and still earn the money. So I can make a living to look after them and collect them from school, cheer the netball matches and moan over Latin homework. I have no choice but to keep working, yet I wonder what kind of person I would be if I had to give up my work and stay at home all the time. Great-aunt Signe and her husband, the Irish poet Francis Hackett, never had children. She used to say 'Our books are our children,' which, as a child, I thought was immensely noble although it made meal times rather dull. Now, I don't know what I think.

I sat in the legendary Blue Bar where some of the greatest wits of America once gathered, drank and fell. I was very tired. I felt like the invisible woman. The bar staff in the small and not very blue place are breathtakingly old. They have clearly served many a dry martini straight up with a twist, but not to this woman sitting alone in a corner. I melted into the oak panelling or, given what I know of American history presentation, possibly facsimile oak panelling. I had imagined a rather fine literary scene for myself, sitting silently, toasting both my great-aunt and the fine Miss Parker – 'One more drink and I'd have been under the host.' No one came near me to assist in this venture. Would those two ladies who battled the inequities of their age have sat alone for twenty minutes and been ignored? Would they not have stomped to the bar and demanded attention? I don't know. I wanted to commune with their ghosts and in a strange way I became them instead. Crowds of people came and left, great packs were joined together with much embracing and 'come here and give me a hug' while at the bar a couple kissed loudly like the bad plumbing on the fourth floor. All the while I was ignored. For a brief moment the one elderly waiter passed right by me. I was tucked in the far corner. I had deliberately chosen a chair directly under the television so that I didn't have to look at it. The sound was switched off so it was not a problem but it was tuned to *Relentless News Are Us* and I couldn't stand the endless flickering intended to suggest urgency. I tried to be oblivious to the news and the waiter was oblivious to me. Entirely new people, people who might never have been to the Algonquin before, arrived, blown in from an evening that promised snow. They stood and shivered, uncertain for a moment, and then found a table and almost instantly the octogenarian waiter and a drink.

I was not there. I was Dorothy or Signe or any one of the women sitting solitary and unnoticed. I'm sure I read that Dorothy Parker died alone and penniless in a New York hotel room. It always broke my heart but now I feel I understand it. I suspect if she had been a man it would never have happened. I think someone would have noticed. Finally, I went to the bar and said to the bartender that I couldn't get the waiter's attention. He said, 'Well, you have mine.'

I ordered my drink but it was not what I had wanted. I wanted to be dignified. I wanted to raise a single eyebrow and find that service was at my elbow. Probably, sadly, even stripping would not have done the trick. Moments after he had left me in the bar, Richard had returned to tell me that he had been waiting in the foyer when a stark naked man clutching his private parts (those jewels that we will all grab unless a man holds on to them tight) had appeared behind the golden lift doors, shouted 'I want a man', and disappeared upstairs again. Jolly japes but there is a part of me that knows with certainty even such a man could have got a drink with no effort in the Blue Bar. I think about those brilliant women, those witty women, those women who took the English language as a personal challenge and I know they would be disappointed. Nothing has really changed. We have gone nowhere.

Richard and I sat down to plan the next trip. The waiter appeared immediately. The whole thing put me in a pensive mood. I have spent a lifetime leading what others regard as an unconventional life. For me it was not a matter of choice. I simply am, in the words of the song, who I am, but perhaps deep down I envied my friends the conventional life after all. Always comfortable in Richard's company, I said I thought in another age we might have married and been very happy. He agreed. We might have had one child he said and then found that the getting of it wasn't quite our thing. It's so English. That exchange of body fluids not being quite the thing, and yet I should have liked the social acceptability of it all. The 'Have you met my husband?' of it all. He would have sat with me till I had got the drinks I wanted and then we would have gone our separate night-time ways. Maybe it would have been better. I never meant to be a person at the barricades. I am very tired of fighting for everything. To me the Blue Bar at the Algonquin Hotel in New York was a holy shrine to learned women. I had no idea I wouldn't be able to get a fucking drink.

# CHAPTER 5

# Joyce – Gladys Nine

*'Have a nice day.'*
Nicole, desk clerk at Hertz

In case anyone else is thinking of doing it – tracking down eleven women in the United States and meeting up with them is not easy. Besides which, life still has to go on and bills have to be paid. Richard and I returned to the UK where our small cowboy film had some degree of success. Ever the bold entrepreneur, Richard had used it as a calling card to get us some paying work. As he is the organiser and I merely smile at the camera, he was now busy with our growing broadcast business. I had, however, begun a journey which was too tempting not to continue, but I was nervous to travel alone. Enter Paul, my very English next door neighbour. Paul is a nice young person with a remarkably good dress sense for a straight man. He is single and, despite heading for middle age, he has never been to America. It was perfect. I wanted to carry on searching and he wanted to see locations from movies and TV shows.

Chronologically, the next Gladys should have been Ginger, Gladys Four, who I thought lived in Ohio or California. I hadn't made any contact with her at all and I was beginning to think it was possible I might never find several of the Gladyses. Paul wanted to go to New York, so I decided to track down the women geographically instead. Having started in my home town I would gradually spread the circle outwards until I had found them all. So far, I had met two out of the twelve who were living the lives of their mothers, a mile from where we grew up. Perhaps I would find them all within a tiny radius. Proof, possibly, that feminism may not have been the triumph women in the sixties hoped for.

A couple of months after my first trip, Paul and I went to rent a car at Westchester County airport in New York. I had tried to rent a car from a local firm but they only rented to 'American citizens', which seemed a little short-sighted. As far as I can see most American citizens have their own car. Ron told me to rent from Hertz. 'I always rent from Hertz when I am on business.'

Corporate loyalty is the watchword of today. Every time I buy my groceries some bored clerk asks me if I have a loyalty card. I don't. I am not loyal to anywhere but the moment always embarrasses me. I look down at my collection of essentials and mutter, not the truth – that I don't have one – but that I have 'forgotten it'. I am too mortified to reveal that I have been disloyally bringing home the bacon from elsewhere. I am foolish, of course. If I were loyal and had a card to prove it then I could gain all sorts of benefits. I use my American Express card a great deal and once managed to gather enough points to get a free case of wine. It was marvellous and had only cost me £30,000 worth of other goods. It is all part of the globalisation of the world. To the British, I think, it is still a very American concept that customer service is conducted with a sanitised and rehearsed script. Everyone is busy wishing me 'a good day' but I'm pretty sure no one actually believes it.

So I went to Hertz for Ron's sake. I was being loyal to Ron who was being loyal to Hertz but Nicole, who worked and may indeed still work at the Hertz desk at Westchester County airport, didn't know that. She didn't know that I represented a good corporate customer. I seem to remember that it is Avis who claim to 'Try Harder'. At any rate it wasn't Nicole. In between spending what could only be an inordinate number of hours perfecting the pearl polish on her nails, Nicole had also taken the time to learn a great deal of 'Hertz Speak'. I knew her name was Nicole partly because she told me, 'Hi, my name is Nicole. How can I help you today?'

But mainly because it was printed on a large name tag above her left breast. Nicole gave me the whole spiel about my 'vehicle requirements', the 'options to buy a full gas tank now' and the 'insurance limitations' which I needed to 'initial' for. She did all this without once looking at me. At various points I tried to interrupt but she had learned her sales monologue and I was frankly an irritation. Paul said nothing. He is a perfect English gentleman and knows that these corporate moments do not require interaction from the customer. I think I fall somewhere between the American ability to be demanding and the English inclination towards reticence. I try to get what I want but do it with superb manners. Still I could not get the unstoppable Nicole's attention. By now she was on the downward pass of her rollercoaster of rhetoric. Finally, I said rather loudly, 'Nicole, I am trying to speak to you.'

Nicole was not bright. She looked rather shocked that I knew her name.

'Hello, Nicole,' I said, looking at something other than the top of her head for the first time. I was trying to develop, at the very least, a short-term relationship with my new friend.

'My name is Sandi and the thing is, Nicole, I hire cars all over the world, all the time.' This, I felt, was both friendly and a bit of a corporate carrot for her. I thought it was good to start by appearing to be a potential gold card member. A woman who, if satisfied, could help keep Nicole's entire fleet on the road.

'And when I hire a car the person renting it out tells me how much it will be and then when I bring the car back it is always exactly double that. So what I was hoping, Nicole, is that you could tell me exactly how much it will be before I leave to save me the shock when I return.'

Nicole looked at me and then looked back down at her computer keyboard. 'There is the basic rental and then you get unlimited mileage and with the full gas tank—'

'Sales tax,' I said. 'There's always sales tax and state tax and federal tax and, I really want to know everything, Nicole.'

This concept of divulging the actual cost of something was new and took some time. I made her write it down. It was indeed double the figure we had both first thought of. I smiled. Nicole banged some keys down on the desk. She hoped that I would 'have a nice day' but she did not smile. I should have known then that we were not about to get the best car in her keep.

Paul and I were left to wander out into the car lot on our own. There we found I had rented the oldest white Ford Escort still in the Hertz fleet. I wasn't sure, but I thought I could just hear Nicole laughing from her desk. Paul, bless him, never said a word but we both knew it was my fault. Like almost every American car, the Escort was an automatic but only in the sense that it changed gear at random and with no particular pattern. I jerked and juddered out of the car park and named the car Betty in a pathetic attempt to feel better about the whole thing.

I took Paul to my old haunts. It was the second time I had done that for an Englishman and I was beginning to feel like a tour guide. We stopped at the Larchmont Tavern for a beer. I didn't even know the tavern was there when I was a kid but clearly it has been around for some time. Although it was only the afternoon, regulars were sitting at the bar, nursing a drink and watching the TV. Rita doesn't like Larchmont because people double park.

'They think they are so rich they can park wherever they like,' she said the last time she and I drove through. From one neighbouring town to another there is clearly a huge social split. I remember not going to New Rochelle with my mother because it was where the lower class lived. So much for the classless society.

I asked the bartender about routes out to Long Island, our next destination. He said it was a very difficult journey and some distance. Rita and Ron had been anxious about us going to the airport alone. They had said it was 'at least' an hour away, which turned out to be twenty minutes. So far everyone we had spoken to displayed terrible anxiety about going anywhere, about how ghastly the traffic would be, how long it would all take and how strange everything would be when we got there. The next journey we were facing was supposed to be a nightmare in every respect.

Long Island is not an island at all but you would need to be God or a spaceman to know that, for it feels like an island. In fact, it is a narrow strip of land, about twenty miles south of New York City, which plunges out into the exposure of the wind and waves of the Atlantic Ocean. We were in search of Joyce, Gladys Nine. Joyce had been the production manager on *The Skin of Our Teeth*. I only know this because I looked it up in the yearbook. Exactly what Joyce did on the show I have no idea, which typifies the attitude of actors to anyone who hasn't got lines to say. She was there, she did something, the play went on, I remembered my lines and didn't fall over the furniture. Joyce was another of the Italian Catholics in our gang with the same lustrous dark hair as Rita, which suggested a life soaked in olive oil. We had not been close at school and the last time I had seen her had been a dozen years before.

As a teenager Joyce had lived with her parents down near the railroad tracks in a house that shook as the commuters trundled past. Some time in 1990 I visited her in a small apartment where the trains too appeared to pass through the living room. She was married to an Irish-American accountant and they had recently had a second son, David. He was perhaps a year old when I met him. He was cute the way babies are but Joyce never let go of him for a minute. He just sat on her hip, whatever she was doing, his head lolling against her shoulder. I was anxious.

Joyce went to get Rita and me a drink.

'The baby doesn't seem right.'

'Sssh,' said Rita.

'He doesn't hold his head up. Shouldn't he hold his head up a little? He doesn't look around.'

Rita changed the subject. We didn't talk about it. Joyce was sweet and welcoming. We never mentioned the baby's head. Well, you don't.

> *Gatsby believed in the green light, the orgiastic future that year by year recedes before us. It eluded us then, but that's no matter . . . So we beat our boats against the current, borne back ceaselessly into the past.*
>
> F. Scott Fitzgerald, *The Great Gatsby*

I wanted to go to Long Island for lots of reasons not the least of which was to see Joyce but also because the island has a long history in American literature. It was in Asharoken that Antoine de Saint-Exupéry penned *The Little Prince*. It was in Northport that Jack Kerouac, that great traveller of American ways and byways, was legendary in his disgraceful and drunken behaviour at Gunther's Bar and it was in Great Neck that F. Scott Fitzgerald started work on *The Great Gatsby*.

The drive out to Long Island was a burden for poor Betty but a surprising pleasure for Paul and me. It was unexpectedly pretty. Many lovely tree-lined streets in among the overdeveloped bits. Ron had advised us to look out for Leonard's on Northern Boulevard. This, he said, is the monolith where Jewish people go if they want to have 'an affair'. I thought he was talking about secretly sleeping with your dentist but as it happens a Jewish affair involves hundreds of relatives and many kosher knishes and knibbles.

Betty, not being a limousine, looked out of place in the parking lot. Leonard's is the Mecca of Empire Ballroom styling. Even through the windows the chandeliers appeared to have cornered the market in crystal. Paul and I wandered in to see if we could get a brochure. I think we screamed 'gentile' the minute we set foot in the place. Many men were busy with many ladders, hanging things from many cornices. A large man with a ten o'clock shadow at nine in the morning appeared in the foyer wearing a tuxedo. It is a difficult look to carry off at that hour.

'Vat you vant?' he enquired with a welcome apparently scratched out not all that long ago on some Russian steppe.

'We were wondering if we could look around?' I said brightly, trying to endear myself to the Eastern-bloc bouncer. I glanced at Paul to see if he could get away with pretending to be a highly successful orthodontist for five minutes. Our new friend, however, didn't even have Nicole of Hertz's way with corporate charm.

'Is clawsed,' he barked, positioning his huge frame so we couldn't even see the ladders. We never got to admire Leonard's. For reasons I can't recall, I went to the Mamaroneck senior high school prom with Stephen Benjamin in 1972. He was a nice Jewish boy. Just think, if I had stuck it out and married him, we might by now be having an affair at Leonard's in Great Neck for one of our little Benjamins. Funny how life works out. And if we had really wanted to push the boat out we could even have drunk Long Island wine.

As far as archaeologists can confirm there has been wine-making in France (that's France, Europe) since 600 BC. I don't think that's true for a moment. I think people have been getting out of their heads since there were first people. They have, however, been making wine on Long Island since 1975. I consider myself to be a bit of an amateur wine buff and, oddly, despite there being over twenty wineries on the small strip, Long Island vintages are not something that have ever crossed my palate before. I glanced over the offerings in a small leaflet about the local produce. Apparently the wines win medals but I have to confess to being a snob when faced with things like Bedell Cellars of Long Island, whose red table wine has a picture of a pick-up truck on the label.

Still, I was determined to see the vineyards. Ron and Rita had both assured me that these were 'at least' two hours away at the far end of the island and that there was no way I was ever going to get there in the time I had set aside. En route, Paul and I looked at a map and realised we were going to pass one with no trouble at all. I was beginning to suspect a general fear among Americans of travelling anywhere other than round the corner.

The Old Brookvale Chardonnay Vineyard is situated in some of the lushest and richest countryside I have ever driven through. Set against a glorious backdrop of mature trees, the vineyard could easily be sitting on some French hillside. Old Brookvale ('Highlight', so they say, the 1996 Chardonnay) consists of fifty-five acres of grape harvest. The locals will tell you that is about one acre for every room in the manor house. Sadly, the place is closed to the public but apparently one of the earlier owners was Margaret Emerson. Her father invented Bromo Seltzer, the ultimate hangover cure, which seems appropriate. I like it when life has a certain symmetry.

Ironically, the place is neighboured by the rich, richer and fantastically rich. Vast houses rattling with people who can afford to bring in wine from France one bottle at a time on a private jet. This is a land of serious money where one family home had a par three golf hole on the front lawn. These people do not need to pop next door for a drop of the homemade brew.

There is, and always has been, a strong link between the demon drink and the writer. If people remember F. Scott Fitzgerald it is as a symbol of the jazz age, of excess and of alcohol. It is an image which suggests he tossed off a novel while mixing a Tom Collins. The truth is he took his writing seriously and spent hours shaping his work through many drafts. His recurring theme was the ideal of aspiration. The belief in upward mobility which seems in many ways to define the American character. The rags to riches story that my family had so spectacularly failed to fulfil. There is nothing left to see of Fitzgerald's time on Long Island. He died drunk and in debt

in Hollywood. My heroine, Dorothy Parker, died drunk and in debt
in New York. I wouldn't want to put myself in the same league but
if it happens to me could someone please note that I saw it coming?

I don't know if the American poet Walt Whitman was a drinker
but I guess he probably was. Lush or not, he was a native Long
Islander. The 'Good Gray Poet' is now considered by many as
America's greatest verse smith. His birthplace on the island is not
easy to find, lying as it does in West Hills opposite a meat market
and between a Rite Aid pharmacy and a petrol station. Pictures
that I have seen of him with his long grey beard make him look
like Father Christmas's slightly less successful older brother. Sadly,
The Visitors Interpretive Center and Library was closed when we
got there, so we didn't get a chance to see the 130 portraits of the
uncamera-shy poet or the desk where he wrote much of his work.
All we could see was the carving above the door which read:

> Stay with me one day and a night
> and I will show you the origins of all poems.

This struck me as incredibly arrogant until I realised what a
devil for the flesh old Whitman had been. His seminal work,
*Leaves of Grass*, was considered obscene when it was first published. One of the first people he sent it to, the poet John Greenleaf
Whittier, threw the collection on the fire. This is not the reaction
any writer wants to his work and makes me glad of the modern
predilection for central heating. But, from what little I know of that
opus, it contains quite a heady mixture of lust, sex, sweat, beauty
and death. Taken in that context, 'Stay me with one day and a
night and I will show you the origins of all poems' strikes me less
as an arrogant piece of poet speak and more as a classic line from
any boy trying to have sex.

A yellow schoolbus-load of kids was dutifully trooping round
the Whitman gardens. I wondered what the teachers would tell the
children about him. Certainly that he lived and worked during the
American Civil War when he served as a nurse to the wounded.

Certainly that in his time he befriended presidents and became a literary figure for the nation. But would they mention how he suffered for his work? How he lost his job at the Bureau of Indian Affairs because of his 'vulgar' verse? That he refused to dilute his work which spoke of his love for other men, his homosexual passions and his long-term 'special friend' Peter Doyle? The website for the birthplace is not exactly clear. It talks of his being 'depressed and moribund' and 'roaming the streets of New York by day, searching for companions among streetcar drivers and ferryboat pilots, and spending his nights in a seedy Bohemian café', but there is no mention of what he sought from these drivers and pilots. The gay community claim him as their own but the curator of the birthplace gives a strong sense that he was just looking for a nice chat or a game of whist. I would have liked to have talked to him. To have shared the burden as well as the joys of being gay and a writer.

The gate to the gardens was open and Paul and I could just see the small wooden house built by Walt's father. I knew from my reading that this small dwelling contained 'the borning room' where his mother let Walt slip from between her legs. Externally it looked like an ordinary unpainted clapboard house but any aficionado would tell you the place had unusually wide doorways, high ceilings and built-in cupboards, all of which Walt's dad got credit for. Built-in cupboards? Wide doorways? My guess is Mrs Whitman had a hand in the plans.

### Amityville, Long Island

> *George and Kathy Lutz moved into 112 Ocean Avenue on December 18. Twenty-eight days later, they fled in terror.*
>
> Jay Anson, *The Amityville Horror*

Joyously for me, Joyce had moved to Amityville. Mention where you are going to anyone in England and they say, 'Do you mean like *The Amityville Horror*?'

And of course you do. The town council is unhappy about it. Their website directs you to much pleasanter possibilities in the community. Everyone is encouraged, for example, to join the thriving Parrot Fancier's Club (Meetings – Second Thursday of each month at the Masonic Temple at 14 Avon Place in Amityville, from 6–10 p.m.). The club, you will be pleased to hear, is 'dedicated to the ethical treatment of psittacines in captivity as well as their preservation in the wild'. I had no idea psittacines were in trouble. Indeed, I thought they sounded like a bit of a bar snack. At the club you can find all the 'parrot-related information' you will ever need, as well as meet Dr Heidi Hoefer, who is willing to microchip 'parrots larger than a cockatiel'. There is more to it than you might think and in my desire to help can I just pass on this message to everyone:

WARN OTHERS ABOUT THE DANGERS OF TEFLON. BUY YOUR BIRD-LOVING FRIENDS A BUMPER STICKER THAT MIGHT SAVE A LIFE. PLEASE READ *MURDER BY OVEN* (available via *www.parrotfanciersclub.com*) IF YOU THINK IT CAN'T HAPPEN TO YOU.

I'm afraid I don't know what the dangers of Teflon are except that you can't get the bird to stick to the pan however hard you try. Still, if the parrot world is not for you, how about the Paumanauke Drum and Dance Team who 'strive to travel the good path through the practice of the Native American Traditions of Modern Pow Wow Drum, Dance and Customs'? Or the Junior League or the Knights of Columbus or the Masons or anything in fact other than driving down Ocean Avenue to stare at the house at 112.

I don't like horror films. Actually I don't like anything scary at all and find the death of Bambi's mother about the celluloid limit of what I can cope with. I have never seen the movie of the Amityville Horror but the story resonates. The house where the supernatural events supposedly took place still stands in a beautiful, leafy, suburban street leading down to the water's edge. It is a white clapboard place with its wide front facing side on to the street. The house has two storeys with further rooms in the attic and a boathouse right on the Amityville river. Anyone who owned such a place would think they had, as the records describe, 'attained a trophy-size piece of the American Dream'.

About the time I was first settling in America, the house was bought by Ronald DeFeo, Sr, a Buick dealer from Brooklyn. The place was called High Hopes and Ronald moved his wife Louise and kids from the city out to Long Island in high hopes of a better, quieter life. Now Ron had made a few bucks out of selling cars but it may shock some people to discover that that didn't necessarily make him a nice person. By all accounts he had a vicious temper which he took out on his wife and his eldest son Ron Jr, known as Butch. (Of course he was. I think every American story should have someone called Butch in it.) As Butch grew he too developed a temper and soon father and son were quite often beating each other up. This was clearly a problem that Ron Sr decided to solve by throwing money at it. Butch started to get whatever he wanted. Aged fourteen, he was given a $14,000 speedboat to cruise on the river.

Soon Butch turned to drugs and became even more of a tricky child. He got a job in the family car business but was paid whether he showed up or not. (Can anyone else see parenting hints in this story – or is it just me?) The young man grew gradually more charming with various episodes in which he calmly threatened friends and family with a loaded shotgun. Then there was a final confrontation over $20,000 Butch stole from the business and things were ready to come to a head.

At three in the morning on Wednesday, 14 November 1974, everyone at 112 Ocean Avenue was asleep except lovely young Butch. It seems he had decided the family had to go. He wasn't willing to sit around and wait for some Teflon-induced killer fumes to off them all, so he took a .35-calibre Marlin rifle from his rather extensive weapons collection, went to his parents' room and shot them. First his father with two bullets, then two into his mother. His two younger brothers, John and Mark, were next with single shots, followed by his sisters Alison and Dawn. The whole thing took about fifteen minutes. Butch cleaned himself up, drove to Brooklyn where he disposed of his clothes and the gun in a storm drain and went to work at the family dealership.

When the police began their investigation it was Butch who alerted them to the murders and who was incredibly helpful in their inquiries but it didn't take long for the truth to come out.

'Once I started,' he explained to the police, 'I just couldn't stop. It went so fast.' So, Butch went to prison for twenty-five years on six counts of second-degree murder. I have no idea why second degree and not first but he's still in some New York jail. So it was horrible, but it's what happened next that annoys the locals. A writer called Jay Anson wrote a supposedly non-fiction account of what happened to the new owners of 112 Ocean Avenue, the Lutz family.

'Their fantastic story, never before disclosed in full detail, makes for an unforgettable book with all the shocks and gripping suspense of *The Exorcist*, *The Omen* or *Rosemary's Baby*, but with one vital difference . . . the story is true' trumpets the back cover of the paperback. The book went on to become a highly successful film telling how the Lutz family was forced to flee the house in February 1976 due to the place being awash with demons and all manner of evil spirits.

There are those who doubt the whole thing. I don't want to be horrid about George Lutz, partly because I never met him and partly because he's probably still alive and Americans will sue you in a heartbeat, but he does seem to have been a bit of an amateur dabbler in psychic phenomena, demonology, witchcraft and so on. Certainly *The Amityville Horror* contains every sort of ghoulie, ghostie and demon you could ever hope to gather for a bit of sheet-shaking and chain-rattling. A veritable panoply of poltergeists. It can't have been much fun living there what with the pig floating outside the living-room window with bright red eyes, the walls covered with slime, the porcelain lion that bit George on the ankle, the endless levitating out of bed for Kathy and the demonic, hooded figures who insisted on hanging about the fireplace. Yet the Lutzes were built of stern stuff and hung in there for twenty-eight days before fleeing into the arms of Mr Anson and the world of publishing.

Today the tale is debunked and derided in the town but the new owners at 112 are still disturbed by the presence of ungodly people; folks like myself and Paul who drive by just to see the house. It is not the image that a town whose very title is friendly wants to present.

The first European name for the village of Amityville was Huntington South West Neck, which is a mouthful on anybody's postcard. By 1850 there were nearly a thousand locals in Huntington South West Neck and the people decided to come up with something snappier. I think they were right. The name of a place does matter. There are towns on Long Island called Hicksville and Plain View which just displays a poor sense of PR. Now, unlike the early settlers, the Huntington South West Neck people hadn't just arrived from somewhere they could simply transform into New Something-or-other, so discussion about a new moniker took some time. The most popular version of the change to Amityville is that there was so much argument about a suitable choice that a Mrs Ruth Williams, wife of Nathaniel Williams, tried to calm everything down by declaring, 'Friends, what this meeting needs is some amity, otherwise we should name our village Contraryville.'

There are two things I like about this tale:

1. That there followed a fairly strong movement to adopt the name 'Contraryville'. This, I think, says a lot about human beings the world over.

2. That it is Ruth's husband, Nathaniel, who is mentioned in all the history books, despite having had nothing to do with any of it.

The history of the town proceeded rather sedately with the usual openings of schools, churches and, for me, the memorable unveiling of the Long Island Home for Nervous Invalids in 1881. I like the idea of being a nervous invalid. I picture myself a weak waif of a woman who is startled each time a syringe plunger is drawn back. The town once suffered a hurricane and once an earthquake, and Al Capone used to summer here, but it is none of these things the world recalls about Amityville.

Time for lunch with a Gladys. Joyce lives in a small neat grey house in the town, in yet another suburban street. The only daughter of Italian descendants; I have no recollection of her parents at all. I think I would have recognised her if we had met by accident. Hair still shoulder-length, neatly dressed with a thin body. She was thin when we were at high school and, despite having three kids, she was still thin. I blame genetics. It's funny about one's lot in life. I inherited a zest for living, absolutely no money and a waistline which makes me look like I swallowed the Michelin man.

You do get a good welcome from an American. Annoyingly, I think Joyce was as pleased to see Paul, whom she had never met, as she was me. I wish I could capture her speech pattern on paper but it is impossible. Of all the Gladyses I would say Joyce has the strongest New York accent. She refers to her home as 'Lawnge Guyland' and talked about what a 'lawnge toyme' it had been since we had seen each other. From the moment we arrived I had a sense that Joyce rarely entertained and was even more rarely the focus of a conversation. She seemed to need to unload and was more than happy to fill me in on her life. We had a meal in her kitchen which contained the largest stove I have ever seen. Built in 1953, it was a kind of oven on steroids, a huge thing. Joyce laughed about it.

'I keep waiting for it to doye so I can get a nooh one but it just keeps going.'

After high school Joyce went to college in Oswego in upstate New York. She was studying elementary education when she met and married her husband Alan. She never pursued her career in education because 'we needed the money', so after graduating she went to work in the personnel department of a construction company in Manhattan. I don't remember Alan but there are pictures of him on the fridge. He has bright red hair and comes from an Irish background although no one is sure where exactly as his father was an orphan. Alan works as an accountant in the city. He at least pursued his career.

Joyce and Alan have three children: Matt seventeen, David thirteen and Kelly five. I wondered, fleetingly, if every Gladys would be at home with three children but no two lives are the same. David was at home. He had been to the orthodontist and had the day off school. He was the baby I had met in Joyce's flat. He didn't eat with us but spent his time on the computer. A sweet boy with glasses and something of a faraway look. He clearly suffers with some physical difficulties and Joyce explained that he is going to need jaw surgery as it is not developing properly.

'He is what they call "low tone",' she explained. 'He is borderline cerebral palsy but no one really knows . . .'

The troubles Americans can have when faced with medical bills, no money and no national health system tumbled to the fore. She and Alan have spent almost every penny at the doors of doctors, for the problems David has are not the kind covered by insurance. Without a shred of self-pity Joyce talked about her life. About the privations and the heartaches and about how David has the reading age of a nine-year-old and every night is a 'homework battle'. David came through to get himself a drink. He hugged his mother from behind and kissed her on the top of the head. She stroked his arm and he stroked back. He smiled at us and went back to his game in the other room.

'For a lawnge toyme we didn't go any place. We just stayed home. PS, everything was so expensive.'

Saying 'PS' and adding a postscript to her own sentences was one of Joyce's interesting speech tics. She did it all the time when telling a story and it made the telling even more mesmerising. I looked out at the small neat yard around the small neat house and knew that fate had confined her to this suburban patch of Long Island. The British moan about the National Health Service but if your kid is ill it doesn't suck your finances dry. As if their troubles with David have not been enough, Joyce's oldest boy had also had difficulties.

'The kids were over near the Carvel,' Joyce said, as if I would know where that was and of course, in a way, I did. The Carvel is the ice-cream stand near the centre of any small New York town. I have never been to Amityville before but I don't doubt for a moment that I could find it.

'There was some trouble and Matt got hit on the head and back with a metal bar.'

The injury was serious and has affected him. Joyce was anxious about him. 'He should be applying for college now.'

Of course he should. It is part of the aspirational American way for almost everyone to go to college now. When I was a kid, finishing high school was still the big deal. People were embarrassed if they didn't get their high school diplomas; now it is all about degrees. Matt recovered from the attack and then one of his closest friends killed himself 'two days before the prom'. Another friend died of meningitis at school. Matt, she said, had become cautious and wanted to stay at home. Marooned perhaps, as Joyce and Alan have been, in their nice, safe house. Understandably, Joyce was worried about her kids growing up on the 'eyeland'. She explained that many of the youngsters from Amityville go away to college, don't make it and come back early. They don't want to leave this narrow strip of land. Maybe we all just want to be at home.

Joyce was the perfect hostess. I explained how interested I was in the area and she took us for a drive. On the surface Amityville hinted at none of the troubles which worry Joyce. The town looked sleepy with its neat bandstand, small shops and closed museum. It was the website image of 'The Friendly Village', a 'Tree City of USA' on which you can hear rather a jolly tune called *The Codfish Ball*. If it had been up to me I would have gone to a bookshop and a place that sold the medal-winning Long Island wine but Joyce's choice was much more interesting. She took us down to the water. Down to the beach area where Matt works as a lifeguard in the summer. We looked out across South Oyster Bay to the narrow sands of Jones Beach where I had once got spectacularly sunburnt on a summer's outing with the Gladyses.

En route we drove past all the waterfront properties that represent the big money in the area. Many of the large houses backed on to canal-like fingers of water running parallel to the streets. Here, boats as big as houses were neatly parked.

'You get a lot of flooding in the winter,' Joyce explained. 'PS, It happens in the spring also.'

To prove the problem, one house had been lifted wholesale up in the air and was in the process of being made eight foot taller than it was before. We drifted past in Joyce's car and could see the men working underneath it. Stripped of its clapboard coating the place looked like a giant doll's house made entirely of wood and paper.

It was an interesting trip. Not just into the area but into Joyce's dreams. Each place had been carefully earmarked over the years by her as to whether or not she wanted to live in it. As we drifted leisurely along she talked about the Junior League to which she belongs. Strictly speaking it is the Junior League of the Amityville Women's Club whose 'primary purpose' is to 'raise funds that are donated to local community groups and national charitable organisations'. It also provides scholarships for students living in the town. It is clearly an important focus for Joyce. Apparently the big

event for the Junior League is their Holiday Homes Tour at
Christmas which she mentioned frequently. Several local homes
are decorated for the festive season and then several hundred
people pay $10 each to look around them. (Tickets available mid-
November at Johnson's Florist, Amy's and Self-Image Salon,
downtown Amityville.) This year there are five homes including
the properties of Mr and Mrs Nick Rosser, Mr and Mrs Skip Weir,
Mr and Mrs Paul Schmidt, Mr and Mrs Norman Rafsol and Mr
Donald Boyd. I don't know why Mr Boyd wanted to keep in with
the women's Junior League and I certainly don't know why the
female members of a women's club had all been happy to have
neither a first nor a last name of their own.

The fund-raising clincher had been the days when the previous
owners of 112 Ocean Avenue allowed their house to be included in
this tour.

'It was great when it was the "horror" house but not any more.
The people don't even like you to stop outside,' explained Joyce.
She didn't like to stop outside either. The people of Amityville are
naturally reticent about the whole thing. The official statement
says, 'In regard to the village's reluctance to discuss the subject,
this kind of publicity trivializes the death of six members of the
DeFeo family,' who were, after all, friends and neighbours of
people still living there. It is understandable but I couldn't help
but gawp as we drove by.

We headed up to the yacht club where Joyce turned the car
around in the drive.

'Everyone is a member except us, of course,' she explained. 'I go
there so often with my friends I think they think I'm a member.'

I damned the yacht club and damned myself. Joyce was a good
woman playing a tricky hand of cards with great style but she did
not need me or my pity. I had been patronising in my presump-
tions about her life.

'We are so lucky,' she kept saying. 'So lucky.'

Paul and I waited for her daughter Kelly to come home from

school. For Paul it was a quintessential American moment as we stood in front of a white picket fence waiting for the yellow school-bus to deposit the child home. She was a beautiful little thing as she stepped down, in a green tartan skirt with little straps over her shoulders. Her long hair was a glistening auburn. A very Irish-looking lass, who would not be out of place in a Dublin street.

'From the first moment I met Alan I wanted a little girl with red hair,' smiled Joyce, as mother and daughter hugged on the street corner. Ah, that gene pool selection thing to the fore. Kelly's book bag was nearly as big as she was but she was proud of herself and stopped on the steps to let me take her picture.

'We are so lucky,' repeated Joyce and I believed it.

She packed up sandwiches for us for the inevitably difficult and worrying journey ahead. As we made our goodbyes, she suddenly said, 'I didn't know if you would stay for dinner – if we would get talking and forget the time.'

And I wished we had. I wished I was not such a restless traveller.

---

*Footnote:* My stomach has become a thirteenth Gladys and is leading an entirely independent life attached to my body. In America, the amount you eat on a daily basis just goes up and up. Statistically, Americans are now the fattest they have ever been. The fattest nation on earth.

# CHAPTER 6

# Lori – Gladys Ten

*All you need in this life is ignorance and confidence; then success is sure.*

Mark Twain

The next Gladys, geographically speaking, was Lori and I must confess to something of a sigh of relief as we headed towards her. Lori and I had kept in touch and I already knew that she was not married and did not have three children. The others had been lovely but I was ripe for a change. Lori has been important in my life. She not only made my confirmation dress but also the full-length gown I wore to the Senior Prom in the summer of '72. I shouldn't have gone to the prom at all. I was only a freshman but, on reflection, the aforementioned Stephen Benjamin was unlikely to get any other date so he asked me. I know the movies make such events very exciting but I have to confess I found the whole business rather tiresome. I think it was an early indication of my impatience with and lack of interest in heterosexual mating rituals.

Rita, however, could not have been more excited about her invitation. I can't recall who she was going out with at the time but I don't think it was important. If our dates had known how far down the list of essential requirements for the dance they came they might never have turned up at all. Rita was a junior and going to the senior prom was something of a pinnacle in her rather heady dating career. She was determined to look better than the best and she was equally determined for me to take an interest. I don't know why she chose me. I expect none of the others had the patience and I didn't have the wherewithal to say no. Consequently she and I visited every dress shop in Westchester in search of the perfect gown. I didn't bother to look in the shops for myself. I was a tiny little thing and everyone knew the only answer was to get Lori to make me a dress.

In the end Rita chose a flowery item with curious capped sleeves. I think it was constructed of entirely man-made fibres and it sparked and floated in equal measure. When she finally settled on it I didn't say that I was fairly confident it was the first dress we had looked at a month previously.

The Gladyses made their lives in Sue and Anne's house and it had been decided that all the members of the society going to the prom would depart from the one house. Sue was not going and was dressed in her usual outfit of jeans and green poncho. Her non-attendance at the event meant she was organising everyone else.

'Okay, I have the camera. Now everybody has to get dressed in here, then I will call you and you can all come down the stairs for the Grand Descension. Sandra, get your feet off the bed.'

Lori and Leslie helped me get dressed in the long blue gown they had designed and made for me. Downstairs we could hear the boys arriving, one by one. Anne appeared in her gown, then Ginger and finally Rita in the much sought-after flowered item.

'What do you think?' she kept saying. 'You think it will be okay?'

'You look great.' Everyone soothed her nerves and prepared to depart. Ginger looked lovely, Rita looked splendid, Anne looked like she'd rather be playing hockey and I looked like an over-dressed team mascot.

'Everybody ready?' Sue called from the bottom of the stairs. It was quite embarrassing really. One by one she made each of us girls who had a date descend the stairs to orchestrated 'oohs' and 'aahs' until we reached the arms of our intended who handed us an orchid in a box. It was a traditional if entirely useless gift. This large, unattractive flower was to be pinned just below the left shoulder on your dress. My gown was of rather light cotton and the corsage caused something of a droop in my creation so that I appeared to have developed dropsy at an early age.

All the boys were wearing rented tuxedos in a variety of lurid colours but only one very wide form of lapel. Their shirts were ruffled and pinioned into place with velveteen bow ties. Stephen Benjamin was in pale blue. He hung his gift of a small ornamental garden on my left tit and leant forward to kiss me. I tried to keep my mouth shut partly because of my orthodontal braces and partly because I didn't want him to kiss me. I was much shorter than my beau and the upshot of our awkward encounter was that he left a wet ring round my mouth, I got a sensation in my neck akin to whiplash and he got a small gash from the pin of my corsage. I don't know if anyone else got injured; I was too busy trying to work out how many more kisses were part of the prom package. As it happens I had rather a busy evening.

The sports hall had been decorated with balloons and streamers. There was music, laughter, a faint smell of old gym shoes and a lurking danger of verrucas. All the girls had made a great effort. Like me and Rita, many of them had been to every dress shop in Westchester. If only she and I had gone to another county for not one, not two but three other girls had bought precisely the same dress as Rita. I don't remember much about the evening except that Ginger and I spent it trying to dance between Rita with her beau and any couple identically dressed. It wasn't a great event. Stephen Benjamin did more of that kissing thing, Rita spent quite a lot of time in the powder room hiding, and my corsage seemed to be unique in having some kind of green-fly problem. The only positive thing was that no one had a dress like mine. I was wearing a Lori/Leslie original.

No one was surprised when Lori went into the dressmaking business for a living. It was only her family who were amazed that it involved the theatre. Lori is a passionate woman and the focus of her passion when I first knew her was entirely to do with the theatre. I have an abiding memory of her standing on the make-up counter backstage at school and scrawling across the wall of the dressing room, 'Welcome to the theater – you fools, you'll love it so! LA.'

Lori did not come from a family with a wide-ranging view of the world. Both sets of grandparents had emigrated to the United States from Italy in the 1920s. Her maternal grandfather had arrived with a wife and child, who both promptly succumbed to some New World fever and died. Meanwhile, her maternal grandmother had married in Italy and subsequently lost her husband. This made her a burden to her family so when the New York widower wrote for a new bride from the old country it was arranged that he could have the widow. It was an unhappy marriage, producing only Lori's mother. I remember the grandmother, who, in her lifetime in the United States, learned not one word of English. After he retired the grandfather returned to the old country. He lived in a *pensione* in Rome but only lasted a month before he returned. It wasn't, as Lori said, what he thought it would be.

Lori's father was a hairdresser and her mother worked all through Lori's years in high school because the family needed the money. The family was not rich, did not travel or go to the theatre, yet Lori would go on to see the world, work in professional theatre for many years and learn to speak both Italian and Thai. From her family, she said, she got 'a good basis of ethics' but everything else in her life came from elsewhere.

Lori lived in a much tougher neighbourhood than my parents had settled in. Their house was an alien world to me, in which her mother shrouded all the furniture in loose covers of clear plastic. Bill Cosby used to say kids with those backgrounds grew up to be either priests or killers, but Lori was unique. Coming from a life where doing well meant not getting arrested, she led the way in her family by going to college. I was, as Lori says, her first 'international' friend. My family opened a new world which she had never even heard of.

Over the years she and I have done some travelling together in Europe. Once we went in search of her distant relatives in Italy and spent a drunken lunch trying to communicate with twenty excitable Italian uncles, aunts and cousins using a Collins phrasebook and the limited English of the local Roman Catholic priest. Travelling, she said, was like a drug. 'The more I went, the more I wanted.'

Having been signed up for a play production class in her freshman year, Lori came under the spell of Regina, the drama teacher, and then the Gladys Society. When she left high school, she went to the University of Richmond in Virginia to study technical theatre. Before long she was the chief cutter/draper in the wardrobe department at the distinguished Cincinnati Playhouse. Then, after fifteen solid years of theatrical success, out of nowhere, Lori gave it all up and joined the Peace Corps. Actually, I don't think it was out of nowhere. Even at a distance, I knew she had been getting restless for some time. The death of many gay theatre friends from Aids had hit her hard and she was looking for some new meaning in her life. She met a Russian émigré and they became friends. It fed into her desire to see more of the world.

Lori talked to a Peace Corps recruiter who persuaded her to apply. She couldn't quite believe it. '"Are you sure? I make little outfits." What could they possibly want me for? So I applied and within two weeks I got a phone call because I had "special skills"! But you always knew that, didn't you?' she grinned at me.

The Peace Corps placed Lori in Jamaica as a sewing instructor but the environment didn't suit her. She developed chronic asthma problems and came home. She was distraught. Determined to make her new life work, she had sold her car and got rid of her apartment. Now she had to live in a tent in a friend's backyard because they all had pets and she suffers horribly from allergies. She decided to forget about the whole thing. Friends got her a job at the Folger Shakespeare Library Theater in Washington, DC.

'But here's the thing – the Peace Corps headquarters is also in DC. It became so clear to me that I needed to do this that I called them and the recruiter remembered me. She said she would try to see if she could get me another placement. A few days later she calls me and says "Do you want to go to Thailand?" I said "yes". "Do you not want to think about this?" "No." My parents thought I was insane. I had been rejected and now I was going again. But that is my personality. You persevere. I did two and a half years in Thailand and it was the best thing I have ever done.'

Lori returned, speaking fluent Thai (apparently she found it hard – 'You have to be so girly') and went straight off to graduate school. Today she is the Director of International Student Services at a New York college and still my friend.

We drove up to see her in her new life on campus. The college (founder and first president, Reverend Mother Mary) stands in the town of Purchase, twenty-eight miles north of Manhattan. My great ambition in life, once my children are up and grown, is to go back to university and I was thinking about education in America as we went. There is an extraordinary magazine in New York City, which you can pick up from a dispenser on any number of street corners. It is called *The Learning Annexe* and contains hundreds of classes which you can take to make yourself a better person. That month's Holiday Issue was on 'Love, Sex, Spirituality and Healing' and there were some fantastic offers. There was, for example, Deepak Chopra, who, in one 'incredible evening, will lead you on an inspiring, in-depth exploration into the world of consciousness and the mechanics of reality making'.

I loved this idea. I didn't know what it meant but it could patently change your life for a mere $39. To be honest, I don't know what reality making is. I would have thought reality either was or it wasn't but Deepak made it sound like basket-weaving – once learned then always a skill at your fingertips.

As I travel the world what I find is how little I know. Consequently *The Learning Annexe* was sorely tempting. How thrilling to learn 'How to Write a Book on ANYTHING in 3 Weeks . . . or Less' or 'How to Write a Hit Song and Make LOTS of Money'. It made me realise how much the experts have merely been blinding us with science when so many skills are so easily acquired. Where, for example, was 'Instant Piano For Hopelessly Busy People', when I was struggling the old-fashioned way with learning to read music? ('In just one session you can learn enough secrets of the trade to give you years of enjoyment at the piano.') I would have gone but I just didn't have the time.

I got many things from my American childhood but an education was not one of them. The Native Americans no doubt knew more than I ever will and even a pilgrim adept at butchering a cow in the correct manner would be one up on my education. Today, learning is highly prized and everyone is expected to absorb a lot but, I suspect, to little purpose. Not just in America but generally. I went to university with girls who could split an atom without breaking a fingernail but had no idea how to wire a plug. It is the age of industrialised specialisation, which fails to equip us for real life.

The US Census provides a fascinating map about the state of American education today. The dark green bits on it show the states where more than 85 per cent of the people have a high-school diploma or higher qualification. The paler the colour, the less education per capita. Worryingly, Texas, home to a possible president at the time of writing, was practically white.

*I think it should be compulsory that by the age of twenty-one everyone in this country has been made to leave the United States for at least a year.*

Lori, Gladys Ten

Driving in America is odd. Any kind of distance is done on a highway or freeway from whose tarmacked surface you can see nothing of the area. Trees line the roads and travelling many miles gives you no sense of geography. It's like driving with blinkers on. You emerge at your exit and the whole landscape can have changed without any warning.

Purchase is not that different from Mamaroneck and Larchmont. It is still part of Westchester County and you enter through similar wide, leafy streets. The college looks like any typical small-town American campus. There are many parking spaces surrounding vast green expanses of lawn leading up to an architecturally mixed bag of buildings. Students wander across the horizon in small groups. They walk slowly as all students seem to, having yet to grasp any concept of life being short.

Unlike Amityville, the naming of Purchase was rather straightforward. In 1661 Chief Shanarocke of the Siwanoy tribe (a branch of the Mohegans, in case you're interested. I have lots more but you need to write to me) turned the land over to one John Budd of Southold, Long Island. John did what all those new people stuck for an enterprise seemed to do – he started a gristmill. I'm not entirely sure what you do with a gristmill but I do know that in the early days they were springing up all over the place. Anyone making gristmill starter kits must have made a fortune. This John Budd was so busy with his new mill that he forgot to register the land, which was rather critical.

About thirty years later, another Native American, Pathungo, reclaimed the land and passed it on to John Harrison of Flushing, Queens, in New York for forty pounds. This John did register the land and thus it became known as Harrison's 'Purchase'.

The place went through various phases, including a rather golden era in the 1860s when Ben Holladay, the 'Stagecoach King', and his wife Ann tried to recreate the Wild West on the estate. They imported buffalo, elk, antelope and deer that rummaged about the place. They built rather a fine mansion but lost all their money in the first great stock market crash of 1873. The next people to take over the mansion, Whitelaw and Elizabeth Reid, were also rather jolly folk and were the first in Westchester to install both telephone and electric light. Unfortunately the place short-circuited and burnt down, which was sad, although presumably they were at least able to phone for help, which was good.

Undaunted, the Reids set about building a stone castle instead. It is the focus of the campus today. An extraordinary castellated affair with panelled rooms imported from an old château in Poissy, France, and bits and bobs of English history shipped in wholesale including some windows from a church in Salisbury. The former Catholic girls' boarding school moved from New York City to the rolling hills of the 100-acre estate in 1951. Now the college is close enough to New York City to be attractive to students but far enough away from Manhattan to make their parents feel calm.

As Lori says, 'They send them to suburbia because they think it will be safe.' No one I know has ever heard of the college although one of the Kennedys went there. One thousand three hundred undergraduates and one thousand graduates roam about in the shadow of Reid Castle busy being educated as 'ethically and socially responsible leaders'. The Catholic heart of the place is apparent in the statuary and there are lots of dead nuns buried in the back. Since the 1970s, however, the place has been an ecumenical home to the liberal arts.

Lori is three years older than me. She is a comfortably large woman with a vast chest which challenged the bra-sellers of Thailand.

As usual, she greeted me as if no years had elapsed. 'Hi,

sweetiepie, another day, another thousand dollars. Once every ten years you show up like a bad rash that keeps coming back . . .'

I had brought her a gift of Cadbury's Flake – a chocolate bar that crumbles the minute you unwrap it. She was thrilled.

'We don't have it here. Your mom actually turned me on to them. The first time, I said, "It comes like this?" It's a mess. You have to work at them. Great when you are cooking.'

At the college, Lori deals with about a hundred foreign students from thirty different countries, providing a resource centre for them, working on cross-cultural acceptance, dealing with immigration issues and acting as an advocate on campus for those new to the States. It isn't always easy explaining America to people who have conceived life in the States by watching *Star Trek* and *Bonanza*.

Photographs of Lori with her friends from Thailand, Thai masks and pictures of Buddhist monks line the wall of her office.

'They are a tiny people. Can you imagine me with them?'

Lori was in Thailand from 1990 to 1992 and the evidence of its importance to her is everywhere. From the Certificate of Appreciation from the United States of America for her work to the large notice which reads, 'The Peace Corps – the toughest job you'll ever love. Ask me.'

We sat in the castle amid panelling once owned by Napoleon III and talked about America, the country she now represents to newcomers. She was abroad during the Gulf War and was ashamed of the propaganda she heard broadcast on the international radio station Voice of America. It made her a lifelong fan of the BBC World Service and I realised I felt pride in that. She spoke of *her* pride in the freedoms of America but echoed what I had thought about some of the education.

'I appreciated the US so much when I came back. I am allowed many freedoms in this country to do, or at least attempt to do, what I want. If I wanted to take on a non-traditional job then I might have to swim uphill but I could make that choice. Somewhere else I might just have got married at twenty-two and had babies. It's a good country but it's not the only good country. There are lots of them. This one just happens to be mine.' She shook her head. 'I find the ignorance of the US college student about geography scary. The kids who think Africa is a country.'

Lori wanted to take us to The Cobble Stone, a local diner, for lunch.

'Can we walk?' asked my English companion.

'No!' she scoffed. 'There are no sidewalks. This is Purchase.'

It was our own geographical ignorance. Over lunch we talked about the past. She was unimpressed by how long we had known each other.

'Why shouldn't we still be friends? It just means being there for someone.'

Lori was happy to look back but I don't think the Gladys connection had been as strong for her as it was for myself, Cathy and Rita. She seemed to live in the present and look forward to the future in a way that I envied. I also felt a twinge of jealousy that, despite all her travelling, Lori was quite clear about her nationality and where she belonged. A simple thing but something I had not yet achieved. I had thought, because of my upbringing, that at heart I too was an American but I was beginning to have second thoughts.

We headed back and wandered across the lawns to the purpose-built apartment complex where Lori now lives. From the elegant old-world confines of the castle we moved to 1960s functionality. Former student accommodation has been turned into a very nice three-bedroom apartment for the Director of International Student Services.

We headed into her computer room to see if we could search out any more of the Gladyses over the internet. In particular, we were looking for Leslie, whom Lori had been very close to at high school.

Lori leads a single life. She and I are both wide-hipped women who would have had no trouble birthing, but neither of us has ever bothered. I had been blessed with kids by another route but it didn't look like being part of Lori's life.

'You never going to settle down with a volunteer fireman?' I asked as she fired up her computer.

She looked over the top of her glasses at me. 'Now that you mention the volunteer fireman, I might give it a second thought.'

Lori has had several boyfriends over the years whom I have met but there seems to be no one at the moment.

'A woman in her forties – the pickings are slim.' She shrugged. I asked her if she couldn't find some nice woman instead.

She laughed. 'Women are always coming on to me but it's just not my thing. I'm just not playing on that team.'

'Twenty-five per cent of the Gladyses are gay,' I told her.

She looked sternly at me. 'Sandi, are you thinking this through? You care about statistics?'

She is a whiz on the computer and the entire time we were talking she tapped away.

We tried to think what we could recall about Leslie. Like Lori, she had been a junior, so she was a few years older than me.

'She was divorced at one point,' Lori came up with. We tried searches in Massachusetts and New York and found a Leslie with the same surname in Worcester, Massachusetts, but the details didn't seem right.

'I would guess that she is at a school,' Lori mused. 'Let's put the name in with "edu" and see what happens. For all we know she has a porn site and we could easily come across it.'

We found a Leslie in herbal medicine and knew it wasn't her and Leslie's architectural page . . .

'I don't think so . . . not her . . .' A different site lit up on the screen. Lori peered at it. 'Georgia . . . Georgia . . .' Suddenly she started to get excited. 'Oh, oh, she *was* in Georgia! She did go down to Georgia. This might be good . . . I'm just having a flash—'

'It's your age,' I replied.

'Shut up!' she boomed and we both laughed. Lori read over the information on screen and announced, 'I believe it's cracked . . . Leslie . . . set and costume designer . . . She's in Georgia. I remember now.'

I was starting to get nervous. 'Do you think she's going to want to see us?'

'I bet it wouldn't hurt.'

There was a phone number and we began to egg each other on to call but neither of us really wanted to. Finally, Lori looked at me and picked up the phone.

'Ballsy, aren't I?'

There was one call to a switchboard and then Lori got a direct line number. Neither one of us had spoken to Leslie in over two decades but Lori placed the call and someone answered the phone.

'Hi, Leslie? This is Lori . . .' I could hear the shriek from all the way down south. Lori grinned at me. 'Oh, it is the right Leslie. We've done a good job . . . I was hunting you down because a friend of ours is here – Sandra Toksvig.'

Lori handed me the phone and I didn't know what to say. I told her about tracking down all the Gladyses and how that meant she was included and I was very English because I was very sorry, etc. I don't know why I mentioned being English. My accent was becoming more and more American as I spoke. My first sensible remark was to ask her where she lived. Her response was a little surprising. She lived in Georgia, as we had established, but she was getting married in two weeks' time. Did we want to come?

'Lori,' I said, 'do you have a hat? Leslie's getting married.'

'That means there's hope for us.' Lori looked at me. 'Well, hope for me.'

'That would be wonderful!' I kept repeating until Lori took the phone back. Everyone was giggling now like the schoolgirls we once were.

'You needed this on a Monday afternoon, didn't you, Leslie?' Lori laughed. 'Congratulations on getting married, you're giving me hope.' It seemed we had caught Leslie just in time. She was now not only costume and set designer at a university theatre but also artistic director in charge of the season. She had been heading out for auditions when we called.

By the time we hung up we were planning to fly to Georgia, rent an open-top car, be very 'Southern' and wear navy.

I was a little nervous. 'Do you want to go to a wedding?' I asked.

'I think it is kind of odd.'

'We've got to have a hat!' I repeated. 'Maybe,' I said, 'we could take some time to—'

'Be bad?'

'Chill . . . as the English say.'

Lori looked at me. 'Since when do the English say that?'

'Are we really going to do this?' I asked.

Lori nodded. 'You know, Sandi, we have a way of making things happen.'

We were both over-excited and I was late getting back. Sadly I missed *The Learning Annexe* class where I was going to learn to 'Speak French in Only 3 Hours!' and for just $8. Still, I could do that some other time. How difficult could it be? French people speak it all the time. I was floating on air. I was going to a Gladys wedding!

# CHAPTER 7

# Leslie – Gladys Eleven

*'I wish I could care what you do or where you go, but I can't . . .
My dear, I don't give a damn.'*

Margaret Mitchell, *Gone With the Wind*

Okay, settle down for a long read. I have enough to say about a
Gladys wedding in Georgia to rival *Gone With the Wind*. Paul and
I returned to the UK and a couple of weeks later Richard, bless
him, flew out to the wedding with me. If in doubt about an escort
to a big occasion always take a gay boy. They know how to dress
and are fabulous with other people's maiden aunts.

Leslie and I had not been close and had not even exchanged
Christmas cards in the last thirty years. Truth be told, when I rummaged in the photo album of my mind, I couldn't remember that
much about her. How bizarre to be going to her wedding. Richard
and I were on an economy drive and flew into Newark Airport
before heading off for a special overnight deal at the Airport Hilton.
The hotel was yet another example of the mass homogenisation of
product throughout the world. It could have been anywhere except
there were signs all over the place indicating that everyone within
spitting distance was pleased that I had 'given them the opportunity to serve'. Being pleased about these things only happens in
America. It is creeping into the UK, but in the old country people
do still seem to serve because that is how they get paid.

I was glad that the Hilton people were pleased, although this didn't actually help with the problem of finding anyone on the staff with whom I could communicate. The Newark desk clerk was handsome and young and nice and very Latino. It had been a long flight. Richard and I were carrying a great deal of luggage (well, we *were* going to a wedding), plus a heavy camera to record it all. I am a nervous traveller and I was thrilled to have arrived at all. I practically fell on the front desk to complete the formalities. When this was done, I enquired, 'Do you have a porter?'

I smiled at the desk clerk as I provided him with his opportunity to serve.

'On the second floor, left out of the lift,' he replied in a thick Spanish accent and smiled back.

I was tired. 'What's he doing there?' I asked.

'Who?' said the desk clerk.

'The porter,' I replied.

'Second floor, left out of the lift,' he repeated, now less friendly.

'Could he come here?'

'Who?'

'The porter.' The clerk opened his mouth but I stopped him. 'I know, second floor, left out of the lift.' I tried a simpler concept. 'Do you have someone who could help me with my luggage?'

There was a long silence. I think he had preferred the banter about non-existent porters. We stared at each other for a while but I stood my ground. Finally he sighed and came out from round the desk. He grabbed the lighter pieces of our luggage and moved away to the lifts. The three of us proceeded to the bedrooms on the tenth floor in total silence. Richard didn't want to get involved and the Latino and I were divided by distant approaches to the same language. I could sense that we were equally disappointed at where we had ended up. This was not what either one of us had expected from America.

It had been an unimpressive return to the land of promise. We had stepped off the long flight and straight into an even longer queue of people. The line of disgruntled immigrants trudged down a dull white corridor with an oppressive polystyrene ceiling about to join the floor below. Through the broken ceiling tiles I could see that the roof void above was actually the same height of the room again. It had been concealed for many years. There was a general air that it was best not to give passengers too much of a sense of space. Each one of us arriving cattle was required to go into a numbered booth to spend time alone with an immigration official. I looked down the line through the plate-glass divisions.

For their initial welcome the USA had provided a uniform front – bored young men with very short hair. They slumped over their work as we waited behind the yellow line to get some individual attention. I took the time to fill in a form which guaranteed that I had not been involved in 'moral turpitude', didn't have any 'communicable diseases' and was not in the country for 'the purposes of sabotage or espionage'. It seemed a strange lesson in honesty. I was honest and said truthfully that I hadn't come to do anything bad but if you were already a bad person then it probably wouldn't worry you to tick the wrong box; to claim to be a cheerful tourist when your head was just bursting with turpitude.

'What the hell is turpitude?' I whispered to Richard.

'Just say no to everything,' he replied. 'Don't cause trouble.'

When it was finally my turn, the bored young man went through the motions. He mumbled 'Welcome to America', but I think we both knew he didn't mean it and he just wanted everyone to move on so he could go home. The trouble was I knew the queue would be full of people coming for the first time. Foreigners with their heads filled with images of *Star Trek* and *Bonanza*.

At the gate, the driver we had booked was waiting with Richard's name on a piece of paper. He was a large black man who talked on his mobile phone continuously but also insisted on pushing the luggage trolley. This made us fantastically slow as we progressed through a British sort of building site – much inconvenience, much dust, no actual work going on. British Airways was 'Sorry for our appearance' and so was I.

The driver was suddenly off the phone and addressing us directly. 'I have a surprise for you folks.' And indeed he did. Some miles away in a frozen car park a stretch limo was waiting for us.

'That is a $75,000 Lincoln Town car stretch,' our new friend informed us.

It was classic mafioso with gleaming black paintwork and banks of white lights etched on the side. We stepped inside and found ourselves in a space the size of my living room back home. Two banks of leather seats faced each other with just enough room, if we had desired, for a reasonable ping-pong table in the middle. I opened a small wooden door in the panelling to reveal champagne on ice, while above, narrow strips of neon changed colour as we drove – blue, green, white, purple.

'The TV gets too much interference,' called Stuart, the driver, from his seat some miles in front. 'But I have a very fine tape of the film *Shaft*, if you want.'

We didn't want and neither did he. The car was great but I was a little financially anxious until we established that we weren't actually paying for this vehicle. Stuart was merely en route and we were a slight hitch in his system. In between his relentless telephoning, he explained, 'It's party night. I'm going "sharking". I am on "the recruit" for a nice piece of lady.'

He told me this in confidence. I was clearly too far from being such a 'piece of lady' to feel offended. Although we had just met he had no doubt that I was no longer sharking and it's true. If there was to be fish involved in my evening then it would probably be lying in the bath with a tuna sandwich. Stuart had driven many 'famous people' all of whom, without exception, I had not heard of. I have never had much time for the notion of 'fame' and Stuart confirmed the ridiculousness of it all. People achieve celebrity for the wrong reasons today. They don't conquer Everest or tingle the world with their spine-chilling talent. They arrive on the public scene through mediocre television and money.

We had turned up on the night the results of the Presidential election were due to be announced but there had been some flaw in the system and no one could agree a winner. There was relentless arguing going on and I began to think that it was time for the world to do things in reverse. The United States endlessly sends monitors to oversee struggling democracies and check their election procedures. Surely now was the time to fly in a bunch of Somalis or Serbs to check the whole thing out? It is a curiosity of the American system that there are no independent senior statesmen. That everything and everyone from judges to dogcatchers is elected and therefore, by definition, partisan.

The contest had come down to a few votes in Florida, a state governed by George Bush's brother with the polling overseen by Kathryn Harris, a close friend of the Bush family. It was not a good day for transparent democracy. I was quite prepared to take the job myself although I did think I would need to see the house first. The big news from Dade County was that someone had been accused of swallowing a 'chad'. Chad was the word on everybody's lips. The new buzz word. Apparently it is the small piece of paper that is punched out from an automatic voting card. I had quickly learned that there are many types of chad – pregnant ones that are punched but not punched out, hanging chads, which cannot bear to leave the mother-ship, and some, presumably, which represent a small country in Africa. Ninety-eight million votes and it had all come down to one man possibly – or not – swallowing a chad. Stuart, our driver, was right. It made America look ridiculous. It is curious that the Founding Fathers (always to blame here. The mothers were too busy baking) legislated for this great hoo-ha.

Election Day is always the first Tuesday after the first Monday in November. Then, six weeks later, the electors meet in their respective state capitals and cast their electoral votes; three weeks after that the House of Representatives gets together in

Washington to count the votes (who would even think of phoning them in?) and then three weeks after *that* the new president finally gets the job. Now this leisurely approach to the whole thing was designed to allow time for many horses to cross the country to carry news of the will of the people. Here we are in the twenty-first century and it takes just as long. Go figure. What I think it shows is a measurement of the process of a modern American lawsuit, which clearly moves at roughly the pace of an eighteenth-century horse and buggy.

Apparently the whole debacle is upsetting many peripheral industries. The tuxedo hire people don't know whether or not to order in loads of cufflinks shaped like Texan boots, which will, of course, be much in demand if Bush finally stands on the podium. I don't know what the Gore people would hold their cuffs together with. Giant lips perhaps.

Florida is an interesting place. Each of the fifty states has certain laws which are unique to that territory. In Florida they actually took the time to legislate against anyone having sex with a porcupine. My mother was once arrested and brought back in a police car for taking a walk in Miami while heavily pregnant with my sister. This is not surprising when in a place like Hialeh, Florida, ambling and strolling is a misdemeanour.

We were not going to Florida nor indeed were we all that interested in where we were – Newark, New Jersey. We were merely on the way to the Gladys Wedding of the Year in Atlanta, Georgia. As usual, I had many books on the subject. *The Fodor City Guide to Atlanta* has been compiled by 'a diverse group of native Atlantians'. This particular tome finds it hard to believe that 'as late as 1993', you couldn't 'get a decent latte in town' but then along came the Olympics and Java jubilation.

There is a certain style of writing that is employed when Americans think they need to be formal. 'No metropolitan Atlanta jurisdiction to date has enacted a restaurant-focused no-smoking ordinance.' That's nice, isn't it?

Lori joined us at the Hilton and we sat planning our weekend away. Certainly Atlanta seemed to offer some strange dining choices. Why not dine at:

'Eureka! Sitting on the patio at dusk watching the lights come up and contemplating the peace of Oakland Cemetery may seem a strange way to enjoy a meal, but it works.'

'Watching the lights come up?' I said.

'They floodlight the cemetery,' explained Lori. She thought it was odd too. We decided it wasn't for us. We could cope with the dead people but we weren't sure about the 'Calamari Dusted in Cornmeal', heralded as the menu special.

Lori and I had a Hilton breakfast where a very fat young man called Dave was pleased to serve us. He was thrilled that we had learned his name, which we had been clever enough to read on his left breast. It is amazing how few people seem to connect the name tag they are wearing with a customer's ability to absorb information. We called Dave's name a lot and got whatever we wanted. I had flown hotfoot from recording at the BBC and was feeling depressed about my weight. I hate sitting in front of TV make-up mirrors trying to decide who that saggy dwarf is staring back at me. Faced with endless encounters with my past I could see what a middle-aged jowly woman I have become. With this in mind, I told Dave that I would have a healthy omelette (white and fluffy according to the menu) with a little smoked salmon in it. When it came it was healthy. It was white and fluffy. It was also accompanied by a small national park of fried potatoes. They were there so I ate them.

Richard had a cold threatening so I dragged him into the Hilton gift shop to seek out a possible remedy. He didn't want to come. It is a male thing that half the fun of having a cold is the drip, drip, drip of complaining that goes with it. The shop was an Aladdin's cave of fine souvenir opportunities, including a pewter picture frame shaped like an apple with the word 'Greetings!' embossed on it and many relief pictures of points of interest in Manhattan.

The woman running the place was a small Cuban; indeed she might have sold me a small Cuban but she was too busy discussing cold remedies with me.

'I read all the magazines, you know,' she confided, indicating the vast array of subject-specific reading matter on the shelves behind her. 'I know about the health issues.'

'Great,' I said. 'My friend needs a nasal spray to clear his nose.'

She shook her head at my ignorance. 'I won't sell them. I read about them and I won't sell them.'

Richard lost interest and left while I purchased a nasal stick without 'spray facility'. Having decided for herself that Richard was my husband, the Cuban woman became my confidante.

'You should tell him, you know. Those nose sprays? They cause sterility in men.'

I was hard pushed to think of a man on the planet less interested in the state of his sperm's procreative ability than Richard. What kind of magazines had the woman been reading? Who researched these things? Isn't the nose quite a long way from the testicles – at least in the general course of things? It was a thought that stayed in my mind.

The whole trip was turning into a lesson in service and the modern myth that it is somehow being provided. The Hilton had thoughtfully laid on a shuttle bus from the hotel to the airport. Just a word of warning to any potential travellers – it doesn't go to any part of the airport anyone actually wants to go to. Lori took charge as we got on.

'We need to go to E,' she told the driver.

'I go to B,' said the man.

'E,' said Lori.

'No, not E. B. Where you want?'

'E.'

'I don't go there.'

'How do we get there from B?'

'You used to take the monorail,' said the man.

'Okay, good,' said Lori, and prepared to sit down for the journey to B to catch something else to E. The man waited till she was settled.

'But it ain't working.'

Lori looked at him. 'So how do you get there?'

The man sucked on his teeth. 'I believe there's a bus.'

'A bus from B to E?'

It was my turn to lose interest. I was beginning to think we should take a taxi. I mean, I knew the bus was free but it was a curious service that dropped you somewhere you didn't want to be.

'I guess I could take you,' said the bus driver finally. This seemed kind but not wildly out of his way. When I had opened the curtains in the morning I'd realised that the hotel had practically been built on the runway. Some other people got on the bus. They wanted to go to E as well and the driver didn't say a word. We had saved our companions hours of amusing banter.

We got to E, where a fantastically helpful man with a desk on the pavement said we could check in before we even entered the building. Richard and I were impressed with this and thrilled at the speed with which he got rid of our bags. We moved off to go inside for some retail therapy but Mr Helpful stopped Lori.

'It's normal to give a tip,' he said, suddenly less helpful and rather cross. He forced some unwilling dollars from us. Why would you get a tip for doing the job you are paid for? No one has ever offered me a tip for anything except to suggest I might do something else for a living.

I had told the others I wanted to go early to shop. There were no shops. Newark airport was under construction. Curiously it was also run by BAA – the British Airport Authority. This struck me as an irony. Britain, the country from which freedom seekers fled in the seventeenth century, was now helping to make their travel arrangements. The place was a modern maze of hoardings proclaiming how fantastic it was going to be. How many dozens of shops there would be at 'mall prices'. You could tell it was all British because there was no work going on whatsoever. The shops would come but in their own good time.

We flew Delta Airlines to Atlanta. Delta now has a commendable policy of having 'mature' stewardesses. These matronly aunts are supposed to look after you. We were very tired and had been given Eva Braun for our needs. How she survived the bunker to harass us I'll never know. Still, the flight was cheap. You could tell it was cheap when you boarded the narrow plane and saw a trolley with dozens of white paper bags containing our in-flight 'snack'. Eva threw a bag at me, which contained an apple, a bottle of water and a very wet white roll with one slice of tomato, half a lettuce leaf, a see-through piece of ham and a fantastically yellow piece of cheese. I extracted the cheese and ate that. I least I think it was cheese. I dropped the bag in front of me and on my way to the loo I stepped on it. Dining at a cemetery was beginning to look like a viable option.

Atlanta airport, by contrast to where we had flown from, was enormous. We seemed to walk back to Newark to find our luggage. The signs for baggage reclaim were a little confusing so we spent some time wandering around the concession stands representing foods of the world. It was an amazing place. You could live there for some time and never visit the same country's cuisine twice.

We finally picked up our stuff and jammed it into the red convertible Lori and I had planned to hire the moment we knew we were heading South. It was a fine car and it would have been fun to drive with the roof off. We set off in the pouring rain. The city was obscured by fog and mist but the conference centre we were seeking appeared in no time. It was a pleasant, modern place done in something Lori called 'prairie style'. Wooden squirrels and woodland creatures crawled over a giant wall. The staff were genial and jovial. Gino, a handsome young black man, showed us to our rooms. He had some genuine ability at providing service but then he was not a real bellhop but a pre-law student at the university who really wanted to be a television 'anchor'. Yet another job that never came up when I was a kid.

I was nervous that we might suddenly run into Leslie. I couldn't think why we had decided to do this. I felt fat and old; I was worried that she wouldn't know me or that she would be shocked by me or something. Leslie had left us a note that she and her groom-to-be, David (surname Pratt – I hope she doesn't change her name), had organised a bus to take us to the wedding later.

We had sort of missed lunch so we had quesidia and buffalo wings (it's chicken – I don't know why) as a snack in the club lounge. Lori now thought she was getting a cold and wanted some boiling water to take a hot lemon powder. The bartender was grumpy, probably because he was an actual bartender and not someone in career transit.

'I have coffee only.'

'Don't you make that with hot water?' I asked.

'I don't have hot water. The food comes from the kitchen.'

'Presumably they don't have hot water either. I mean, that could come with the food . . . from the kitchen . . . which we ordered . . .' I tried and realised I was being annoying. 'Do you have tea?'

He eyed me with irritation. 'I don't have water for tea. I have coffee.'

We all had coffee and sat watching a giant TV. Some woman was espousing hateful and homophobic viewpoints. Apparently, she is called Dr Laura and is famous in America for doing phone-ins where she solves the world's problems. Reap and you shall sow. It seemed *she* was having problems. She has come down hard on the gay community in the past and now they were coming down on her. She is not a medical doctor at all but has a Ph.D. in physiology, which I think is a bit like knowing a lot about gym. The largest religious group in the state is Baptist and much is made of its historical escape from religious intolerance. The TV also covered the fact that the Georgian Baptist Convention was taking place in town. They too were full of anti-gay rhetoric. It seems that religious freedom is only for those who agree with the establishment. Religious intolerance may have been something to escape from but it was also something to pack in the bag and bring along for the ride.

I turned my attention to my maps. Atlanta is located cheek by jowl with Athens, Rome and Birmingham. You do wonder how difficult it would have been for them to think of a name of their own for a new town. Perhaps the many pilgrims had other things to worry about. The only original name I had found was Cabbagetown which, the guidebook told me, got its name after an amusing incident when a cart carrying cabbages overturned in the street. Must have been a heck of a slow news day.

> *After all, tomorrow is another day.*
> Margaret Mitchell, *Gone With the Wind*

Georgia was the last of the thirteen founding colonies of the United States. Named after King George II, it became a state on 2 January 1788 and has many claims to fame. There is, for example, Blakely, Peanut Capital of the World and home of the last remaining Confederate flagpole; Ashburn, where you can see the largest peanut in the world; Athens, home to a one-of-a-kind double-barrelled cannon, designed in 1863 to fire two balls connected by a chain; Brunswick, 'World Center for Processed Seafood Dishes'; Gainesville, Poultry Capital of the World and Calvary, where every autumn they celebrate Mule Day. I was quite keen to head out to Sandersville, 'Kaolin Center of the World' but only if it were twinned with somewhere leading the world in morphine. Some of the places had given a little more thought to their new name such as the small town in the County of Bulloch called 'Hopeulikit'.

Following my lessons on New York from Rita's daughter, I can tell you the following:

Georgian State bird – Brown Thrasher
State Tree – Live Oak
State Mineral – Staurolite (Fairy Stones)
Flower – Cherokee Rose
Insect – Honeybee
Fossil – Shark Tooth
Fish – Largemouth bass
Wildflower – Azalea
Gem (1976) – Quartz
Game bird (1970) – Bobwhite Quail.

This last one presumably doesn't apply in Albany, Georgia, which is the self-styled 'Quail-Hunting Capital of the World'.

The Civil War between the South and the North still rankles with the locals. Like many Southern states, Georgia used to depend on cotton production for its livelihood; a production made possible by the many slaves owned throughout the state. When in 1863 President Abraham Lincoln declared the emancipation of all slaves there was bound to be trouble. Seven Southern states, including Georgia, seceded from the Union and formed the Confederate States of America. Soon there was war, the Civil War, known to Southerners as 'The Great Unpleasantness', in which 125,000 Georgian troops fought. Huge and bloody battles raged at Shiloh, Vicksburg, Chattanooga and Gettysburg.

Lincoln was killed two years later – shot to death at the Ford Theater in Washington, DC, by an actor called John Wilkes Booth.

Typical actor's question – 'Yes, Mrs Lincoln, but what did you think of the play?'

Since that time and the loss of the war, Georgia has been mainly Democratic but is still an odd mix of political beliefs. It brought America Jimmy Carter, the Democrat too principled and I think good to be elected twice. It was the first state to extend full property rights to women (1866) yet it fêted men like Lester G. Maddox. Maddox, a successful Atlanta restaurateur, closed his business in 1965 rather than comply with a federal court order to serve blacks. Instead of being reviled, he went on to become governor two years later. Then, two years after he left office, Atlanta became the first US city to elect a black mayor. Make of all that what you will.

Atlanta, itself (the correct pronunciation is to drop the last 't' and say 'At-lanna'), is the capital of the state. It lies in the foothills of the Blue Ridge Mountains, a few miles south of the Chattahoochee river. (Boy, the Native Americans knew how to name things.) It exists entirely because of the railway. It was like this. Back in the early 1800s there was a small city called Zebulon. It lay about fifty miles south of the present capital. Here lived one Samuel Mitchell, a leading light of the community. One night a stranger, Benjamin Beckman, stopped at Mitchell's farm and was offered shelter. As is often the way with house guests, Beckman became ill and stayed on. When he was better he declared a liking for one of Mitchell's horses to help him continue with his journey. Now Mitchell wanted Beckman out of there but he didn't want to trade the horse. So Beckman said that in the recent 'Indian Lottery' he had won Lot 77, a piece of land in the wilderness near Fort Peachtree, fifty miles north, which was worth $41. Beckman traded the land for the horse.

Meanwhile, the Western and Atlantic Railroad was expanding. They wanted to join up in the South with the line from Savannah. According to the engineers the perfect spot for the terminus was in the middle of Lot 77. Sam Mitchell, who could have made a fortune, gave the land to the state in 1842. He declined to have the place called Mitchellville but there is a street named after him.

The terminus had no name. At first they tried naming the place after William Lumpkin, who had been state governor and head of the railroad. But Lumpkinville didn't roll off the tongue, so they tried Marthaville, after his daughter Martha. It was officially adopted but it seems the people didn't like it. Two years later it was called Atlanta. It appears no one knows why. Maybe it was a feminine part of Western and Atlantic.

The South lay before us and Richard, Lori and I were determined to explore, so the next morning we headed out. The day began as an odd exercise in non-communication. Gino, the nice bellhop who is pre-law but wants to be a television anchor, had been trying to help me but it was hard. Our back left tyre on the rental was slightly flat and we needed to pump it up before heading out.

'Do you know where the nearest petrol station is?' I asked.

'Yes, ma'am,' he replied. 'Are you taking the bus?'

I could not think why anyone would take a bus to a petrol station. There was surely nothing, not even on special offer, that would make the journey worthwhile. He had misunderstood me. We did not speak the same language.

There was much landmark history in the area but we decided instead to drive forty minutes north to 'The Largest Flea Market in the South', It was a tough call as we could have visited The World of Coca-Cola and amused ourselves as suggested in their leaflet by 'guessing how many bottles there are on the assembly line'. Instead we headed for the Pendergrass Flea Market. Their leaflet had a sure ring of success about it as the place was advertised as providing both 'Heating' *and* 'Air-conditioning', although presumably not at the same time. For those of you who want to travel in our footsteps, it is 'conveniently located on I-85 at Exit 137, US Hwy 129'. Apart from Highway 129, I have no idea what it is convenient for.

It was still raining as Lori steered the convertible up Jimmy Carter Boulevard and past a hotel which offered 'B'Fast and Pool'. I didn't know if 'pool' meant swimming or snooker and we didn't stop to enquire.

On the way we seemed to pass nothing but fast-food outlets.

Strangely, we were not drawn to any of these or indeed to the other retail options such as the Dinette Center or my personal favourite, The Plastic Bag Mart. As we got closer to our destination, advertising hoardings began beckoning us to Horsetown – the Largest Western Store in the US, and an inviting offer of Top Soil for Sale. All along the highway large signs warned us to 'Keep Off the Median'. I asked Lori about this.

'What's the median?'

'It's the grass in the middle of the highway. You get a lot of immigrants who don't know any better and they stop and have a picnic there,' she explained.

I could see immigrant alfresco dining could be a problem but I doubted many of them would grasp the concept of the median and where it was located. I wondered what they would make of signs encouraging everyone to 'Adopt a Highway' or 'Stop for a Jiffy Lube' or even an 'Express Lube'. There must be something different about American cars. The preponderance of quick oil-change places on every street corner suggests vehicles gasping for a bit of new lubrication.

We passed some great restaurants – the Lettuce Souprise You, with two carrots making the Ts of lettuce, and the Chick-Fil-A, but stopped for coffee at a fast-food joint called the Golden Griddle. It was a high-class affair littered with instructions about not bringing firearms in or causing trouble. Definitely not a place for turpitude. Despite this, the welcome available was second to none. We sat up at the counter and were served by a collection of wonderfully cheerful people called Oliver and the like, all of whom had had their teeth entirely reconstructed in gold with diamanté infills. Our main waitress was called Pythia, pronounced, she told us, with a hard P.

'It's a Greek Goddess,' she said.

'Oh really?' we asked. 'Which one?'

'I have no idea,' she replied and took our order. Great place. Great people.

It was a long way to the flea market but as Lori said, 'I am happy to drive for ever if I am questing for something.'

Questing we were, and the Pendergrass Flea Market is something. I would recommend it to everyone. The leaflet does not lie when it tells you that you can 'Walk through more than 2½ miles of storefronts centred around a turn-of-the-century old town main street'.

And I guarantee, whatever it was you were looking for is in there somewhere. It's not very nice but it is in there. We parked our rental car amid a sea of pick-up trucks. These were big vehicles. Some so large they gave the suggestion that the people didn't just arrive in them – they were also their homes.

'Is this what they call "white trash" country?' I asked Lori, ever questing for some sociological understanding of America.

'Will you be quiet?' she hissed. 'These people have guns.'

We had arrived in a part of the South which can only be described as redneck country. Men wearing plaid shirts and even the occasional pair of ancient dungarees wandered about calling each other 'Bubba'. We entered across a large wooden porch which had a fading Thanksgiving display and two wooden rocking chairs as if it were a genuine 'down home' experience that we were about to enjoy. The turn-of-the-century old town main street turned out to be a kind of set through which many people were happily strolling as if it were the real thing.

There was no soft sell about any of it. Everything was 'A Bargain!' and 'Utterly Unique!' I think I got the measure of the place from a display of bumper stickers which boasted the Confederate flag plus quotes from one or two of the more amusing things Hitler had said. There were also stickers that contained fairly straightforward sentiments clearly designed to be read at high speed.

'You came to this country. Now speak English or get out.'

The purveyor of friendly car sentiment was a friendly sort of guy. His other merchandise included numerous blowpipes, a

200,000-volt stun gun for just $36 and a Road Warrior knife with a 12-inch serrated blade – 'Yours to Take Home and Treasure' – for a mere $24. It was a scary display and the owner watched us the whole time we were checking it out. He made no move to serve us. He knew potential customers when he saw them. To me the knife looked like a great King Arthur fake but a large man with no neck picked it up and exclaimed, 'Heyell thajt's shiaaarp!' We moved on.

All around us the accent had changed completely. Everywhere people were greeting each other in deep Southern drawls.

'Aye remember yooo. Yoooo cut mah Tiffany's haijr.'

Up at Jeremy's Critters, they were offering a special today of a Hand-Fed Cockatiel. Psitaccines, I thought, and told the man about the Teflon. He wasn't interested. A dozen rabbits lay disconsolately on top of each other in a cage no more than two foot by one. They were miserable and didn't move. I couldn't tell if they were for pets or pies or both.

But I felt calm, for everywhere I was comforted by large signs telling me how much Jesus loved me – although patently not as much as he loves truckers. Jesus was available in a range of merchandise including powder compacts, fridge magnets and chiming clocks. My favourite was the 'Touch Lamp' which did as advertised. When you touched it, the thing lit up and displayed the entire Last Supper in an amber glow. A man offered to make me a personalised licence plate with a picture of myself actually with Jesus but I declined. There were too many other purchasing possibilities for my dollar.

I was tempted, however, to get my own gravestone. This is a purchase which I think is often made too late in life. The one thing you wear for eternity and it is usually chosen by a grieving relative already counting the cost of the canapés for the wake. There were many styles on display and the offers were excellent. For the day I was there (and that day *only*) I could benefit from the Lay Away plan *and* get Free Lettering! There is something pleasing about associating the words Lay Away with funerary artefacts but not as pleasing as the rather ironic placing of the stall opposite.

This was the home of Nancy Clark who gave psychic readings. Nancy was clearly serious about her work although there were many signs proclaiming the fact that she didn't give refunds. Seated on a sofa at the back of her small tent-like room, Nancy was busy giving a young girl the future low-down. It was obviously an intense experience only marred by a man, whom I took to be Nancy's husband, sitting on a plastic chair beside them, counting money and speaking on a mobile phone. Perhaps Mrs Clark was busy looking ahead while Mr Clark did a spot of reality making. I hovered, but Nancy was in an intense session and I wasn't sure that I wanted the future laid out for me.

As well as the pets, the weapons and the tombstones, avenues of junk radiated out from the turn-of-the-century main street. There were many 'historic' Coke bottles for sale in this home of the 'real thing'. You could collect hundreds of different styles through the ages. They looked just like the ones Lori and I had drunk out of as kids. Now we were history. The place was exhausting, but we did find a small oasis down at one end where a jovial man was selling quilts.

'Are they handmade?' I asked him.

He nodded. 'They are by somebody,' he said.

We wandered past 'antique' furniture from the 1940s and I teased Lori about the lack of history, but she said, 'A lot of the furniture got destroyed in the Civil War and what there was probably stayed in people's families. The concept of the heirloom is big. Your history, where you came from, helps establish who you feel you are in America and they are unlikely to sell it off in a flea market.'

'Funny, I haven't seen any books,' I commented.

Lori looked at me over the top of her glasses as if I couldn't possibly be serious. She's right. This was not a place where anyone had ever come to buy a book.

She went off to get some lemonade in Bubba's Food Court. I couldn't face it. The court offered much high-cholesterol fare – chilli dogs, cheese jalapeños and peanuts, endless peanuts, but it was also full of quite young people who were all enormous. A woman my age wandered past with a small child. The roll of her stomach was quite literally banging against her knees. Her bottom was so large it didn't seem it could possibly be part of her. I felt sure it must have snuck up in the night and attached itself when she wasn't looking. It is a picture of excess I have not seen any-where else in the world. The United States contains 4 per cent of the world's population and uses 25 per cent of the world's resources. Certainly the people in Bubba's were doing their bit to keep up the statistics. How sad – a people who could have any-thing, including health.

Anyway, my eye had been attracted to a nearby stall. Here a ten-inch white plastic chapel with a grey pitched roof, bell tower and three rather fine stained-glass windows of coloured film stood amid a sea of battery-operated products. Above a small set of red double doors was a miniature clock. A woman behind the trestle table the chapel rested on eyed me with some difficulty. She had a fairly mobile pair of eyes which seemed to wander as she spoke to me. There was a sense that although the Good Lord had placed her vision equipment in the standard place above the nose, actually they longed to drift over her left earlobe. It was slightly unnerving.

'What does the chapel do?' I asked the woman, because almost everything we had come across so far 'did' something. The dinosaur clock which roared on the hour, the plastic water foun-tain which lit up, played a tune and had a ballerina dance about on top and quite possibly, the gravestone which lit your name in neon when flowers were placed near it.

'It's fantastic!' she said. 'Every hour the windows light up, the doors open, an angel comes out and dances to a tune and then the bell rings the exact time.'

She didn't have any batteries to prove this, but by the market standards the thing was rather expensive – $20 – and I was inclined to believe her. She smiled at me and removed a cardboard box marked 'Musical Inspirational Chapel' from underneath the counter.

'You're lucky. It's the last one.'

There had clearly been a positive rush for them. She struggled to get the tall, slim church into the tall, slim box.

'Funny, I cannot get this into the box,' she muttered.

Her eyes wandered about as she struggled and it occurred to me that the difficulty perhaps lay in her mother having married her cousin. The lid never did close but she handed the box to me with a beaming smile.

'That's going to give your whole family a whole lot of pleasure. It is an heirloom for tomorrow.'

In fact, when I got it home, the item was rather better than I had hoped. It took a staggering amount of batteries to power up but there were many more extras than she said. The chapel plays a random selection of four hymns and there are hours of fun to be had sitting in the dark with the stained glass illuminated, trying to guess which of the four listed tunes it could possibly be. The clock also happily strikes the hour as advertised but the actual number of strikes is marginally random. It might not be a good time-keeping device for those relying on aural input only. The box suggests that the chapel would 'make a comforting night light for children'. I'm not sure about this. I think if a plastic building suddenly lit up at one o'clock in the morning, an angel shot out, played 'O Little Town of Bethlehem' and struck eleven, a child might be damaged for life.

We hooked up with Richard again who had been threatened with expulsion by the security people because he had been filming with his video camera. I don't think you can sink any lower than being chucked out of a flea market. As we headed off, I looked into a small stall near the entrance. An African gentleman was sitting beside his display of Nigerian crafts. He was the only black person we had seen and he looked lonely. We had been served by many Vietnamese and Chinese people but I thought it unlikely that in the land of the pro-Hitler bumper sticker, many people popped in for a bit of an ebony elephant or a straw hat.

We headed south, back to Atlanna and tall buildings and the suggestion of civilisation. Along the way hundreds of companies beckoned for our attention with huge advertising hoardings. There was a 'Sofa and Loveseat' available for only $599, a 'Rooms to Go Outlet' (oddly closed on Tuesdays and Wednesdays), 'Previously Enjoyed Cars' (as opposed to second-hand) and a 'Diversified Cabinet Distributor', which might be a thriving business but I felt lacked something as a catchy title. Everywhere signs told us what to do and what not to do.

'Trucks with 6+ wheels ONLY use four lanes.' (At one time?)

We drove into the vast, modern city, confident that it must be awash with places to eat but could find nothing. Navigating was confusing. Everything seemed to be called Peachtree something. There were no peach trees, indeed few trees of any kind. (Peachtree Street was the main thoroughfare and it had become severely rutted by all the traffic so the good burghers built a Peachtree West next to it, which is in fact not west but . . .)

We went off to get some culture. A magazine in my hotel room had described *Gone With the Wind* as 'the world's bestselling novel (second only to the Bible)'. I thought this was remarkable – not just the sales figures but the description of the Bible as a novel. The Windy author, Margaret Mitchell, was a true Southern girl. Legend has it that as a child she was so steeped in stories of the Confederate past, she didn't know the South had lost the Civil War till she was ten and her mother confessed. *Gone With the Wind* is the quintessential Southern novel and I wanted to see Margaret's house. I had only seen the movie but already I liked her. Apparently she had been refused admission to the local Junior League due to a rather scandalous Apache dance she had done at a charity ball.

The Margaret Mitchell house is set back from the road (on one of the endless Peachtree streets) and looks like a classic American clapboard house with a white porch across the front, inviting you to 'set awhile and visit'. I was excited, and there isn't a better companion for these things than Lori. I have travelled with her in Europe and she is very good at relaxing into the moment. We wandered in looking for a true slice of the South.

The entrance to the house is via a newly minted office of white walls and giant glass store fronts. Behind the desk a cheerful young woman sat waiting to take our ten dollars to breathe the air that once was Margaret's. The place was all efficiency mixed with charm. Margaret would have been thrilled, apart from the large poster behind the woman, showing the house clearly quite horribly ablaze.

'You had a fire at the house?' I asked politely.

She nodded and smiled. 'Oh, yes, nineteen nineties, burnt practically to the ground. It was tragic,' she confided. 'They had all sorts of plans to use it for the Olympics.'

Lori and I both thought about that for a moment. She, perhaps, recalling the Olympic disappointment and me trying to think what sport they could possibly have had in mind for this particular venue. Through the glass display hall I could clearly see the house still standing there.

'So they rebuilt it?' I said rather stupidly.

'Certainly did,' said the helpful woman. 'It was gorgeous . . . (there was a long pause) . . . then, the darned thing burnt down again.'

This struck me as either fantastically unlucky or suspiciously like the work of a literary critic with an obsessive soul and a box of all-weather matches. Clearly the woman now felt she had done enough to be helpful. There were other tourists behind me.

'That'll be ten dollars to see the Margaret Mitchell house,' she repeated by rote.

'Except it isn't actually her house, is it?' I persisted in a rather annoying and pedantic way. The woman looked at me with irritation.

'It is . . .' she replied very firmly '. . . very like.'

We paid and wandered off to look at the displays. It seemed Margaret began her scribbling as a journalist for a local newspaper, the *Atlanta Journal*. This was not a time when women did that kind of thing, so she must have been a gutsy girl. The small museum had blow-ups of some of her articles. They were written in a snappy style, heavy on the human interest – men who'd lost their memories and didn't know how they'd got to Atlanta, families in desperate circumstances and so on. The photos on display showed Mags to be a jolly woman in the flapper style, not unlike a Southern Dorothy Parker. There were several tightly strung wires suspended at an angle from floor to ceiling in the main display hall. After a while, a small knot of tourists gathered rather edgily around them as the young woman from the ticket desk moved in to double as tour guide.

'We are about to enter the home of Margaret Mitchell. Does anyone have any questions?'

'What are the wires for?' asked a man with many cameras.

It wouldn't have been my first question but I think it helped to assess the level of the group.

'They are for future displays,' was the reply. Provided of course they didn't burn down. We headed outside, across a small dull patch of garden and into the house. The ground floor was entirely devoid of furniture. It had been laid out like an art gallery and contained only black and white photographs of Atlanta and a few of her sons and daughters. The lighting was very modern – little focused halogen lamps on thin wire runners littered the ceiling. It was probably not how Margaret would have had it. This, it seemed, was the 'corporate area' where Atlanta dignitaries are entertained.

There was a rather fine portrait of John Henry 'Doc' Holliday – a member of the Wild Bunch and some distant relation of

Margaret's. It transpires he gave up dentistry partly because he had a weak chest and was told to go west and partly from unrequited love. He fell hopelessly for Margaret's cousin Melanie, who took one look at him and decided to become a nun. It is the kind of decision that would make any man question his powers of attraction to women. Women becoming nuns or lesbians or sometimes both can have a strange effect on the male. He buggered off to shoot people and Margaret named her goody-goody character in *Gone With the Wind* after her cousin.

The guide spread her arms around the empty art gallery. Margaret, we learned, 'did not live here'. Of course. No one did. It was all brand new but we nodded anyway.

'Margaret lived in a small apartment. Even when she made lots of money she still lived in a small apartment.'

She didn't, it seems, want a big apartment because then people would come and stay with her. I decided I liked Margaret even better. At the foot of the staircase was a square foot or so of mosaic floor tile in a colour and pattern too dull to recall.

'This floor was salvaged from the terrible fire to this house and has been painstakingly reconstructed by experts. Are there any questions?'

I wanted to ask 'why?' but I couldn't bring myself to. Having a bog-standard floor, which Margaret Mitchell may or may not have stood on while fumbling for her front-door key, reassembled by experts with many years of training and huge college loans still outstanding, struck me as a desperation to find history, any history.

We entered the apartment. It was indeed very small. So small, in fact, that the radiator, a fat hot-water affair, was suspended from the ceiling.

'This was the apartment where Margaret Mitchell wrote *Gone With the Wind*.'

It was very nice but it was not actually Margaret's. More like a rather good theatre set.

'Is any of the furniture actually Margaret's?' I asked.

'It's very like,' said the woman. 'We know she had a blue settee. There . . .' she pointed emphatically '. . . is a blue settee.'

We all dutifully turned to the settee. It was indeed blue. It had never carried the honour of Margaret's *Gone With the Wind* buttocks but it was no doubt very like. In the bathroom we were invited to 'Go in and look behind the door. There you will see a piece of plaster which has been preserved from the apartment before the fire.'

I was bold. I went in and looked. Preserved behind the door, behind a piece of fire-shielding glass, was a section of plaster not unlike the piece of wall which had recently fallen unexpectedly from part of my house. It was a light brown/grey colour. It looked like plaster or, at least, it was very like.

We got to the bedroom and I was becoming desperate. The guide was becoming confidential.

'When Margaret invited guests she would sometimes show them something which was rather shocking.'

Suddenly I was alert. I love anything from history that might be even mildly shocking. (I remember the thrill in the fifth form when a history teacher inadvertently introduced me to *Gargantua* by Rabelais and I read that the finest loo roll available to man or woman is a live goose. I've never tried it but not a luxury hotel reservation goes by without me living in hope.) Perhaps the guide might break into the celebrated Apache dance which led Margaret to shame with the Junior League, perhaps . . .

From behind the bedroom door (well, not the actual bedroom door but certainly something very like) the guide brought out a framed print of a naked woman sitting up in bed. It was rather a delicate thing, low on real detail as it was a copy of a pencil drawing. The woman portrayed was not even sufficiently naked to assess her natural hair colour. The poorly framed print was passed round the hands of the tourists with some reverence. This was, after all, Margaret's measure of pornography in the bedroom. I didn't have my glasses but I thought the woman looked in need of chiropractic treatment.

'Is there anything, anywhere in the house which Margaret Mitchell might have seen even just once during her life?' I was heard to cry amid questions about exactly how the plaster in the bathroom had been preserved. The guide had tired of me by now and became rather smug.

'On your way out,' she declared in the manner of an announcer of the sole winner of the lottery jackpot, 'you will pass a wooden ice box which belonged to Margaret herself and you may . . . touch it for luck.' We did pass it and, God help me, I did touch it.

Beyond the walls of the very like apartment was another collection of black and white photos of existing Georgian writers sitting at their places of work. Now that was thrilling. It was real and I loved it. Real writers battling with the endless formation of words, shaping them into something never said before. I think Margaret would have loved it but I don't know. Truth be told, I don't know that much about her. What I have gathered about the writing of the book seems less romantic than I first believed. I had always been told that she wrote her great saga of the South while bored on a coast-to-coast train ride from New York to California. I've done that trip and it's very nice if you have something to occupy you. I was ten at the time. The train we went on had a bubble-shaped observation car where you could sit and watch the scenery. My brother and I played there because it was mostly empty. People don't tend to place train stations in the grandest geographical sites and through great swathes of the Midwest you had to be a real prairie dog aficionado to stay glued to the window.

Anyway, I could see that such a trip might lead some old schoolmarm to write a piece of romantic slush instead, but it wasn't true. Margaret married a steady fellow called John Marsh while she was a journalist. Then she hurt her ankle and retired to their small apartment. After that, nothing really. She spent nine years (1926 to 1935) writing *Gone With the Wind*. Nothing before and nothing after, till she was killed in 1949 by a local driver while crossing the road to see a film version of *The Canterbury Tales* at the local movie house.

*Gone With the Wind* won the Pulitzer Prize in 1937, which is great, but (and I don't want to be picky) nine years in the writing seems an awfully long time to me. How bad could her ankle have been? I suspect Margaret would not have done well in today's instant success instant access world. Certainly *The Learning Annexe* would not have been for her.

In the *Gone With the Wind* Movie Museum across the street there were many posters and little heating. Something had gone wrong with the plumbing and the place had a rather appropriate air of a morgue about it. Hidden in one corner was the story of the driver who achieved notoriety by running over and killing Miss Mitchell. It seems he was famous the moment it happened and when arrested was pursued by the press. While having his fingerprints taken, a photographer told him to look up and smile. It's what we are all conditioned to do when there is a camera three feet away and he did. It was this quickly released photo which allegedly showed a lack of remorse. It wasn't true and he said it wasn't true. He served some months full of remorse and was quietly released back into the community. It says something about the Atlanta police department. First, that nothing has changed in the relationship between press and police where celebrities are concerned and second, perhaps, that taking fingerprints from a driver who freely admits hitting someone suggests an unnecessary degree of diligence.

We finished off in the Margaret Mitchell gift store where I bought a copy of the book and a fridge magnet kitchen clock with Clark Gable and Vivien Leigh embracing on the front. The man who sold it to me was breathtakingly camp. He told me his job was a dream. Where else could he watch *Gone With the Wind* six times a day, five days a week? In a home for the mentally unstable, I thought, or at least something very like.

The only really useful piece of information we gathered on our tour was that at Margaret Mitchell's request, the original manuscript for *Gone With the Wind* was burnt upon her death. Rather prophetic I felt.

Richard's guidebook reading led us to the Georgian Terrace for some food. We were thrilled when we pulled up to see that there was not only a smart doorman but also valet parking. We had been saved from the land of Bubba. The doorman, however, had other ideas. We might as well have pitched up in a pick-up, playing the banjo and helping the dog look for fleas the way we were greeted.

'What do you want here?' he growled.

'We want to eat,' replied Richard, the perfect Englishman.

'Can't. Restaurant closed. Can't eat here.'

I suggested that there must be somewhere near by to eat. That it was a big city, but he denied it.

'Nope. Not here.'

We set off depressed and went round the block. At the side of the Georgian Terrace, indeed in the basement of the building, we spied an Italian restaurant which was patently open but we lacked the will to go and face General Sherman again. Snobbishness is a curious thing. America is famed as the land without class, where anyone can do anything, where any mother's son can become president, and yet it is riddled with status issues. Just as we had somehow presumed ourselves above the pick-up people at the flea market, now we too were disdained. I don't know what the doorman based his opinion on. In England it is easy – it's done on accent. There is a wonderful line in *My Fair Lady* where Higgins sings, 'The minute an Englishman speaks he makes some other man despise him.'

The Georgian Terrace is famous. It's where Vivien Leigh and all the stars of *Gone With the Wind* stayed when the movie premiered in Atlanta. But Hattie McDaniel, the brilliant black actress who played Scarlett's maid, did not attend the opening. The Georgian

Terrace was not an integrated hotel, indeed there weren't any in Atlanta, so she stayed at home. She stayed at home until she went to collect her Oscar for the part. The Georgian Terrace didn't want her and they didn't want us. Although I was hungry I felt at least that we were in good company.

We drove on past acres of what looked like financial institutions set in a sea of nothingness. When I asked Leslie the next day where the hell the heart of Atlanta was, she replied, 'It's like Gertrude Stein said, "There is no *there* there."'

I could quite lose my heart to anyone who can quote Gertrude Stein and she was right. There is no there there.

The bus for the wedding was due between 5 and 5.15 p.m. It left promptly at 5 although no one on board knew if everyone who should be there was there but the driver said he 'ain't waiting for nobody', which set everybody off in a holiday mood. It was a white student bus carrying about twenty people, none of whom we knew. It was full of old people wearing smart clothes and clutching large packages. They looked uncertain and unchatty. The seats faced into the centre of the vehicle and everyone sat eyeing us suspiciously as though we had chosen the wrong wedding or at least the wrong bus. Richard rested his camera on the floor and started filming our companions. He did it quite subtly but I wished he wouldn't. I didn't want anything to draw attention to us whatsoever.

The journey took a long time. It was raining so the windows steamed up. No one spoke. For about forty minutes no one spoke. Outside we passed the National Center for Disease Control, the Center for American Cerebral Palsy and other places of interest, but I kept quiet. Finally the driver came to a halt and made a call on his mobile. He was lost. I had imagined if you got married in Atlanta then it all happened on a glorious day in some piercingly white church beside an ante-bellum mansion. Leslie, it turned out, was getting hitched in an Indian restaurant in a shopping mall.

Through the glass in the door I could see the restaurant in the distance. It was entirely outlined in neon and was difficult to miss.

'It's behind you,' I said out loud to the driver. This caused some shifting in seats because I had spoken. Then even the old people began to see the restaurant. It was obvious they felt the driver should be told but not one of them did. No one said anything and I didn't want to cause more of a scene. Lori, who had dealt so brilliantly with the shuttle-bus driver who wanted to go to B or E or whatever, had run out of steam. She too was suffering from nerves. By now the driver was through to the restaurant on his mobile.

'Where are you located?' he asked.

'Behind you,' I said again, feeling like someone at a pantomime, but it was not a popular contribution.

The driver nodded for some time, received much instruction and then turned around having realised the restaurant was behind him.

The Palace Indian restaurant was outlined in light. How anyone could have missed it was a marvel. It sat sandwiched between a Mobil petrol station and a Boston Market fast-food restaurant. The Banquet Hall had a neon sign outside which boldly declared it was OPEN. Neither Lori nor I wanted to go in first. Cars were driving in and out of the rain-swept car park which was emptying for the evening. It had enough spaces to accommodate the whole of Atlanta were they suddenly minded to join us for a bit of brinjal bhajee.

Lori and I and the rain pushed and prodded at each other till we finally went inside. It was not the most glamorous venue I'd ever been to. A high-ceilinged, slightly cold room with seating for about 120 at mainly round tables of ten. Three white men with straggly beards and a poor judgement in head-dress were playing Indian music at the front of the room. None of them was Indian and I suspected the furthest east any had travelled was New Jersey. One played a sitar, one was mad for a bit of bongo, while the other had some sort of floor accordion which wheezed away.

People at weddings should wear hats. Lori and I failed here but the band made up for it, wearing their hat choices with a confidence that bespoke a lack of mirrors in the building. Fez or turban? Always a tricky choice, and on white people always a mistake.

The place was filling up with quite a lot of elderly relatives. There was a bar but it was not doing a roaring trade, probably because most of the guests would be fighting some kind of age-related diabetes. Weddings are curious things. I think older people feel they ought to go and younger people feel it would be nice to go – or is it the other way round? I didn't feel either. I was just nervous. Each table had rank after rank of empty brown beer bottles in which rested orange-coloured arrangements of a single flower, a few leaves and what looked like some kind of tangerine-coloured salad pepper. It was hard to know if it was a starter or a decoration.

The barman had red or white wine and dark or light beer. I tried the wine which was undrinkable and made me long for all I had missed in the pick-up-truck-decorated cellars of Long Island. I laid out Leslie and David's wedding gifts on the table at the side. I'd had no idea what to buy this woman from my past and her man whom I'd never met. I had settled on a miniature carriage clock from Harrods for her and silver cufflinks for him. I figured these days it's probably good to get separate gifts in case the couple divorce.

It was a large family gathering and Lori and I knew hardly anyone. We tried to greet Leslie's mother. I called her by her surname as I had no idea what her first name was. When I was a kid grown-ups didn't have first names. She was an elegant woman with short grey hair, wearing a grey velvet dress. I expect she was very preoccupied for she had little time for niceties like saying hello.

Lori recognised another grey-haired lady called Nancy and her husband for whom she used to baby-sit. Nancy had worked as a reporter for the *Journal News*, a local paper in Westchester. Then

she taught journalism for a year at Lori's present college. She only
did one year because 'They kept giving me freshmen. You can't
teach freshmen journalism. You are too busy teaching them the
basics of English.'

I remembered reading that many first-year American college
students take remedial reading as their first course but I decided
not to mention it. All I remembered from high school was some
testing system called SATs where everyone sat in big halls and
did multiple-choice exams that were then checked by machine. I
wondered about those results now. Checking things filled in by the
general populace didn't seem to be what the country did best.
Perhaps some people failed because their chads had dimpled.

Nancy had an interesting wedding dress sense. She wore black
trousers with quite a smart jacket and a nice blue scarf and then a
very old pair of boating shoes. They were brown and falling apart.
She could have stepped straight off the deck of a small yacht and
indeed with all the rain that would have been appropriate.

Just then the service was announced and a few people began to
line up in an open V, like geese escaping south for the winter. The
upside of all this was that the music stopped for a minute. I had
already figured out that the band would play all evening and yet
I would never get the tune.

We'd been told that no photos were to be taken during the ceremony. There was to be no flash and no noise. This made the
room a little tense. Leslie appeared, looking lovely. She had
always been beautiful, with sleek brown hair and marble white
skin. She was wearing a classic white silk wedding dress with a
short veil. It had a fitted bodice, no shoulder straps and corset
lacing at the back in gold trim. The skirt was full with a small
train and she had those white satin shoes you only ever see at
weddings. Damn her eyes, she had kept her figure and looked
gorgeous. She also looked older but of course she was. What did
I expect? A teenager going up the aisle? Of course, it wasn't an
aisle. She had come from the back of the room out of what

appeared to be the kitchen. I'm not sure it would have been my choice to spend my last single moments next to a man preparing chicken tikka masala. I mean, you might get that yellow dye they use all over your nice white shoes. One or two people started to clap as she progressed past the bar but no one else joined in because of the noise ban.

I finally identified David, the groom of the moment. He was a slightly podgy man with longish dark hair. He was wearing a maroon-red Indian suit – long shirt to his knees and silk trousers with a grey waistcoat over the top and very flat brown leather sandals. It was a bizarre combination. He looked like a well-fed extra from the movie *Gandhi*. Leslie's two stepdaughters from a previous relationship (I had gathered a few morsels of background information) were also wearing traditional bridesmaid dresses in silk but carried larger versions of the curious beer-bottle flower arrangements. The ceremony was to be conducted by David's brother.

These days pretty much anyone can marry their friends and family if they want to. I found a website which offers 'ordination' for just $29.99 and I was rather sorry I hadn't sent off for it. David's brother was said to be a Buddhist monk but he looked more like a Mormon with an insurance salesman's haircut and a sober dark suit and tie. He had his words written out on index cards. He said a few things about love and then announced that Leslie and David would each read a poem. Behind us the kitchen was hotting up and I thought they had better be quick or the poppadoms would be toast.

The Mormon monk fumbled in his inside pocket and pulled out pieces of paper, which he handed to the bride and groom. Leslie was beaming. You could feel her happiness. It pulsated in the room and made me that ridiculous tearful thing that women often become at weddings. David, however, appeared to be on valium. His poem was called 'Silent Movie' which caused a ripple of laughter. I joined in. Not because I thought it was funny but it was better than being quiet. Leslie's verse seemed to be about 'precious love' while David's recurring theme was more of a Laurel and Hardy 'How did we get into this mess?'

Finally they kissed and people felt free to clap. Then we were all asked to line up and congratulate them. Lori and I joined the line late and last. Leslie smiled and hugged us together. It was a strange moment and I felt extremely awkward. I didn't really know this person at all. I don't know what we talked about – how far we'd come, how lovely it was to be invited. I stood with my hands behind my back having suddenly turned into Prince Philip opening a cheese factory. We went to sit down.

'Don't you think we should talk to David?' whispered Lori. He stood separately from his new wife under a ventilation fan. It seems to be what happens at weddings. A man and a woman are joined in holy matrimony and then don't speak to each other for the rest of the evening. We dutifully lined up for David. It had been socially correct but, as it happens, he couldn't have cared less and looked elsewhere the entire time we were talking. I decided he probably wasn't going to be our big friend. It was odd. I think if old friends of my partner's turned up, having travelled thousands of miles, I might have shown a passing interest.

Leslie had been thoughtful and put us at the long table next to hers. She had also placed two families with young children. The booster seats on either side of us struck me as a bad sign for conversation. The other people were very straightforward and didn't even try to be our friends. It was curious and seemed very un-American to me. The man and woman sitting directly opposite us had a small boy called Wills. He was about two. I knew he was called Wills not because anyone bothered to introduce themselves but because throughout the ceremony all you could hear was an exasperated but utterly unenforced 'Oh Wills!' as the child attempted to wreck everything in a quarter-mile radius. Perhaps his mother didn't normally look after him for she clearly had no idea what to do as he ran riot, sticking his fingers in the sockets of fairy lights and attempting to eat several table decorations.

Leslie's brother, Eric, had been at our table but moved when Lori made the mistake of asking him a direct question.

'So, Eric, where are you?' I know she intended it as a general question of geography. Eric had been at school with Lori's brother so she knew him to say hello to. A thick-set man with a thin moustache and the build of an American football player, he took the question badly.

'Why do people always ask that? Why does it matter where you are in the world?'

It didn't really. It had only been chit-chat. We found out from someone else that he lived in Idaho and repaired computers. Perhaps something in that was a source of shame but I couldn't spot it. He had no partner or wife that we could see and stolidly moved to the other side of the room where no one could make further enquiries.

There was a woman at the table called Susan. She was from Connecticut and had been at college with Leslie. She had three young sons one of whom, aged about eleven, would not let go of her. He hung round her neck while she dandled a two-year-old on her knees. Her life was patently not her own. There wasn't a husband around and her conversation was limited due to the filial goitre condition from which she was suffering. She never asked us anything about ourselves. It seems to be an American thing to talk at length about yourself (unless you're doing that computer thing in Idaho) but not to show any particular interest in anyone else. She had been 'in theater' in her youth. 'I acted and stuff but then my family came along.'

I thought it a curious expression, 'my family came along'. It made pregnancy sound like a bus you weren't expecting. She had moved to Connecticut and now she 'did' real estate. There was an edge of disappointment and defensiveness in what she said. She had clearly sacrificed her theatrical ambitions for her boys. I found myself saying, 'Well, real estate is a kind of performance.'

I couldn't think how these words had come from my mouth but they hit the spot.

She nodded vigorously. 'Absolutely. You have to sell a property to people and you have to understand the spirit of a house to know who should fill it. You have to get the match right.'

This was so far from the British concept of house selling that I couldn't grasp it as a thought. American realtors will show potential home buyers the schools and churches, and local shops. The British estate agent doesn't even want to make an appointment for you to see the house. American realtors have a much greater sense of 'the community'. When we moved to Mamaroneck, the woman who had let the house to us never seemed to be out of the place. She really wanted us to 'settle in' to the town. Today, I don't know how much of that attention belongs to the 'have a good day' school of superficial interaction and how much of it is real.

Just when I thought we were getting along, Susan became preoccupied with her children and we were dismissed. I decided it was my fault and that I lacked the ability to make friends. Lori and I went outside for some air and saw that some of the other shops in the strip mall were still open. It was 6.30 and an announcement had been made that dinner would be at 8 p.m. With no one to talk to we wandered off to the shops.

The RadioShack was open to sell us computers and telephones but the nearest store was a CVS pharmacy, a giant supermarket selling over-the-counter drugs. It was a fantastic place with each aisle running one hundred yards from front to back. The use of anaesthetics was discovered in Atlanta by a doctor who had enjoyed experimenting with recreational drugs in medical school. Coca-Cola also started life here in 1886, at the hands of a pharmacist called John S. Pemberton. It was made with fifteen different ingredients and was guaranteed to 'refresh' you, mainly because, as I understand it, it originally contained cocaine. Just think, Pemberton sold the rights to the whole thing for just $2,300. Even today I imagine the crying of Pemberton descendants can be heard long into the Georgian night.

The pharmacy was awash with mind- and body-changing possibilities. Here you could see something of the American lifestyle in microcosm. There was not a haemorrhoid preparations section, there was a haemorrhoid preparations aisle. You could walk for three or four minutes knee-deep in pills and potions for the poor posterior. What can have happened to a country that has such trouble with its bottoms?

I wanted to buy some sleeping pills and there were acres of those too. Thinking about sleep then put me in mind of how I might stay awake through the evening. I was turning into Judy Garland as I bought both sleeping pills and 'Revive with Vivarin' – an Alertness Aid with Caffeine. The place was also full of Christmas tat, including rolls of fake brown bricks in case you wanted to build your own Christmas village scene. I thought we probably had time and no one would really notice at our table in the corner but in the end we decided against it. We were the only customers and it was the manager who rang up the till. It felt like a quintessentially American experience to shop at night under neon in a giant, empty place. I would have quite enjoyed it except we had come for a wedding.

Back at the event in question we had not been missed. We were, however, just in time for the speech and a toast to the bride and groom. I had learned several things about David. First that he was a film student and second that he collected unusual beer. (He had 500 beer bottles in his collection which explained the table centres.) He was also a fan of Bollywood movies, that particular Indian fare of rich sets in front of which people fall in love, while elephants hover in the background. This explained the Indian restaurant.

'So are you going to go to India for your honeymoon?' I asked Leslie.

'Oh, David doesn't actually want to go there,' she said. 'He just likes the movies.'

David's closest friend from his school days was the best man.

He had written his speech out single-space on three sides of A4 and was unable to find his place on the page at any point during the talk. It was, as is customary on both sides of the Atlantic, supposed to be a hilarious account of David's rakish youth. Consequently it was incomprehensible. As far as I could gather, the two men seem to have been arrested under amusing circumstances but only David's immediate family was able to get the joke. I have spoken three times for female friends at their nuptials but it still isn't the norm for a wedding. No one spoke for Leslie. She was David's now.

After this it was time to salute the couple. Apart from selecting the venue, David had also chosen some special beer for the toast. It was obviously extremely special as it had both a metal cap on the bottle and a cork underneath it. It was dished out sparingly having come all the way from Belgium. Someone said a few nice words, everyone raised their glass and drank. This was followed by the unified sound of over a hundred people retching as quietly as they were able. It was raspberry beer and it had come all the way from Belgium because no one in the Low Countries would have wanted to drink it.

Lori and I discussed what we would do if we ever got married. Neither of us ever has. I think we both felt a little sad and spinsters of this parishish. Despite being gay, or maybe because of it, I would love to get married. I would love to have my family and friends celebrate and welcome my partner.

'I'd still like that one other person who "fits",' mused Lori and I guess that is what we all want. The other half of our jigsaw puzzle. Richard had bought the *National Enquirer* at Newark airport, in which there was a large article about the American comic and famously out lesbian Ellen De Generes. Allegedly she had found a new love after Anne Heche buggered off. Anne and she had been 'in love for life'. Two years on and it was over. If lesbians could marry would it change things? Would it help give a framework for commitment? Lori couldn't understand why I couldn't just have a ceremony but the truth is that I couldn't stand the pain of it not really meaning anything.

Lori and I discussed what we would do for a wedding. It is, after all, something of a theatrical affair. In general, I think we felt that Indian restaurants were out. The food was finally served but I couldn't really eat. Just twenty-four hours earlier I had been cracking jokes in Birmingham and now I was eating bits of Bangladesh in a shopping mall. It was quite surreal and only became more so as the alertness aid kicked in on top of the raspberry beer and the wine. I think I was becoming slightly hyper when the belly dancer appeared. If the crowd, who were mostly old with old money, had hated the beer, the belly dancer got an even better reception. You could almost hum along to the rattle of teeth as collective jaws hit their plates of poppadoms.

She was very young, very thin and had stuck a jewel in her belly button presumably with a bit of Blu-Tack. She had long orange hair, which I thought was a nice touch as it matched the table decorations. Her body, much of which was revealed, was heavily hennaed and tattooed. I am not a great fan of belly dancing. It is something mine does just getting out of bed and I don't really see the skill in it. Apparently this woman was very good indeed. She approached the fake parquet dance floor with the blade of a large sword balanced on her head. This was not a sword for beginners. It was at least three foot long and wide enough to make light of a substantial loaf. I had a sneaky feeling I knew where she had bought it. There was much whispering among the guests. 'Don't try this at home kids.' Most of them were by now in shock. Each one spent some time telling Richard they didn't want 'people in England to think this is normal'.

The woman danced for quite some time showing a remarkable agility at maintaining the sword on top of her head and not taking off an ear lobe. It was a skill that might perhaps have amused the troops in the many Civil War battles fought not minutes from the strip mall we were in. I couldn't really think of another use for it.

The chances of you happening to have a yard-long sword about your person to impress at a disco seemed limited. Anyway she did it very well and then she did it again and then a bit more. Then she touched the floor behind her bottom with her nose and pointed round the room a bit to get other people to dance with her. There was much shuffling and looking down from the other guests and I found myself standing with my arms firmly crossed over my chest. I don't dance at the best of times. I certainly wasn't going to start with cutlery on my head in a Georgian Indian restaurant in front of people I had never met before. It presented an interesting social dilemma. Would it have helped me win friends and impress or just have confirmed their opinion that I was not quite the thing?

Of course David, who was responsible for us all being there in the first place, got up and did the sword thing and then I think Leslie felt compelled to dance around him. She looked great and you could tell it was love otherwise I don't think she would have done it.

Lori and I decided that the belly dancer ought to do brises as well as weddings. For those of you who've never had the joy of attending, a bris is the ceremony of Jewish circumcision. We thought the dancer could provide her own cutting equipment and then dance around afterwards to cover up the baby's cries. I managed to chat with her afterwards. Well, there wasn't exactly a queue for her autograph. I always think it is a sign of your place at a social function if you end up gossiping with the entertainment. She also taught belly dancing but this, pleasingly, was not the limit of her skills. 'I also do goddess posturing,' she explained.

This was not a statement for which I could think of a single suitable follow-up question other than, 'What?'

I was, of course, being breathtakingly ignorant and she eyed me with pity. 'Goddess posturing!' she said, using the technique of repetition often employed by the English when talking to foreigners. 'I've studied the poses of the goddesses on Grecian urns and now I teach them to bring people serenity and to help alleviate stress.'

I only wished we were staying longer.

The bus driver reappeared in the pouring rain like Lord Roberts arriving at the Relief of Mafeking. Richard and Lori found me under a table, wide-awake, with a butter knife on my head, trying to pose as Pythia, Goddess of the Griddle or very like.

We were herded back on the bus. Packed to the gills with artificially induced caffeine, I had many things I was prepared to talk about. It had been a very strange experience for all of us but somehow it didn't make the conversation any easier. We had begun as interlopers and sadly so it remained.

The next morning I was buzzing on a combination of caffeine and Sleep Rite. I didn't know whether to sleep or salsa. The TV offered me five channels direct to God, two sets of cartoons, a kid's movie, CNN and an opportunity to pay to see *Sorority Shower Cam*. I opted for CNN where someone was presenting a serious analysis of the problem with chad droppings. I was hung-over, fat and sad. The perfect state to be in on a journey in which I was questioning everything in my life. The hotel had provided a magazine called *Appalachian Life* that promised me 'History, Humour and Culture'. It also had a long article about Margaret Mitchell, about her life and her good husband who brought in the ready money while she wrote. I decided I wanted a husband who would look after me and leave me at home to write the one great novel for nine years. I certainly know that I have it in me to be a recluse. I have had to be jolly for so long that it might be quite pleasant not to bother for a bit.

CNN moved on to more arguing in the Supreme Court about whether the re-counts count. A very angry, very white Republican woman appeared.

'You'd have to beat me and drug me to get me to believe these re-counts are being done fairly.'

'We are good people doing a good job,' countered a very sensible black woman.

Elsewhere, Dick Cheney was in hospital with chest pains and Bush had boils on his head. Those Republican boys didn't seem to be able to stand the strain of the vote counting. How well we would all sleep in our beds if they got to run the place.

I went to the wedding breakfast where I tried some unspeakable food. Lori told me not to be so judgemental.

'There are certain foods,' she said, 'which you have to grow up with in order to like. Comfort food.'

I think she was right. I also think that unless you are on a major highway towards 'carb-loading' then grits and biscuits with gravy have no place on the morning table. I put both on my plate from the buffet because I like to have a go at everything culinary. I have in my time eaten both locust and zebra and enjoyed neither but I'm proud of my attempts to eat local. Grits are pure white with a thin porridge texture and a slight seediness. They taste of absolutely nothing. When president-elect William Howard Taft visited Atlanta in 1909 he was served a thirty-pound barbequed possum and only took one bite, so I was not the first person to decline to eat Southern delicacies.

For reasons I can't fathom, the same people who had sat with us the night before and not really spoken came and sat with us now and didn't really speak. There were no assigned places. They didn't need to sit with us but perhaps they too didn't know many people. It was like the first days in the school cafeteria where you gravitate towards any face which seems vaguely familiar. Wills, the uncontrollable child, had not been subdued by sleep. Indeed, it was possible he too had been munching his way through a packet of Vivarin. His father, a bespectacled businessman with neat hair, had no concept of how to feed children at all. He had piled a plate full of everything the buffet had to offer, placed Wills on his lap and then simply allowed him to rummage through it with small fat little hands.

Gravy and sausage were spewed about in equal measure until Wills took to sucking on a whole sausage which dangled from his mouth as if he'd suddenly bitten the sexual appendage off a small dog. There were no dogs limping in the area but he was a swift child and I thought it a distinct possibility.

Leslie came and sat with us for a moment but she had many people to see who had come from miles away and we were soon given back to our table. A general conversation about grits ensued as I couldn't think of anything else to talk about. No one wanted to discuss the election any more and certainly no one seemed inclined to question the current state of the weather in England.

'What are grits?' I asked, struggling with a mouthful.

'It's wheat,' said Wills' father, while the food in question flew from Wills' hand and on to the man's trousers.

'No, it's corn,' said Susan, the estate agent, who used to be an actress but has three boys and 'couldn't possibly now'.

'It's a product of corn,' someone else ventured, 'but it really needs something to flavour it.'

Like real food, I thought.

'Cheese or maple syrup or maybe both,' Susan suggested.

The biscuits and gravy were worse. It isn't a biscuit at all but a small sweet white roll. It's called a biscuit because it uses baking powder, not yeast, to rise. When they say 'The South will rise again' that is the ingredient everyone is thinking about. This 'biscuit' is then blanketed in a thick white gravy not unlike something we would think covered a cauliflower quite nicely. This gravy too tastes of nothing and is a possible contender for the maple syrup and cheese cover-up.

A waiter called Alemu Kamedu served coffee. He was from Ethiopia. Apparently, 'Alemu' means world and 'Kamedu' means weight. His name meant weight of the world. It was a lot for one man to carry. I told him that my name means 'defender of men' but I didn't go into the irony of that particular choice by my parents.

I can't say we got to know Atlanta. My personal tips are *don't* eat at Anthony's. It is much sold as the full Southern experience and described everywhere as 'an oasis of green in the heart of Buckhead'. It turns out the place is green because they have surrounded it with astroturf and I suspect put some in the food. *Do* eat at Canoe. It lies on the west bank of the Chattahoochee river and I had the best meal I have ever had anywhere. Do also visit the largest tin chicken in the South. It's a 57-foot National Landmark for Kentucky Fried Chicken where you can also have your picture taken with a full-size, white plastic model of Colonel Sanders. I don't think I've time now to go into the artist we met in a forest, who, in partnership with Leslie, had tarred and feathered a headless mannequin wearing a Victorian ballgown as a political statement against ante-bellum womanhood. It's a long story but it did make me feel better about life in general.

I learned little about Leslie except that she is a charming person who seems, until now, to have had better luck professionally than personally. I would say she has not always been fortunate in her choice of men and I can only hope the Pratt she has married is an improvement. How odd to flit into someone's life for so important an occasion and flit out again.

As we flew back the newspapers were full of the election and the possibility of the whole saga ending up in the Supreme Court. Some people are now saying if the contest is between George Bush's intelligence and Al Gore's honesty then the correct court for the case would be small claims.

Bumper sticker: 'Texas – I'm going in, cover me'

# An Interlude of Terror

*I will show you fear in a handful of dust.*

T. S. Eliot, *The Waste Land*

September 11. That's all you need to write. It is, like Pearl Harbor, a date written in infamy. From now on there will be two halves to modern American life – the stuff that came before September 11 and everything that came afterwards. It changed America and, of course, it changed anyone trying to write about the place. I had come to seek out an America of the past and now could not help but be gripped by the present. I should have been in New York on 13 September 2001 but by then America had closed its air space to all European traffic. I should have been heading for a weekend on Martha's Vineyard with a bunch of Gladyses but it didn't happen.

Despite having made a good start on my Gladys quest in 2000, many things had conspired to stop me completing my mission. Other work had arisen, the publication of my new novel had kept me on the road and I had been busy moving house to be nearer my children. Travelling up and down from London to the country to see them almost every day had become too much. You cannot compartmentalise time with your children and I wanted to be round the corner.

I was in Italy on the day of the tragedy, on holiday on the shores of Lake Maggiore with my partner Alice. We were having a tranquil time, taking the small ferries across the still waters and imagining ourselves as a tiny piece in a rather beautiful jigsaw puzzle picture. In the afternoons we returned to our hotel. Here we helped bring down the average age of the clientele by about forty years and also made them feel better by going for the obligatory afternoon nap. That particular afternoon we had lain on the bed watching Italian television. Apart from being able to name twelve different types of pasta, my Italian is poor but we had gathered that they were showing some biography of Bruce Willis, the movie actor. Gripping as Willis' life may have been, we fell asleep and awoke to the sight of the first plane crashing into the Twin Towers.

'That's a heck of an effect,' I said.

'What movie was that?' asked Alice.

Still convinced this was all part of the walk through Bruce Willis' action-packed life we watched idly on and chatted about our day. Then they began to show other footage, raw news footage. I spent a year of my life working in a television newsroom. I know the difference between reportage and make-believe.

'This is happening. This is actually happening.'

The world had turned into a Bruce Willis movie where bad guys did unbelievably horrific things.

I'm not sure that at first we all quite absorbed what had happened. Despite the events and general world panic, I still tried to get to America as quickly as possible. I refused to let this event get in my way. I phoned Rita. At first she was upset but calm. She too was determined to carry on and would still be going to the Vineyard to meet the others. Then, with each succeeding call, she became more and more unsettled. She needed to be with her church, her children did not want her to go and, in the end, she did not want to go. It was the beginning of rampant fear on both sides of the ocean.

It was not until late in October that I finally managed to get back on my journey. My neighbour Paul was once again my travel companion and keen to see more of America. Richard and I were due to make some films for the BBC and he couldn't get away. Paul and I arrived at the Washington Square Hotel in the heart of New York around midnight on the night of Hallowe'en. It had been an uneventful flight. A few extra security checks but nothing out of the ordinary and, despite the news of airlines looking like the Marie Celeste, a very full flight indeed. At the hotel, a handsome young man of Asian appearance was in attendance behind the desk. We were tired and went through the credit card routine as quickly as possible.

'So, where are you from?' asked the clerk.

'London,' we said. It is not London at all but it is near. I remembered Lori's remark about the number of Americans who think Africa is a country and I thought it would do. The young man tapped on his computer with confidence and spoke confidentially to us.

'Must be nice to get away from those race riots,' he said.

I thought I had misheard. 'I beg your pardon?'

'The race riots,' he said confidently. 'I hear there is a lot of racism.'

I looked at Paul to see if I had somehow missed a huge section of news back home. He shook his head and said, 'No, I don't think so.'

The young man laughed at us. 'Yeah, people rioting in the street about Afghanistan. The race riots,' he repeated with more emphasis.

'No. Not one,' I said.

He looked at me sympathetically. Clearly I didn't even know what was happening in my own country.

'I'm from Pakistan,' he said, as if that gave him greater knowledge of where there might or might not be race riots in the world. I felt a sigh seep through my body. It was coming up for one o'clock in the morning but the desk clerk was ready to be on the *Larry King Show*.

'Of course, I think this is all just for the governments,' he expounded. 'They are the ones who are going to benefit.' I won't go into his full thesis of conspiracy theories but we did stand there long enough for me to contemplate phoning home to check the status of civil obedience. Paul and I popped out to buy some bottled water from a Duane Reede drugstore on the corner. Duane Reede on Fifth Avenue was the first shop I had ever bought anything in in America although I doubt I had ever seen the clientele it attracted in the small hours of the morning.

We found our beverages and went to pay. The Hallowe'en festivities were still going on and there were two men ahead of us in the queue. One was tall and dressed in fishnets, a baby-doll nightie and something of a 1950s woman's wig. Behind him was an elderly tramp. I was impressed that both had made such a convincing effort for the dressing-up season. Then I noticed that the tramp stank of urine and was buying many packets of incontinence pants with a built-in waist strap. This seemed to be too close to method acting for the world of pretend. The man in the baby-doll winked at Paul and purchased some lip balm. Outside, clowns and devils walked past in a great throng.

'Hallowe'en, I guess,' said Paul.

'I don't know,' I replied. 'It could just be New York.'

Half a dozen of New York's finest were hanging around the steps of the hotel when we returned.

'Excellent security,' I commented.

A young officer built like Joyce's cooker tipped his hat at me.

'That's what you're paying for, ma'am.'

It turned out we were staying in the place the local cops all use as a restroom. I was a little nervous and inexplicably it made me feel better. What they might have done to save me in the face of a descending 747 I have no idea. I lay on my bed and watched *Star Trek* with the lovely Captain Janeway. I thought about Lori's foreign students gathering their notions of American behaviour from the show and I realised something strange – no matter how many times I have seen *Star Trek*, and I do love it, I never seem to see the same episode twice.

I will confess to having been somewhat anxious about coming. Rita had phoned me in London to pass on an FBI statement warning of 'impending further attacks'. The Governor of California had announced that he had 'credible information' that state bridges were to be targeted so he had stepped up security on all river crossings. Then the FBI had announced that the 'rumours' of impending attack might now be false just to scare everybody. I sent silent congratulations to whoever had started the rumours because they were certainly working for me.

My room was very small indeed. Not only could you not have swung a cat, I don't think you could both have been in residence at the same time. My miniature window looked out on to a brick wall some six inches away. In the morning I couldn't see the sky or, indeed, tell if anything else had fallen out of it in the night. I thought I'd better check the news before I ventured forth but as usual the TV seemed to carry nothing but ads. I could only presume nothing else earth-shattering had happened or the world wouldn't still be worrying about pocket-sized remedies for bowel disorders.

Everyone said that New York had changed. That everyone was kinder. That the restaurants and theatres were empty as the natives stayed at home in the bosom of their families and the tourists stayed away. I was prepared to be treated kindly in the street and sense a new reaching out among the people. I don't know why but I actually found it comforting to find that this wasn't entirely true. It was a good sweeping hook for media stories but I am not sure it was what was happening day to day.

Paul and I wanted to walk. We wanted to walk south down to what everyone was now calling 'Ground Zero', to the place that had been the Twin Towers. I don't know whether it was ghoulish or not. My brother Nick, a foreign news journalist, had flown out to Kabul to cover the story. I think when someone close to you heads off with a flak jacket on, you probably want to find out why.

To see what it was that had involved my family in such a remote corner of the world. The first sign that we were getting near the site was a local fire station. Here they had clearly lost many. An entire wall beside the open doors was covered in handwritten messages, flowers and photographs of unbearably young men smiling with pride in their uniforms. Behind us in the street two fire engines wailed past as we stood and looked at the impromptu memorial. Where the Wall Street mogul had once been king of New York, now it was the fireman or policeman of my youth. Everywhere a roaring trade was being done in FDNY and NYPD baseball caps. Tacky T-shirts with the Twin Towers on were for sale on every sidewalk to 'honour the dead' and make a few bucks for the vendor.

I saw a police officer standing on a street corner. He looked impressive and I stopped to take his photograph. That was when I saw he had a little white cart parked near by. He stood with his cap in his hand where he had tucked his morning post into the inside brim. He was a 'correction officer', a traffic warden. People nodded to him as they walked past. The city had really come to something when even the guy with the parking tickets was getting respect.

The closer we got to the site, the quieter the city became. At the Chelsea Vocational College, groups of young black men littered the steps and pavements. Maybe it was my mood but they seemed subdued and listless. Maybe it was always like that at the college. Every downstairs window was covered in tough plates of grey mesh busy both protecting against crime and obscuring what little light might have got through the filthy glass. It was hard to imagine anything less vocational looking.

Soon there was an acrid smell in the air. It burnt the eyes and the back of the throat. It was unlike anything I have ever smelled before. Was this burning flesh or had there not even been enough left for that? Another block and the world went from colour to black and white. We had stepped into an old film noir movie. A thick film of dust lay on every surface. About a block from the site, on a corner, stood an ancient shoe shop. It was the kind I remember from my childhood when there was a complete honesty about the window display. They sold shoes. Shoes you could walk in. Shoes that would keep your feet dry. They didn't sell dreams or aspirations, just good sensible shoes and that's what there were in the window – row after row of them. Not laid out with any nod to art whatsoever. Just in ranks like a large Imelda Marcos closet.

It was hard to imagine that such an old-fashioned place had survived so close to the heart of the financial district of this great city. It was impossible to decide whether the dust on the shoes had always been there or whether it had arrived on the coat-tails of September 11. The women's shoes were mainly for the wider fitting. The sort that provide a good covering for a problem foot or bunion. One blue tasselled pair of loafers was labelled 'SAS Guaranteed Comfort Shoe'.

It was hard to imagine the SAS selecting a slip-on for their operations, but who knows? It was all very odd.

We walked on and the smell got worse. Soon we started seeing people in gas masks. A young man got out of his truck wearing a huge respirator with twin Barbie-pink vents sticking out from either side of his mouth. He looked faintly ridiculous. I suppose I would expect a young man like that to be rather more cavalier about his mortality; to cock a snook at Mr Bin Laden. But he wore his cerise protector when not everyone else had bothered. Several men were painting a newly constructed narrow wooden walkway towards the site. It began at one end of the street and ended at a dark green mesh wall that surrounded the heart of the towers' collapse. It was hard to see what the walkway would be for. It was so narrow it could only be used for one-way pedestrian traffic and it didn't seem to go anywhere. Two men were painting it white while two other men added orange stripes. They were being slow and careful in what seemed to be a pointless exercise. The white paint was filthy as soon as it was applied and the orange striping appeared to be an unnecessary extra. The men all wore hard hats. I don't know why. There was nothing above them but blue sky, but then I guess that is what people had thought on September 11. Hard hats and gas masks – everyone protecting themselves against something unknown and not understood.

Handwritten signs on scraps of paper and cardboard hung haphazardly on the hoarding. There was nothing very official-looking about any of it. My favourite on a torn piece of A4 simply read, 'It is unlawful to touch this sign.'

There was a general sense of people having to make it all up as they went along. Plumes of smoke or dust still rose from the scene. A soldier was guarding the gap in the hoarding, which occasionally swung open to allow a sanitation truck through. He had thick glasses and was wearing traditional army green camouflage. This too seemed a little pointless. There was certainly nothing green for him to blend against in the event of an invasion. Quite tempting to run up to him and yell, 'I see you!'

He saw me too.

'Don't take photographs,' he commanded. 'This is a crime scene.'

And, of course, it was but that is not what it felt like. Crime scenes are places where there is a single body at an odd angle drawn on the floor in chalk. Crime scenes are places where men in raincoats mutter and put bits of fibre in plastic bags. This was much too big for that. Above the mesh, the jagged remnants of the aptly named skyscrapers could just be seen. All the steel that was left was bent and bowed and blackened. A monument to man's inhumanity to man. A police officer in his classic blue uniform trundled past in a golf cart wearing the new regulation pink mouth protector.

Many writers tried to capture what they felt after the event but the one who spoke to me most was Ian McEwan. He said that the greatest crime that had occurred on that day, was a failure of the imagination. That if any one of the terrorists had had the imagination to envisage what the victims and their families were about to go through, they would never have been able to carry out their deed. It is a writer's understanding of the world. Without imagination there is only death.

It was, as you might expect, a moving place to visit but in a moment the New York character that I have known for many years appeared. Beside the hoardings was an office building. It was the largest and nearest place to the scene to remain unscathed and still in operation. Three wide steps led up to the front door and passers-by were taking it in turns to stand on the top step and take a closer look at the remains of the towers. Signs indicated that the place used to be a photographic shop but now it had been turned into the temporary headquarters of a real estate development company which was offering luxury apartments to anyone interested. A moustached man appeared in the doorway and began screaming at me and Paul.

'We're trying to do business here!' he yelled. 'Get off my steps.'

Then he officiously barged into the street to grab some barricades and drag them in front of his door. How nice for him to be alive to do it. I hoped the apartments he was selling were important in the great scheme of things.

A block away they were digging up the whole road. I couldn't tell if it was necessary because of what had happened or because, without any traffic around, this was now a good time to dig up the road. Local people had used the metal barricade around the works to lay flowers. The flowers were rather sad. They were the kind you buy in England at petrol stations. Tight little blooms still wrapped in cellophane. They were all dead now but you knew even if they had been unwrapped and placed in water they would never have looked nice. False, forced flowers. There was nothing joyous about them. Nothing even reminiscent of life. In my mind I kept replaying the images of the people who had jumped for their lives. The man who jumped with an umbrella as if it might have saved him. How impossible to imagine the heat and the horror. To finish your life with not even a DNA sample left.

At the Red Cross Disaster Relief Center a block away, a man in a Red Cross pinny marched up to us.

'Can I help you?' he demanded. He seemed brusque and irritable and I couldn't tell if he meant it or not.

We politely declined and he stomped off. Perhaps there weren't enough people to help, perhaps he hated the tourists the place now attracts or maybe he was just having a bad day. Across the road half a dozen people were standing around in gas masks. The door to the centre had many signs offering help, the largest of which was obviously important and was printed twice.

'NO Restrooms!' it declared with some vehemence.

And I thought about that. I thought about the general sense of irritation in the area that people were coming to look, to see what had happened, but I think it was a natural desire. If we are all destined to stand shoulder to shoulder and fight the good fight, can we not also be allowed to go and see why? After the planes hit, New Yorkers queued up to give blood, make food and fill the coffers of a charity fund. The Disaster Relief Center would have been happy to help if blood or oxygen or something grand were needed but they didn't want to help with the small stuff – they didn't want to let you go to the toilet. The British are the same. Everyone tells you how great the Brits are when their 'backs are against the wall' but wouldn't it be nice if we all helped out when there was no wall there at all?

We drifted away and found ourselves outside City Hall with its small surrounding park. There were American flags hoisted everywhere but the place was locked up tight. Metal gates and railings hemmed in the park and a large metal barrier had been raised in the road. In bright red it had the word STOP writ large.

The sun was shining and we needed to get away. We managed to find a cab and headed north. On the way we passed a shop called the Funny Cry Happy Gift Shop, which I liked. I thought how unhappy it would have made my old English teacher. Not even a sentence – just a whole lot of descriptions. In Greenwich Village we passed the Rubyfruit Jungle restaurant, a lesbian hangout where I once heard Neil Sedaka give an impromptu performance because he likes to sing for the girls. Paul was looking everywhere for a road under a road which he had seen on *Friends*. It is another British image of America – all those jolly Americans bantering with each other and having a lovely cosy time. When we reached Midtown we got out and walked. In a shop selling costumes, a giant plastic rat in the doorway seemed to be grinning at me.

Q: What is bin Laden going to be for Hallowe'en?

A: Dead.

Paul asked me, 'What was the best thing to be for Hallowe'en when you were a kid?'

'Catholic,' I said.

'Catholic?'

'Yeah. The next day is All Saints' Day and you'd get that off as well.'

It was 1 November and Paul and I sat at a pavement café and drank coffee in the sun. Beside us two women were chatting in German, while across the way a French couple and a friend were sharing a copy of *Le Monde*. Something terrible had happened, but a few blocks away life went on. I knew New York would survive when we saw the first piece of hoarding around Ground Zero. On it someone had neatly stencilled,

'Osama bin Laden missed us, don't you make the same mistake. The Dakota Steakhouse. Honor America. Join us for cocktails.'

My sister rang my mobile. I was five minutes from her and she rang me via London. We headed down to South Street Seaport for lunch and for a brief moment to pretend that everything in the city was normal. The setting was great – a café on a wonderful wooden boardwalk, ancient tugs tied at the dock and a most authentic smell of fish. The lunch was less great. Plastic cutlery, plastic plates, plastic cheese – the whole plastic experience.

Afterwards we couldn't resist the gadget shop on the pier. Here I quite fancied a pair of dull metal glasses, which were for sale for hundreds of dollars. They were not just ordinary spectacles. Inside each eyepiece was a tiny individual screen for watching television. A young sales assistant was keen to assist.

'Aren't they great?' he enquired.

'Yes,' I said. 'But they wouldn't be much good if you were having friends over to watch the game.'

He thought about this for some time and then nodded. 'No. You would each need a pair of glasses.'

Indeed. He didn't understand me and I didn't understand him. We weren't about to bomb each other over it but of these small acorns . . .

CHAPTER 8

# Sue – Gladys Five

*Dogs are Shakespearean, children are strangers.*
*Let Freud and Wordsworth discuss the child,*
*Angels and Platonists shall judge the dog.*

Delmore Schwartz, American poet

I don't know what that poem means. I'm heading for New Jersey to see a woman about a dog. As the horizons of my trip expand geographically so too do the occupations of the Gladyses concerned. Sue moved to New Jersey some years ago to open a dog-training centre and boarding kennels, a notion in the parade of possible professions that never even crossed my mind. As usual I had left everything to the last minute and even as we headed towards her canine world I wasn't at all sure that we would be able to hook up. Every time I called I got the answerphone message which reminded callers that the kennels insisted 'humans must be accompanied by a dog'. It went on to say she was probably out with the dogs and would the caller please leave their own message. I left one saying I too was gone to the dogs but could we have dinner anyway. It was only after I hung up that it occurred to me that she might not find that funny – she might even find it offensive. It's very tricky with people you knew but don't really know now. I was also a little nervous about Sue. She was a comfortable-looking person even in her teens with long, dark centre-parted hair and a penchant for wearing what appeared to be the same clothes every day. Sue had been one of the techies in the high school drama department. One of the slightly grubby technical people backstage who climbed ladders a lot and always had a pair of pliers about their person. Although she was not the oldest in the group she always seemed to be in charge – certainly everyone did what she said. Rita and I once went out with Sue on her family's small motorboat in the waters of Long Island Sound. It was the summer of '72 and I remember it as incredibly hot, although that memory may be faulty. I think lots of people recall their childhood summers as being bathed in golden sun.

The boat was a ubiquitous craft in the area known as a Boston whaler. A stubby little flat-bottomed affair noted for its stability in the water, it was about twelve foot long with a central seat for the steering wheel and not much else. It was a boat used for fishing or idle day trips. Sue took me and Rita out on one of those hot days. Rita wanted to tan and I wanted to drive but Sue had other plans.

'Sandi, throw that boat cushion in the water!'

'Why?'

She looked at me and gripped the wheel of the boat. 'Just do it!'

I picked up one of the flat boating cushions by the cloth handle on the side. When we had first arrived at Mamaroneck Harbor, my brother and I had both taken our motorboat driving and boating safety licences. I knew that these flat cushions were not just to keep your bottom from chafing on the seats. They also floated and could be used as temporary lifesavers. I threw the cushion in the water and it bobbed up behind us in the wake.

'Hold on!' shouted Sue, as she spun the boat round, neatly grabbed a boat hook from the floor of the craft and scooped the cushion out of the water without slowing down.

'Neat!' I said.

'Sue, could you warn me in advance when you're going to do that?' asked Rita, looking up from the seat where she was reclining.

Sue looked at her and slowed the boat down to idling.

'Rita, get in the water.'

'No!' Rita shook her head.

'Rita, get in the water.'

'I don't want to.'

'Rita! Jump!'

So she did. I was very glad it wasn't me. Rita bobbed up behind us. Sue gunned the boat away and seemed disinclined to turn back and scoop Rita out of the water. I didn't want to annoy Sue but I was sure this wasn't a great idea.

'I don't think she swims that well, Sue,' I managed, hoping that would help. Without a word, Sue swung the boat around and headed back to Rita. We fished her out and went home. I never really knew what that was all about. That was the trip Sue told me I should shave my legs. I was wearing shorts and had tiny blonde hairs on my bare thirteen-year-old legs. I went home and shaved them and cut myself badly. I was starting to be a grown-up. Being a bleeding grown-up.

So everyone did what Sue said but underneath the tough exterior and barking orders was one of the kindest women I've ever met. It was Sue who got me up early one Easter morning to deliver baskets of sugared eggs secretly to all the other Gladyses. It was Sue who persuaded me once that we should deliver anonymous roses to Ginger because it would make her feel better. I always dragged along behind Sue – a kind of Robin to her Batman. When I left for England she and her mother came to say goodbye. Sue did not say much but she handed me a cushion on which she had embroidered the quintessential American dolls, Raggedy Ann and Raggedy Andy – rag dolls in American red, white and blue that carry a secret message. Underneath their clothes they have a heart embroidered with the words 'I love you'.

Sue's mother shook her head. 'I didn't even know she could sew,' she said.

Wherever I have settled over the years that small cushion has always found an important place.

So you understand I approached seeing Sue again with a mixture of caution and delight. I also approached in something of a roundabout way.


## New Jersey

*More chemical products are made in New Jersey than in any other state.*

Carole Marsh, *My First Pocket Guide to New Jersey*

The New Jersey Turnpike is aptly named for it goes from New York to New Jersey. Paul kept singing the Paul Simon song about how we'd all gone to look for America and trying to remember what Simon had said about his home state highway. Paul was still excited about seeing as much as possible. As we hadn't actually heard from Sue we had decided to drive right across the state first and visit Philadelphia. On the map it didn't look that far. The fact that we had bought the book of maps for $3 from a man on the corner of Lexington Avenue who was also willing to sell us his grandmother and the Tower of London should have been a warning. It was really too thin a book to have as many as fifty states in it. Even California didn't look that far away.

I entered the Garden State, as New Jersey is called, thinking about my great-aunt Signe, the one who was friends with the Algonquin crowd. She was a remarkable woman who had graduated from Cornell University in New York in 1916. This was unusual in a girl and even more unusually she became a writer. She married Francis Hackett, an Irish poet from Kilkenny who had emigrated to America when he was eighteen. For many years they lived in the States and they did that rather clever thing of having patrons to look after them while they wrote. As we drove past Hopewell, New Jersey, I recalled that this was where Charles Lindbergh's baby was kidnapped in 1932. I had visited Signe at the home of Lindbergh's wife Anne. A fine writer in her own right,

Anne Morrow Lindbergh was charming and the house was grand. Signe was living there while she scribbled. How wonderful. Fed and watered and given clean paper. No need to deal with the grinds of life. What more could a girl desire?

My trip was dotted with great women whose stories leapt out at me with every passing mile. Stories I had been told in my American schooling.

'Monmouth,' I pointed out to Paul as we drove south.

'So?'

'The battle of Monmouth? Molly Pitcher?' He didn't know.

Nearly a hundred battles of the American Revolution were fought in New Jersey. From the turnpike it's hard to see why. Certainly the garden part of the state is not entirely visible. Nor can you see why it is also known as the Clam State. We didn't stop at Monmouth because I don't think there is anything to see, but it was there that Mary Ludwig Hayes got the nickname Molly Pitcher. It was during a particularly hot battle on 28 June 1778 and she was helping by carrying pitchers of water from soldier to soldier and cannon to cannon. At one point she stopped to help load one of the cannons. The story goes that while she was reaching for a cartridge she had spread her legs apart in the effort and a cannon ball shot from the enemy went right through, carrying away the lower part of her petticoat. She is said to have looked down calmly and observed, 'It was lucky that didn't pass any higher or it would have carried away something else,' and gone back to work.

The world needs women like that. Actually, the world is full of women like that but we just don't get to hear about them.

I was waxing lyrical on this when Paul yelled, 'Mind that car!'

This is not necessarily a helpful remark on a turnpike which is full of cars all of which need minding. It didn't take me long, however, to realise he was anxious about the car in front. In almost every country in the world the traditional way of proceeding down an eight-lane super-highway is to drive your car in just one lane at a time. The driver ahead seemed to prefer to try many lanes at once in a great sweeping move.

'Driver must be asleep,' I said, and attempted to pass him. Indeed, he was asleep. Absolutely off the planet, leaning against the window in that attractive open-mouthed position that all sleepers have. Now here is the dilemma. If you are driving next to someone on a busy American motorway who is asleep do you

A. Hoot your horn and wake him up?

B. Drive on?

Actually not an easy decision. Choose A and he may startle awake and crash, choose B and you have failed your Good Samaritan test. We chose B and drove on. I can't say I felt happy about it but we did see him some time later at a rest stop. I don't know why he needed the rest stop. He had had plenty of sleep on the road.

I was beginning to feel tired myself. My beloved Dorothy Parker was born in New Jersey two months early because her mother was exhausted by the trip from New York. I knew how she must have felt. It was just as well that I was not heavy with child or I would have dropped several at the service station. Due to her accident of birth, New Jersey claims Parker as one of its own but I have no idea if she ever went back. I can't say it's a place it had ever occurred to me to visit. First, however, Philadelphia.

*I'd rather be here than in Philadelphia.*

W. C. Fields' tombstone

We arrived at the Alexandria Inn in downtown Philly through some ingenuity and very little map reading. The place was full of mincing, lisping boys.

'Hi,' said the concierge, Greg, in the sort of highpitched voice that can make dogs gather. 'God! You're from England and how is that Queen of yours? How is her mother? Isn't she amazing? Say,

have you seen the new *Ab Fab* series yet? We just can't wait.' Greg
went on for some time about all things British so that I had leisure
to read his many tattoos and admire his small triangular badge
with a rainbow on it.

'Sorry, Paul,' I apologised quietly to my straight English companion. 'It seems to be a gay hotel.'

'How can you tell?' he asked.

I am going to skim through Philadelphia as, basically, I
shouldn't have been there in the first place but if you've never
been then here are my quick tips for the place. Don't eat dinner at
Inn Philadelphia, however much Greg at the Alexandria Inn begs
you to, but do visit the Benjamin Franklin Museum. I think by
now you will have guessed that I am a big fan of both the poorly
presented place of history and the unique object found nowhere
else in the world. I am as likely to travel hundreds of miles to see
the world's largest tin chicken, as I am to seek out a holy fingernail which bleeds on alternate Tuesdays in Lent. For someone
who loved the Margaret Mitchell Experience, the Benjamin
Franklin Underground Museum is well worth the detour. I had
actually been there once before, when I was twenty-one, and
now again because it stuck in my mind. Really, it's an absolute
must.

> *If you would*
> *not be forgotten,*
> *as soon as you are*
> *dead & rotten,*
> *either write things*
> *worth reading,*
> *or do things*
> *worth the writing.*
>
> Benjamin Franklin

I don't think anyone doubts that Ben was a genius. A fine
printer, a great diplomat, an inventor and the man who should be

given credit for creating the soundbite, so you'd think someone would have preserved something he once owned – anything in fact. But no.

The entrance to the museum is promising. There is a replica post office, replica printing house and other replica bits and pieces where you can meet 'living history interpreters'. Basically these are people who dress up in silly hats and try to pretend they knew Ben or whoever you are visiting. The concept that history needs inter-preting strikes me as peculiarly American. Many years ago I was introduced to a Californian woman called Karen who went on to marry Mike McShane, a comic I had done much work with.

'What do you do, Karen?' I asked early on, having run out of conversation.

'I'm a conservative historian,' she replied. This rather flum-moxed me. Ever on the look-out for a career that had never occurred to me, here was something new.

'What does that mean?' I enquired. 'Do you deal with the his-tory of the conservative party?'

'No,' she said. 'I reinterpret history from a conservative point of view.'

Extraordinary idea. I could see history getting a bit skewed because you forgot something or someone steered you a bit wrong but reinterpreting from a political perspective . . . well, I suppose it's what politicians do every day. Rum business, truth. Personally, I think Ben would have been appalled.

We abandoned the living history people and marched out back to the underground museum. The entrance is through some glass doors and then underground (as advertised) via several long slopes. I expect the slopes wind their way down gently in order to accommodate the usual throng of visitors. I don't know if Mr Franklin is going out of fashion but Paul and I had the place to ourselves. We could have skateboarded in and not bothered a soul.

The first corridor had a sedan chair on display. It was a nice sedan chair and was a replica (on loan) of the sort of sedan chair which Ben might or might not have ridden in at one time if he ever did, in fact, ride in a sedan chair. It was, as it were . . . very like. An enormous black woman in a security guard uniform appeared at my shoulder.

'There is a movie in there,' she wheezed. She really was very large and could hardly walk in her Perma Press pants. Her shirt stretched across her chest, held together for modesty with only three buttons and her security badge. She appeared to be suffering some form of breathing difficulty. You had to wonder whether there had been any kind of aptitude considerations when she applied for the job. Is an ability to walk without injuring your thighs a requisite part of guarding historical valuables? We didn't really want to see the film but she was so breathless I didn't want to start a conversation either. We were a long way underground and if she had a seizure I doubted anyone else would happen by for some time.

The cinema was quite large and Paul and I had it entirely to ourselves. We sat and watched the film. Ben's life was fascinating but I could still hear the vast guard wheezing outside. I was sympathetic but I was also quite tempted to commit a crime for I felt sure that with a guard of such immense proportions there was a fairly high chance of getting away with it. I venture to suggest I could have run off with the sedan chair on my own.

I was, however, keen to get on for I knew what lay ahead. After the film and the sedan chair you head off through a room full of mirrors. Here neon signs flash in the reflections with individual words like 'writer', 'printer' and 'postmaster general'. It's supposed to be a room that 'reflects' the great man's life but you begin to wonder where the museum part is. That is when you enter the *pièce de résistance*. The room worth travelling for. The Bell telephone room has not changed in over twenty years. When I was twenty-one the place seemed rather modern. There are banks and banks of telephones on individual stands. In the early eighties these digital phones with push-button dialling in the handset were very new. Now they are very old. Each visitor goes to a phone and looks at a list on the wall. It is a directory of famous people through the ages and their phone numbers. You ring the number of, say, Mark Twain, and he tells you what he thought about Benjamin Franklin. This is the centrepiece of the museum and hours of fun for the whole family. I don't want to spoil it for anyone who is thinking of going but I can tell you that everyone I phoned only had nice things to say about Ben and that Dick Van Dyke appeared to have recorded all the English messages.

It was a heady experience of living history and I think we had been spoilt by the time we got to the house of Betsy Ross. She was the legendary seamstress said to have made the first American Stars and Stripes flag. We sped around the homestead in which time I learned that they weren't really sure she had ever lived there or indeed, ever made the flag. Everyone else seemed impressed.

'Look at those knickers!' said a woman, pointing out a display of old underpants to her child. 'Isn't that amazing; they're done up with buttons.' So is my cardigan, I thought and we left.

We didn't linger long in Philadelphia. Basically the city is much poorer and more depressed than New York. 9/11, as everyone is now calling it, had clearly had a big impact on the city. When we arrived there were state troopers crawling all over the place and it wasn't exactly visitor friendly. Independence Park was all closed up and there were huge security checks if you wanted to visit the celebrated Liberty Bell. Through a plate-glass window we could see queues of people going through body scanners, personal searches and all sorts to stand beside the bell. You could sense terrorists from very far away managing to yank the American chain. We didn't bother. You can see the thing through the window. Basically it's a big . . . bell.

There were bag check places set up in shops, one of which was offering 'Gas masks at $24.99. No return.'

I thought no return was an unfortunate phrase. It suggested a finality about your purchase which, anyway, gave you the face of an elephant.

*Rarely is the question asked: 'Is our children learning?'*
George W. Bush, 11 Jan 2000

We rose the next morning to find Bush addressing the nation. He looked rather startled as if he were surprised to have been woken up. Since my last visit he had not only been elected president but had taken his country to war. After all the election uncertainty I kept trying to find out what the actual vote count had been but no one seemed interested any more. There had been some magical transformation in the White House and the idiot jester of the court was now revered as the king. As far as I could work out, one Supreme Court judge cast the final vote to elect him, which in terms of history means that Supreme Court Justice Sandra Day O'Connor created the presidency on her own. 'Dubya', as he seems to like to be called, had quite a knack for the bon mot, calling Nigeria an 'important continent' and remarking how more and more American imports are coming 'from overseas'. Still, he followed in the footsteps of the previous Republican genius, Ronald Reagan, who believed that 'facts are stupid things'.

In other news a small girl of six had been kidnapped from some leafy town in New Jersey. Her family had previously used the house just for weekends but had moved there full-time after 9/11 because it felt safe. Now a ransom note for their child had been found attached to a flagpole. The relentless cameras showed her father almost speechless at the obligatory press conference. You don't know what will get you in the end but no one in America felt safe any more.

Our bargain-basement map was vague about actual routes out of town but we left Philly driving north on the 611. It was a dismal experience. US flags were still everywhere but here was a

side of American life you rarely see on TV. Endless shops
where everything was a dollar, pawn parlours and rows of dark
brown terraced houses whose porches were either depressed
or collapsing. A man pushed a small child on a trolley piled
high with black rubbish bags while a large crowd of black men
wearing white gloves attended a huge funeral. It was an odd Al
Jolson image.

You'll want to know a few things about New Jersey. It's not a
big place and operates as a kind of crossroads for the east. It is a
place where many people live while actually working in either
New York or Philadelphia.

Bird – Eastern goldfinch
Flower – Violet
Tree – Red Oak
Memorial Tree – Dogwood. I don't know memorial to who or what or
    when, in fact, it would be appropriate. Answers on a postcard,
    please.
Animal – Horse
Shell – Knobbed Whelk, which I think is quite unpleasant
Dinosaur – Hadrosaurus. This is getting silly.

We were due to meet Sue for dinner. Actually it was a pleasant trip
and I would recommend it. We came up the east side of
Pennsylvania through somewhere called Bucks County. It's a
pretty place full of folk-art galleries, coffee shops and farmers'
markets. We stopped in Doylestown to see the rather curious con-
crete castle of Henry Mercer. Here I hummed the words of their
native son Oscar Hammerstein while trying to buy clean underwear. It turned out not to be that sort of place. In Doylestown you
can get great pastry but not underpants. Underpants, a woman in
a shop told me, you buy out of town at factory outlet stores. There
you can buy as many underpants as you want. We drove out of
town and found a large knicker selection but only in man-made
fibres. I was desperate for clean knickers and put on a new pair in

the changing room at the shop. I normally wear cotton and I swear I sparked as I walked from the premises.

We drove north, me sparking, Paul trying to work out which direction the sun was in so that we could continue north. We crossed small rivers by covered bridges. We stopped and took photographs, not just of the wooden structures but of the enormous number of warning signs at the entrance to each bridge. A montage of legal precaution in this most litigious of countries.

We were heading for a place called Clinton, New Jersey. According to the leaflets I collected it is 'Historic Clinton', the 'quintessential small American town'. I don't know if I can vouch for all that as I really only saw a motel and the Cracker Barrel restaurant. I do think, however, that it says something about the place that the people of the town petitioned to have the name changed when Bill Clinton became president.

Sue had not taken offence at my phone message and after several hundred miles with no guide but the sun and the electrical impulses from my underpants, we found her exactly on time on the porch of the Cracker Barrel restaurant in Clinton. Who needs planning? The restaurateurs had gone to some lengths to make the almost new building on the edge of a highway and a shopping mall look old. The entire front of the building had been clad with a long wooden porch. As we pulled up, Sue was sitting there amid a mass of white rocking chairs which were for sale. Indeed the whole shop was selling some kind of homey 'on the porch' vision of America. A Martha Stewart image without the need to do any of the work yourself. Sue smiled at me and stood up for a hug. Still a comfortable woman with longish hair and a centre-parting. As I might have expected she had made little concession to the more girly aspects of grooming and her hair had been allowed to go the grey it wanted. From a distance she looked like her mother. She stood and smiled out of the corner of her mouth. We hugged and it felt good.

The Cracker Barrel restaurant, it will not surprise you to learn, is

a franchise. A franchise where no alcohol is served because it is
'family dining'. There is a curious American notion that alcohol
must be banned from anything connected with the family, or parents
will succumb to its evil temptation, leaving the children to trawl
through the pudding menu at will. At Disneyland in both Florida
and California there is no alcohol served anywhere. They tried to
institute the same principle in Paris but the French just laughed.

If you like mashed potato then the Cracker Barrel is the place
for you. Everything, including I think a few desserts, comes with
mash and everything appears to have been fried, not once but
several times. The menu was vast with little choice. In the end I
ordered 'chicken fried chicken', which basically seemed to be the
low-cholesterol option in that it had only been fried twice.

'Do you want it just as it is on the menu?' asked Michelle, who
was my waitress for the evening and hoped that I would be
having an enjoyable meal and if I wasn't I was sure to say so that
she could make it enjoyable.

'Yes,' I said, doing that English thing of trying to be no trouble to
serving staff. 'Doesn't everybody have it just as it is on the menu?'

Michelle laughed. 'No, everybody changes everything.'

'And you keep smiling,' I said.

'It goes with the job,' she said and smiled. I liked Michelle. I was
sure she was going to make my meal enjoyable but now, after our
conversation, I didn't know whether she was smiling because it
was her job or because she actually liked me. I have no idea why
this was worrying me, as the chances of me ever repeating my
dining experience in that establishment in that part of the world
were slim.

The whole interaction with serving people is very complicated
in America. Basically it comes in two forms. The first is a kind of
therapy for the customer whereby the waiter takes an enormous
interest in their food selection and never fails to say that something
is a 'good choice'. Served and server do brief bonding and one
goes home feeling better and the other gets a good tip. The second

is where no words are exchanged because the food is too cheap and too fast and you don't speak because no one is pretending either one of you has fluent language skills. I don't know which I prefer. I suspect I am too British now for the therapy version.

Exactly as I remembered, Sue had little time for general conversation and we swept into her life and her business. Before she entered the dog world full time, Sue worked as a stage manager in the theatre. Indeed she stage-managed a play in London at one time and organised some auditions for a hideous corporate show I once directed in the United States. (Never ask me about contract industrial cleaning – I am something of a world expert.) Since I had known Sue, she had always had dogs but now they were her life and indeed, other people's.

She looked tired and blamed it on 9/11. Everyone else did too but in her case it was true. 'Pet assisted therapy' is very big in America and something she works with a great deal. After the Trade Center 'incident', she was asked to go down and help at a centre by the water on the New Jersey side. She kept describing the place in the same way over and over again. 'It's a rock concert down there, a complete rock concert.'

This is about the worst thing a professional theatre person can say about an event. It means it is badly organised and is flying by the seat of its pants. It seems Sue arrived with her dogs only to find two other teams of dog people had also been called. She was asked to coordinate things and there appears to have been much political backbiting. It was all volunteer work, something Sue has filled much of her life with. She underplayed this during the meal, which was typical. It wasn't till we got to the office that I saw a dark blue plate on the wall, The Governor's Award for Volunteer Service 2001, and learned of her invitation to breakfast at the New Jersey Governor's mansion. Not just a good volunteer worker for the state, but the best. Before 9/11 she had worked in hospitals, helping people who need to walk with a brace and cane learn their skill by leaning on a specially trained dog, helping children who need to take medicine but won't and many other things her animals are trained to deal with.

At the 9/11 centre the work had been varied. Sue told us that immediately after the disaster, when it had been people filling out missing person forms and providing DNA samples and so on, it was different – there still seemed to be some hope. The dogs were used to pry the children away from the adults so the adults could get on with what they needed to do. Often they would use a dog to distract a child and get it to leave its parents and come to the care centre. Frequently it was the rescue workers themselves who needed to stroke the dogs. They told Sue the truth of what they were seeing, which was being sanitised on TV, and she had many sleepless nights.

Now things are slowly changing. People are collecting death certificates and everyone has to give a formal deposition: 'When did you last see the person?' 'What makes you believe they were in the area?' etc. She said some people just sit on the floor, hugging one of her dogs while they sob and try to get through it. They have children who have elective mutism and she teaches them to do tricks with a dog. Fools them into speaking by saying, 'Oh listen, I have to get something. Could you just tell the dog to sit?'

Dealing with grief and pain, her concern is focused not just on the people but on the animals.

'Dogs are sensitive,' she explained. 'They are trained to do many things but not to have adults throw their arms around their necks and sob and wail for half an hour.'

After a session like that she has to take the dog out and play with it for twice as long as the session took. The dogs too have had to deal with the grief. She spoke of the huge problems with the specialist search and rescue dogs who worked at the disaster scene in the beginning. No one could fly anywhere so the New York authorities were forced to use only local teams. Everyone, man and beast, worked fourteen hours a day as they all scrambled about in the hope of finding anyone alive. By the end the dogs were exhausted and, not surprisingly, depressed. Rescue dogs are schooled to expect a reward when they find someone alive but there was no one to find. Occasionally the workers would hide someone just to please the animals but it wasn't real. It didn't feel real. The only animals getting true satisfaction were the specialist 'cadaver' dogs. They are trained to seek the dead and had no problem finding body parts.

Now people are riding across on the ferry to visit the site. It is part of what the Americans call 'closure'. Sue won't let her dogs go on the journey.

'One dog with one hundred and fifty people who are at best going to behave erratically, in a confined situation where I can't remove the dog from the situation if I need to? I don't think so.'

As we left the fine eating establishment we passed through the general store which was awash with many down-home retail opportunities. I was spoilt for choice but settled for a three-foot-tall turkey dressed as a pilgrim in autumnal colours. I strapped him in the back seat of the car, where he could look out, and decided to name him Franklin. I think that would have pleased Ben.

## Milford and Frenchtown, New Jersey

> *Three lasses of Milford, of courage no doubt,*
> *A-milking one day the three sallied out,*
> *The cows were collected and all standing still,*
> *Not far from the house, as you go to the mill.*
> *Their three passions higher and higher did grow,*
> *When Kate gave to Hannah a terrible blow,*
> *Sukey flew off, and with tongue did berate*
> *With heaviest curses both Hannah and Kate.*
> *The battle soon ended, for Hannah was small,*
> *And Kate, a stout hussy, could out-box them all.*

Local poem by unknown author

I like the idea of being a stout hussy. Indeed, I like the idea of being a stout hussy living around here. I had an image of New

Jersey as a state full of factories and much chemical manufacture. Well, that is indeed going on somewhere but not where Sue has settled. The next morning she took us out from our motel to her dog country club.

'Paul is not very good with dogs,' I explained, as she drove me in her car and Paul followed behind in our car, Betty. 'They always seem to choose him to jump up at.'

Sue didn't really say anything. I think the notion that any dog would jump without her permission was entirely alien. We drove past classic red barns, sweeping fields and neat wooden home-steads. It was the America of the farm movie. The place where a young lad in torn dungarees grows up wishing to be a big league baseball player and eventually triumphs, only to realise that there is 'no place like home'. There is no place quite like Sue's home. It's in a lovely six-acre spot of woods with a small tribu-tary of the Delaware river running at the foot of a hill behind her house.

This neat, not very large two-storey house was surrounded by chain-link fence holding back many dogs of many types. Some were guests and some were Sue's. She did point out which was which but the excitable things kept moving and I never quite got the hang of it. Here, Sue has turned an interest into a liveli-hood. People as mad about their dogs as I am about my children pay her large amounts of money to care for their pups while they are away. The dogs arrive with special diets, special toys and permission to sleep on the furniture. The inside of the house was well lived in. It would never win any *House & Garden* prizes and had the faint aroma of a well-satisfied clientele. They should be. It was costing them more than the Alexandria Inn in Philadelphia. This does not mean that Sue and her husband are rich. This means that keeping a property for dogs is an expensive business. They chose New Jersey because it is cheaper than New York.

'We researched the area and knew there would be a demand,'

said Sue. I couldn't even begin to imagine how you would start such research. Who would you ask? What kind of questions would have been appropriate? Apparently it's a simple matter of demographics which goes to show why I have never had a business of any kind.

The local area is in Hunterdon County. It was once known as Lenapehoking and was home to the Lenni Lenape tribe. I quite like their name as I think it sounds like a second-rate Jewish comedian. 'Ladies and gentlemen, let's give it up for Lenni Lenape!'

'Thanks very much, folks. I've been Lenni Lenape. I'm here till Thursday. Try the veal.'

Apparently it means 'genuine or original people' which is simple and clear about who you are. Makes you wonder if the Palestinians would have done better if their name meant 'Bog off, we've always lived here'.

Ty, Sue's husband, is lovely. He is a sound engineer at a large church in Manhattan. A job I have never investigated in detail but I do find hard to imagine. He is a small round man and he is also black. I think it is fair to say that neither Sue nor her sister Anne did what their mother expected. One married a black man and the other came out as gay. It may be, in terms of familial disappointment, that Sue has done well to avoid children and devote her life to dumb animals. Sue and Ty have not had an easy time in this mixed marriage. They have no doubt that being an interracial couple lost them the house they first wanted to buy and that people have, over the years, treated them differently. It has been a strain.

Sue was good about Paul and put the dogs away before we entered. You could hear them upstairs. I like dogs but it sounded as though there was quite an entourage and even I was relieved. We sat down to watch some videos of dog shows. It was like being at Rita and Ron's house watching the children on tape except this time there were fewer selections from *Annie*. After a while Sue decided we had to meet one of the dogs; I forget the name. This dog would be fine. It bounded in and was fine and then jumped on Paul. And the next and the next . . .

Frenchtown and Milford were well worth the visit. Pretty, sleepy places, but can't say you'd go there to see any historic sights. It was once a centre for the wagon-spoke industry and celebrated for growing peaches. But the peach crop was unreliable and the wagon-spoke industry died away because . . . okay, it's not my area but I imagine people stopped using wagons. The most famous thing in Frenchtown so far has been the chicken farm. Kerr Chickeries was founded in 1907 by Richard W. Kerr who (you will remember) developed chick gender identification and artificial insemination techniques, later used by the entire industry. Funny how people's lives take different paths. The chicken business was big around here. In 1923 alone, more than three million chicks were sent by mail from the Frenchtown post office. I don't know if each one needed a stamp.

Never mind the chickens, let me take you to Lebanon, New Jersey. More specifically, let me take you to a dog-training facility in the basement of a shopping mall in Lebanon, New Jersey. Okay, it's not what you might expect. I have to confess there have been many moments in my life when I can't think how I've ended up in a particular location. I remember painting a remote lighthouse with John McCarthy once and realising that not only was it a strange thing to do but, following a stint in children's television, it was the second time I had done it. The Lebanon Plaza shopping mall, where I found myself that evening, was a place not awash with choice. Basically, you could either get your nails done or have Sue teach your dog to eat biscuits out of your mouth. The indoor training facility for the kennels was new. Indeed they had only recently had their Howl-a-ween party there for the clients. It was all very nicely done with dog paraphernalia everywhere. Framed photos of dogs winning awards, dogs jumping through hoops and several dressed as action heroes decorated the walls. There was even a stencilled paw print on the light switch. Here many types of dog turn up to learn to be obedient. Many types of dog but only one type of owner. The keen owners were all the same breed – middle-aged women mostly without wedding rings. They wore sweatshirts with pictures of dogs on them and were learning competition obedience and dog elocution.

'Would you please remember, people, that "sit" is a one-word command.'

I certainly would. The first time Sue had barked the word at a recalcitrant dog, everyone in the room had ducked down on a bench. Sue was in her element, for I realised that in that basement in Lebanon she had found her dream job – having people listen to her as she told them what to do. Sue had been ill but she still taught with energy and humour. She was kind but concealed it beneath her trademark gruff exterior. During our short time together I had tried to talk to her about the difficulties in my life.

'You can do anything you set your mind to,' she declared. 'If you don't have something, it is because you don't want it enough.' And that was an end to it. I wondered if it was a tack that would be effective when I tried to persuade the BBC to make my programmes.

I watched her work. She gave very clear explanations and managed to get a variety of dogs to do quite complicated things on hand signals. I tried to imagine my shih-tzu at home doing anything even remotely obedient and could just see him rolling over on his back, paws in the air, crying with laughter at the thought. I have always had dogs but I wasn't sure the training was for me. The women kept putting dog biscuits in their mouths and then removing small pieces to reward their animals. I asked one of the women why she couldn't just keep the biscuit in her hand.

'You want them to look at your face,' she said and spat out a small quantity of mashed meal for her pooch.

It was a strange moment sitting in a New Jersey cellar watching schnauzers skim over miniature horse jumps. I couldn't for the life of me think why I was doing this but I was glad Sue was happy. It was a contentment which I hoped would run in the family. My next port of call was to be her older sister, Anne.

# CHAPTER 9

# Anne – Gladys Six

*Men travel faster now, but I do not know if they go to better things.*

Willa Cather, American novelist

A woman who bought a coffee in a paper cup from a Drive-Thru McDonald's has sued the company for injuries and won. It seems she put the hot coffee between her legs when she drove off. The coffee spilled and burnt her thighs. She sued them, as far as I can gather, for selling hot coffee. Someone once burnt me badly on a British Rail train when they dropped four cups of coffee on my left leg. I didn't even get to my destination on time.

Paul and I were back at Rita and Ron's house in New Rochelle and things were, to say the least, a little tense. Mostly this was my fault. I don't 'do' good organising. Indeed, I don't really do organising at all. This is born out of an intense dislike of the telephone and a general desire not to be responsible for plans. When Alice, my partner, and I holiday, my only contribution in choosing our destination is limited grunting and the signing of cheques. In emailing Rita about who I had to see next I had been more than happy, at her suggestion, to pass the necessary arrangements on to her. The upshot of this was that she had laid many plans for mice and men and that, for the next portion of the journey, she was now not only in charge but coming along. I think travelling with someone is a true test of how well you get on.

Paul and I ditched Betty, the redoubtable car, and met Ron at Grand Central Station. This time I was struck by how much more Russian than American the place seems – that vast marble hall with giant Fabergé eggs for chandeliers. But since 9/11 it has been dominated by a huge American flag hung from the ceiling like a giant's bedspread hung out to dry. We had an hour to kill and tried to get rid of our luggage but the man at information told us, 'We don't offer that any more.'

Everyone was scared. We sat and had a coffee. With the addition of Franklin, my three-foot turkey, and various factory outlet purchases, Paul and I were now laden with luggage. We were not so much in need of coffee as of a Sherpa with a smile. Ron met us at the information booth. He carried a small shoulder bag with his things in it. He smiled, he hugged us and then headed off, luggage free, as we struggled behind him. I was reminded of the chair at Sunday school and the difference in approach to manners. The commuter train to New Rochelle left from one of the hundreds of platforms. Unlike any public transport in the UK you could still get a seat on the 5.20. It was a train I had sometimes taken with my dad.

'Where's the bar car?' I asked Ron.

Many was the time I had watched my dad ordering a scotch for him and a coke for me as we trundled out to the burbs. Now it seems you can't get a drink on the New Haven line unless you're going to Connecticut. Maybe they figure if you are going that far you deserve a drink. I wished we were.

From Rita and Ron's house, every now and then, you can hear the great *whoo!* of an old train whistle. It is the romantic American sound of journeying. We were due to head north to Boston and New England to scoop up three more Gladyses. Rita was now on board as a fellow traveller but the theory proved more comfortable than the fact. Travelling, I had decided, was a tense business for

Americans and it became clear why only about 5 per cent of them own a passport. I don't think most people go anywhere, besides which 9/11 hung heavy in the air. Fundamentally no one felt safe outside their own yard.

The morning started with a serious discussion about how to treat your mail. As well as fear, chemical warfare now floated on the horizon. Ron picked up the post from the outside box and brought it in saying he knew a woman who, fearful of anthrax attack, now sprayed bleach on all her mail. He tutted at this and I thought he was going to say how ridiculous she was. Apparently she was ridiculous but only because that 'doesn't actually get rid of the anthrax'. You have to . . .

'Put the mail in the microwave,' said Rita.

'I hadn't heard that,' replied Ron. 'I don't think that's right. I think you have to iron it. Steam and iron it.'

'I don't iron anything,' said Rita, who is a funny woman. 'I am not going to start with the mail.'

She noticed some sweets on the bench in the kitchen and wanted to know where they had come from. Ron shrugged. He was still eyeing the post with its free opportunities to win a million dollars. Could the Taliban be so low as to have infected *Reader's Digest*?

'Don't eat the candy until we have traced its source,' she said firmly to the room in general, but to me in particular. I was, after all, the woman who drank water from a bottle without checking the seal.

'There is a woman in my exercise class,' Rita continued, 'who was going to let her kids go trick or treating at Hallowe'en and then throw away the candy.' Rita paused for a moment. 'At least, I think that's what she was going to do. I couldn't hear exactly what she was saying. We do the exercises in a loop and she kept getting ahead of me. Anyway I think everyone agrees that anyone could buy tainted candy.'

Tootsie Rolls and junk mail – the Taliban had America pegged.

Ron was also grieving for the Arizona pitcher who the night before had 'given' the game away to the Yankees in the twelfth inning. Apparently the pitcher threw a ball and the other team hit a home run. Ron was delighted for the Yankees but sorry for the young man. He tapped the newspaper picture of the distressed pitcher.

'He's only twenty-two,' sighed Ron.

'You shouldn't have that pressure when you are twenty-two,' said Rita.

'How much does he earn?' Paul asked.

'Not that much. About $400,000,' said Ron and went to remove the sweets from the bench.

Seemed like a lot to me for throwing a ball. I could cope with the pressure. Now the series stood at 3–2 to the Yankees and they were all off to finish up in Arizona. The championship was played as the best out of seven games, which I felt gave my British companion Paul plenty of time to get the hang of it. There was a general consensus in the press coverage that New York deserved to win in order to make up for 9/11. I watched a television talk show where two old men in suits were discussing the matter.

'I must be a liberal,' said one man, 'because I wanted to comfort the pitcher who gave the game away.'

The other man snorted with derision. 'Yeah, well, I'm a conservative because that young man is just a "loser". This ain't ballet, you know.'

And I realised I didn't know. I had no idea what that meant.

Down in the basement Rita and Ron's son Paul was practising the trumpet. It was an astonishing sound.

'That's . . . quite a tune,' I managed politely.

Ron stopped to listen. 'He's playing "God Bless America".' I was impressed that he could tell. 'You see that, Sandi . . .' Ron pointed significantly to the floorboards where the sound was coming from, '. . . that would never have happened if it weren't for September eleven.'

'In that case,' I said quietly, 'we must redouble our efforts to find Osama bin Laden.'

We had originally delayed the start of our journey because Rita had an exercise class she felt committed to. Then she didn't go to the class because she had a bad headache but we didn't leave any earlier anyway. It seemed to be stress. Part of it was Julie, the youngest child. Julie did not want her mother to go and Rita was worried about her.

'I think it's puberty,' she explained.

'She's not quite ten,' I said.

'It could be puberty.'

We finally left Julie to the pains of maturity and departed in Ron's car at about 11 a.m. It wasn't an easy departure because Ron had many maps to give us. He kept bringing them out of the garage where he seemed to have opened a small map concession shop. Mostly he showed them to Paul. Maps were, like baseball, complex male things. By the time we left we had about six of them all charting the way from New Rochelle to Boston. Rita sat in the back of the car. She was happy to come but never drove anywhere unless it was local. It was a very smart car with a leather interior, which Rita said Ron had bought to stave off a mid-life crisis. I was beginning to think I might have one of my own. I was just backing out of the drive when Ron ran after us.

'Here, have this!' He passed Paul a new map. This one was hand-drawn. Ron had made it himself in case the others didn't live up to expectation. I steered us out of the neighbourhood and headed for the 95, the freeway down the road.

'What's the route?' I asked Paul, manly bearer of all maps.

'You get on the 95 and you stay on it till Boston,' he replied evenly. 'Then if you want to go somewhere else you get back on the 95. Everywhere we want to go is on the 95. It is the road to all New England Gladyses. Never go anywhere except the 95.' Paul put the maps in the glove compartment and never mentioned directions again.

I took us up the 95. We moved quickly away from Westchester. After that there seemed to be miles and miles of road with just trees and no people. It gave the most incredible sense of space. Although we had missed the true glory of the fall colours there was enough left for it to be wonderful. Many of the trees were still on fire with red and gold leaves. My driving wasn't going all that well. I found it odd in America. I didn't mind being on the right-hand side of the road: that was fine. So much American travel is done on freeways that it seems all the traffic in the country is only going in one direction anyway. The tough thing is the free-for-all attitude of everyone on the road. To use an indicator was clearly a sissy thing to do and there seemed to be a presumption that I only got in the wrong lane to annoy others. I refused to get caught up in the tension, so occasionally I drifted off the 95 just for the devil of it and then took my time to drift back. It was a bad idea. Rita was getting very annoyed in the back of the car.

'Is it like an English thing that you don't ask directions?' she asked irritably. I didn't like to tell her how we had got to Sue's using the sun and finding magnetic north with my underwear. We located Boston without ever looking at a single map.

*Boston is what I would like the whole United States to be.*

Charles Dickens, English tourist

*I am heartily ashamed to have been born in Boston.*

Edgar Allan Poe, Bostonian poet

Edgar Allan Poe always referred to his home town of Boston as 'Frogpondium'. He thought the place ghastly and provincial. Others will tell you that Boston is the one place in America where you can truly find civilisation and culture. As far as Ron had predicted we would be lucky to find anything at all. We entered the city with some trepidation. Ron had been very clear.

'Boston is a nightmare to drive in. You will never find anything.'

We were looking for the Harborside Inn. I take things at face value and figured it would either be an inn on the side of the harbour or we would find a landlord with a perverse sense of humour. I headed confidently for a confluence of water and boats with buildings built alongside. We found it straight away. Actually, I quite liked driving there. Boston has no grid system and winds and twists about rather like London.

We checked into the Harborside Inn. When Lady Frankland went to Boston in 1768 she carried with her 'six trunks, one chest, three beds and bedding for the same, six sheep, two pigs, one keg of pickled tongues, some hay, three bags of corn and other such goods as one should think proper to carry thither'. I had a wheelie bag with a dodgy wheel and a laptop with a broken strap. The glamour of travel was beginning to pall on me. Our accommodation, apart from being an inn down near the harbour, was also part of the heart and thrust of 'The Big Dig'.

Above the unplanned pattern of the city, a freeway on gigantic green metal struts roars past. The plan now is to put the whole thing underground and an incomprehensibly large engineering programme is digging out the very bowels of the town. This is not a project with one or two Irishmen and a shared spade. Night and day, the city is consumed with the sound of earth moving. It is huge and involves a great deal of digging. It is called The Big Dig. I have no idea how they thought of the name. So far, the cultural side of Boston was eluding us. Outside the Harborside Inn there was much labouring behind movable chain-link fencing. So much earth was being shifted that you could go out in the morning and not be able to find your way back to the hotel entrance by the afternoon.

It was late and after trying to watch yet another baseball battle on TV, everyone went to bed. I slept soundly till about 4 a.m. and then I pinged awake. It is an hour I have become used to in my travels in the States. It is the hour when my body decides that whatever my brain may say, it is time to be up and at 'em. Actually, I think my body is right. It is quite a good time to look around. Devoid of people and hustle and bustle you see a place stripped back to its architecture and the ghosts who linger about in the early hours.

Boston is not huge. It is a walking city quite reminiscent of European towns. It is a must for the student of the revolution and a seeker of anything vaguely cultural confined to the American shores. The 'Athens of America', the 'Cradle of Liberty' and the 'City on a Hill'. Here the Pledge of Allegiance was written and here hoop petticoats were once condemned as being against God's law.

The name, as with so many others, has an English connection. The story goes that in the seventh century there was a tiny fishing village on the River Witham in Lincolnshire, where a Benedictine monk lived. They also say he was the bastard son of King Ethelmund but this isn't that sort of book, so I won't go into detail. Anyway, the monk used to get up early every morning and pop down to give the fishermen a bit of a blessing to set them up for the day. They named him Bot meaning boat and ulph meaning helper – Botulph. The place became known as Bot Ulph's Town then Bottleston and finally, because people are fundamentally lazy with pronunciation, Boston.

Then on 7 September 1630 John Winthrop and his merry band of Puritans arrived from Boston, England and named their new home after the one they had just left. The local tribe called it 'Shawmut', which loosely translated from the Wampanoag language means 'the place you go to find the boats'. Which only goes to show that people are universal in not having a wide-ranging imagination. The brethren who escaped England to seek religious freedom founded a town where you were free to practise whatever they said you could practise. Boston has always had a religious image and often a repressive one. The city had the first official censor in the country and did so till 1975. From the 1920s to the 1970s the words 'Banned in Boston' printed on the front cover of a book could guarantee millions of sales for an author.

I wandered out, happy to get lost. The guidebooks will tell you that the streets were laid down on top of old cow paths. I think this is unlikely unless they had cows wandering at will all over the place. This is not the home of the Brahman heifer and I suspect it is more likely that they simply tarmacked over the places where the original footpaths had once meandered. I think you can sense this as you walk around. There is Purchase Street, once the property of a man called John Harrison. It was an important byway in the past, as people used his property as a short cut to get to the sea. Harrison, however, was a bad-tempered soul. He plied his trade as a rope-maker and used to hang his ropes to dry across the path to stop people and their carts getting through. This annoyed everyone. Finally, officials bought the land from him and gave it over to the city. The tradition was to name such a thoroughfare after the original owner but there had been too many rows and everyone just called it Purchase Street. There was a John Harrison connected with Purchase, New York, where Lori lives. I don't know if it was the same one or just something about the name.

Finding one's way around Boston isn't easy and that's George Washington's fault. He made his last visit to the city in 1789. Everyone in America was fighting to honour the old general and most cities did this by naming something after him. Boston, too, wanted to get in on the act so they created a Washington Street but one with a difference. Their Washington Street (of which there are hundreds across the country) ran right across the city. Then to mark it out, every street (with a handful of exceptions) that crossed the tribute road had to change its name as it crossed. Thus when Court Street crosses over Washington it becomes State Street, Winter becomes Summer, Boylston turns into Essex and so on. It is a curious bend of the knee to an old leader which confuses the tourist and, perhaps, even to the resident is lost in the mist of time.

I walked up Beacon Hill to look out over the park and admire the statues around the Senate House. Boston is a great place to stroll if you love words. It was here that bloomers were invented by the Boston lady Amelia Bloomer. On Beacon Hill you can pay tribute to the statue of Major-General 'Fighting Joe' Hooker. Fighting Joe was not the greatest general who ever lived. He was defeated by General Robert E. Lee at Chancellorsville in 1863, even though he had double the number of troops. But it is not for his army manoeuvres that he has gone down in history; he went down for rather more. During the Civil War he allowed women to follow his troops in their own tent encampments and they became known as Hooker's Ladies or Hookers. Hookers, happy to take down their bloomers.

I was thinking about a conversation I had had with Rita which had disturbed me. I had been reading Karen Armstrong's book about Islam and, for want of other subject matter, had brought up the topic of religious fundamentalism with Rita and Paul as we drove. I was keen to consider those young men who were so addicted to their religion that they were willing to die for it.

'They're crazy,' Rita said, dismissing them. 'Fanatics.'

'But don't you want to know why there are people in the world who hate America so much? Wouldn't you want to talk to one and find out?'

'There's no talking to those people. They don't believe in anything.'

This seemed an odd stance to me. It was the very deep nature of their beliefs which seemed to be causing the trouble. No one ever became a suicide bomber because they simply had a hunch about something. But Rita's view was one I heard expressed everywhere I went. It was on the television, on the radio and in the newspapers. There was no talking to the enemy. There was no point. Walking the streets of Boston before the blessing of the sun was an interesting place to dwell on the matter. Apart from perhaps Salt Lake City in Utah it would be hard to find an American city more steeped in past religious extremism than Boston.

Boston was founded by the Puritans who were altogether different from the pilgrims. Both lots wore the funny black hats but the Puritans were strict in body and soul beyond belief. If there was one thing they couldn't stand it was a Quaker. Those people, so called because they trembled before the Lord, were most unpopular in Puritanical Boston in the 1650s. To be fair to the Puritans, the Quakers, although a lovely peaceful people, did have some strange practices in the early days. They never cut their hair and were apparently quite keen on blackening their faces with charcoal before dancing naked in the street. There are also countless stories of them urinating in public and shrieking. I don't know how much of that is true. I expect a lot of it is rather extreme propaganda. Yet another example of how difficult it is for people to get along.

The Puritans did what they could to get rid of the Quakers. They were jailed, their books were burnt and finally they were sent to Barbados which I don't think sounds too bad. But the Quakers were an ornery bunch and they kept coming back. So the Puritans started whipping them, cutting their ears off and piercing their tongues with a red-hot poker. Now presumably they couldn't even say their irritating 'thees' and 'thous' or indeed hear when told to leave but even this didn't seem to do the trick. Finally, in 1658, the Puritans passed a law saying that any banished Quaker who returned would be put to death. Four Quakers were subsequently hanged for returning, including Mary Dyer whose statue stands up near Hooker's.

It wasn't until the Toleration Act was passed in 1689 in the British Parliament that things calmed down. After that the Quakers were allowed to own land, build churches and, people being what they are, their numbers immediately began to dwindle. By 1744 there were only eleven members of the Society of Friends left and by 1808 they had all packed up and gone. Proof, if proof were needed, that it is better just to let irritating people get on by themselves and eventually they will go away.

I had this image of America being founded for religious freedom. Of people escaping in leaking boats to eat beef jerky for months so they could call their God when and where they wanted but it isn't the whole story. The American past, as in so many other countries, is littered with intolerance and extremism and endless misunderstanding. Nothing really has changed.

At about 6 a.m. I was outside one of the oldest buildings in the heart of the town, the Customs House. A plaque on the side proclaimed it as having been host to the scene of the Boston Massacre. Many a time as an American schoolchild I had been shown a reproduction of the famous engraving by Paul Revere depicting that cold March eve in 1770 when the British redcoats had shot down unarmed Bostonians. It was only as an adult that I had learned the story was actually rather more interesting than that and had more to do with alcohol than freedom fighting.

That cold March evening, one poor schmuck redcoat had drawn the short straw for the night and was standing sentry at the Customs House. At closing time, a group of Bostonians spilled out of the Bunch of Grapes Tavern on King Street (now appropriately renamed State Street). They were probably pretty jolly and started mocking the lone sentry. Brit-baiting was a popular pastime following various acts of taxation, run-ins with customs officials and many public meetings at Faneuil Hall across the way. A crowd grew and the sentry couldn't get away. The captain of the guard pitched up with some soldiers to try to calm things down but by now there were several hundred in the mob and, as the tabloids would say, 'It was getting ugly'. News spread and someone went to ring the bell in the Old Brick Church behind the State House.

Now here's the thing – the church bell in those days was only rung to call people to service, for special occasions or because there was a fire. Lots of people in the crowd heard the bell and thought there must be fire. So they shouted 'Fire' and indeed that's what the soldiers did. Funnily enough, one of the lawyers who defended the redcoats was John Adams, later to be the second president of the US. He got them all off, leaving only two to be found guilty of manslaughter. (This wasn't so bad in those days. You just pleaded 'benefit of clergy' – recited a verse of scripture and had an M branded on your thumb so you wouldn't do it again.) It was a misunderstanding. It was about people not talking to each other.

The more I read about the past the more I realised what a skewed picture I had been presented with as a child. I didn't know that just as many Americans joined the British in the fight as joined the Sons of Liberty and that an equal number remained neutral. Only half of the nearly four million people in America at the time were of British descent. The rest had drifted from other parts of the world or were there in bondage.

Across the way at Quincy Market, even at that early hour, breakfast was being served. Quincy has been the central market of the city since 1826 and sits inside brick buildings where you could once have heard the boom of Founding Fathers banging on about independence in Faneuil Hall. Today it consists of endless fast-food opportunities, only some of whom seize the opportunity to serve before the cock crows. We were about half a dozen gathered to break the fast under what I hoped were newly hung Christmas decorations. The Pizzeria Regina was just kicking into action. A positively historic food provider, they were proud to be celebrating seventy-five years of pizza production with a competition to send someone to Italy, which I thought was sweet. They were also suggesting pizza as a 'stocking stuffer' for your mailman, which I was less sure of. It had never occurred to me to present a postal employee with a stocking of any kind, least of all one that oozed garlic.

Around me everything was about choice. There was none of

that British approach to catering where you can 'have our breakfast or go hungry'. I stood in front of the Bagel Bite and mentally
tried to compose my request. It wasn't easy. There were at least
eighteen different types of bagel, which could be prepared in
myriad ways with innumerable toppings, and several dozen coffee
options. After some minutes I thought I was ready. I joined the
small queue. I knew that I did not want the 'healthy option'. I
tried to look the small Mexican woman behind the counter in the
eye and declared boldly, 'Could I get' – No 'pleases' or 'may I
have', I was practically a native – 'Could I get a sesame-seed
bagel, toasted on both sides, with cream cheese and smoked
salmon, red onion, chopped not rings, with no lettuce, a little
cracked pepper and lemon and a tall American coffee with no
sugar?'

I drew breath and smiled. She never even looked up.

'What kind of cream cheese?'

I don't know what I chose. The first one on the list I think. I
felt deflated as I took my paper bag of purchases to the small
rotunda in the centre of the market and sat down. Here wooden
square blocks to sit on at wooden square blocks to eat at had
been laid out. Grown-up pre-school furniture. I realised I was
thinking like an American. No European ever even heard of pre-
school. I pulled out my breakfast. Coffee, one hot sandwich, a
plastic tub of melon and orange, a small fork (plastic) and
twenty-eight napkins. Twenty-eight napkins. I counted them.
Enough napkins to imagine that the world would never run out
of paper.

I don't know what the tub of orange and melon was for. I took
it as a reminder that really I should have had the healthy option. I
didn't want it but it had been free. A pigeon entered and joined the
early morning throng. I tried him on some of the violently
coloured fruit. He didn't want it either so I put it in my rucksack
out of guilt, thinking I might offer it to the others later.

When I met up with them at a more civilised hour, Paul was

wide awake and keen to do the whole American Revolution experience.

'We should definitely go to Liberty Square,' he said, looking at the map.

'Where is it?' asked Rita.

I had been up since four and had read the guide book from cover to cover. 'It's nothing to do with the American Revolution,' I said.

'Corner of Kilby, Water and Batterymarch streets,' said Paul.

'It was named after the French Revolution,' I tried.

Rita and Paul both looked at the map.

'Oh, I see it,' said Rita. 'We could go there.'

'It has some kind of statue,' said Paul.

'It's to Hungarian freedom fighters,' I said feebly.

Oh well, one revolution, another revolution . . .

I had had enough history by then and wanted to see the site of the Great Molasses Disaster instead. I think a lot of the truly important events are lost in history. It was 15 January 1919, when a fifty-foot-high iron tank containing 2.3 million gallons of molasses exploded in the North End of Boston sending a fifteen-foot tidal wave across Commercial Street to the harbour. Twenty-one people drowned in the sugar mass, many more were injured and six buildings were swept into Boston harbour. What a fantastic way to come to a sticky end. We did walk up to the North End, but to see Paul Revere's house and his church.

Paul Revere is one of the most famous characters in American folklore. It was he who rode to warn the troops that 'the British are coming' and waited for the famous 'one if by land, two if by sea' signal from the North End Church.

Except, that's not actually what happened. He didn't ride out by himself. There were three of them – Revere, William Dawes and Dr Samuel Prescott. All three were captured by a redcoat patrol but Dawes and Prescott escaped. They went on to alert everyone while Revere went back on foot. The history books never mentioned Paul Revere until Longfellow wrote a poem in 1863 called 'The Midnight Ride of Paul Revere'. Instantly fiction blended to fact and fame was assured. Maybe the names Dawes or Prescott didn't scan so well.

Paul Revere's house (*c.* 1680) is probably the oldest wooden building in town. It's next to a pizza parlour where the intense smell of tomato sauce must have driven the family demented. Across the road was a large edifice advertising itself as the Italian Catholic Church.

'What the heck is that?' asked Rita.

I imagined it was a Catholic Church for Italians but no one was waiting for my opinion.

The small dark green house was unique among the historical sites I had visited so far. It did actually have many things in it that had belonged to Paul Revere and he had actually once lived there. I like history when it comes to life and you discover that the great men (and sometimes women) of the past were just human beings. That is certainly true of the gentlemen who led America to freedom and separation from Mother England.

For a start, they weren't all that keen on each other and were given to quite a lot of name calling. Samuel Adams, Father of the Revolution, was deemed by his contemporaries 'a poor student, and a failure at everything he attempted in life'. Before he became a famous Founding Father, he was a rather celebrated debtor and nearly went to prison for stealing public funds. Like so many students down the ages, Adams graduated from Harvard University by waiting on tables. He then failed at every job he tried – counting-house clerk, shopkeeper, salesman, brewer, until he found all these skills combined to make him a successful politician as one of Boston's selectmen.

Paul Revere was a silversmith and engraver by trade but he was considered greedy by his neighbours and described as 'a poor artisan who copied everything he did from other artisans'. The greedy part seems clear. He once charged his mother when she borrowed half a cup of sugar from him and his detailed bill sent to the state of Massachusetts for his midnight ride is on display at the State Archives in Boston.

Up in Paul's bedroom, a man in a tricorn hat was waiting to interpret history for me.

'This was the bedroom of Mr and Mrs Revere. They were a happy couple and Mr Revere fathered sixteen children.'

This seemed like a lot. Certainly it seemed like a vast brood for two people to have and still be a happy couple.

'Sixteen children!' I repeated. 'It's a wonder he could still ride a horse.'

'I beg your pardon?' said the guide.

I repeated what I had thought was a rather fine quip only to find it even less successful the second time.

'I said, it's a wonder he could still ride a horse.'

The guide was almost stern with me. 'Oh no, ma'am, he was a very good rider.'

Some respectful tourists from St Louis, who had said nothing about the fecund Mr Revere, eyed me with suspicion. The guide turned his attentions to them.

'Where are you folks from?'

Folks? That was the word George Bush had used to describe the terrorists being hunted down in Afghanistan.

Having done the house, we felt obliged to do the church. It's a pretty, white, wooden structure. Rather plain with a good bell tower if you fancied sending a signal to Charlestown. Inside there were white box pews: high-sided enclosed benches for individual families to keep out the wind and the riff-raff in equal measure. A trim middle-aged man drifted about with a label on his chest. It gave his name and said he was the 'docent'.

'What's a docent?' I asked Rita.

'He's the guy who knows about the church,' she explained.

I had never heard of the word. 'Why is that a docent?' I persisted. She was getting annoyed with me now. 'That's his job.'

Docent – another job I had never thought of. I sat in a pew trying to work out where the word had come from. I knew you could be a 'docetist' which was a second-century heretic who believed Christ's body was only a semblance, but that seemed an unlikely person to work in a church. Still, Ron taught Bible studies and he didn't have a Bible . . .

It was time to get ourselves together and go and meet the next Gladys.

> Oh, if only Jupiter would give me back my past years.
>
> Virgil, *Aeneid*

When you go back and review the past it has an interesting effect. As I travelled I realised that I had spent thirty years confident that the one year I spent with the Gladys Society had been the best time of my life. In a way I think such a belief holds you back. I had been so convinced of my fundamental Americanism that I had failed to see how very English I had become. Allied with this was my notional retention of Danish nationality as a mark of respect to my beloved father. Consequently, despite my passionate interest in politics, I realised that I had spent my entire adult life living in a country where I could not vote. Both a loyalty and a sense of duty to the past had stopped me applying for the British passport to which I am entitled. Now it was beginning to matter to me. The beloved Denmark that my father knew was changing and I could no longer take pride in its socialist kindness. I was aghast as it lurched further and further right in the political spectrum, horror-struck as I watched the parliament pass laws which seemed to me not just horribly conservative but to strike at the very heart of human rights. I didn't want to live in Denmark so the truth was that I had no business holding Danish citizenship. I did, however, want to live in Britain and be involved in its politics. Not only was it something I would enjoy, it would enable me to do the one thing that matters most to me – to make a difference. I think it can happen that a person develops an image for themselves as a child that doesn't sit well as an adult but which one fails to shake off.

I was in a state of questioning some fundamental things about myself as we headed off to visit Sue's sister, Anne, in the Bostonian suburbs. Anne had not been involved in the original play at school. Her membership in the Gladyses stemmed mainly through her sibling. She had not been very theatrical although she did play clarinet in the band in the spring musical. Going to see Anne I was reminded that the year had not been all golden and that actually there had been a darker side too. Anne had been one of the older members of the group and probably the most serious. Apart from playing the clarinet her main interest at school had been sport. When she left high school she went to study political science in Maine for four years. I would have thought that was enough political science for anybody and it wasn't surprising that after that she wanted to go back to her old love of hockey and physical education. I like the American approach to further education. It is not a finite thing but can stretch and twist and turn across many years and a multitude of disciplines. Then Anne met someone called Cindy and realised her personal preference in life. It was at a time when I didn't see Anne but had become friends with her mother Pat. Towards the end of her life Pat would come to London fairly often and I would take her drinking in clubs. She loved that and she would talk to me about her daughters, about her rather more genteel upbringing and how she had borrowed every book the library had on offer to find out why her daughter had turned gay. Sue had not found it easy either. I remember her telling me with horror that Anne had brought Cindy to the house one Christmas, right near the beginning of the relationship, and sat on the sofa with her arm around her. 'That wasn't necessary,' Sue said.

I thought it probably was but I didn't say so.

Anne had always been kind to me but we were not friends in the same way as I was with some of the others. During the year at high school, I'd had a great time doing all sorts of 'theater'. Then things started to unravel.

My parents had been busy with the new baby, my sister Jeni, and I had often been left to the care of my close and older group of friends. This care had included going into the city to see shows, sitting around backstage at the high school theatre and rarely, if ever, actually going to any classes. I had worked out that as long as you turned up for homeroom in the morning, then as far as the school was concerned you were attending. Everyone went to such a variety of classes that it was impossible to keep an eye on who was doing what. Certainly your guidance counselor didn't seem to have time for you unless the police had also called for an appointment. I don't know why I started cutting classes. Perhaps it was the appalling social studies classes or perhaps I just found better things to do. Then my parents made the unexpected decision to go to a parents' evening. I don't know what possessed them, but I do know they were hard pushed to find a teacher who knew me. It's not how they had hoped the evening would go. I had always been such a good girl. My fate was sealed, my cards were marked and I was off to the first British boarding school that would have me.

Anne picked me up in her brown Ford Pinto to take me to the usual Friday night for the Gladyses at her house. It was unusual that no one else was in the car. For once in my life I was allowed to ride in the front. Anne was a senior and we didn't have that much to talk about. She was always nice to me and let me sleep on the floor in her room if I was scared at night, but we weren't exactly close. She often kept to herself and was less openly theatrical than many of the others. She parked in front of her parents' garage and turned to me.

'So, what's the matter with you?' she asked, and I began to sob. She put her arms around me and I sobbed and sobbed. My life was over and she was the first one there to help me.

Despite Rita's thorough organisation for our trip, the instructions to Anne's house were not entirely clear. She lives in a suburb of Boston and the instructions out to Jamaica Plain contained few if any actual street names. There were, however, quite a lot of instructions about 'turning left at Dunkin' Donuts'. It had proved impossible to pass a Dunkin' Donuts in the car without Rita saying how happy the place would make Ron. I could only think that the man must be in a permanent state of euphoria as they are every-where. You could not take directions from anyone without including a left or a right at a Dunkin' Donuts.

By the time we even got to the general neighbourhood it was pitch black outside. Relentlessly we turned left at a Dunkin' Donuts and kept coming back to a large clock tower illuminating the entrance to the public transport system. It didn't help that we couldn't read the few instructions we had. I had left them in my rucksack where they were now covered in melon juice from the fruit I had completely forgotten about.

'I think we should be eastbound on Potter,' said Rita from the back.

'This is Woodbourne,' I pointed out as we passed the same street sign for the eighth time.

'Maybe she said Woodbourne,' said Rita, who I think by now was just trying to be amenable.

I phoned Anne. It was our first phone call for thirty years but I was beyond nervous into a new state of hyperirritation.

'Anne? This is Sandi. Okay, we are quite lost.'

Probably she detected a certain note in my voice. 'What do you see?' she asked quite reasonably.

'I have the Sydney Opera House ahead of me and Big Ben is on my right.'

There was no pause at all as she shot back with, 'On your right? No wonder you are lost. It should be on the left.'

I knew in that moment that she and I were going to get on. In the end, Anne was reduced to standing in her street waving a torch to bring us in like lost sheep on an airfield. I was impressed. I might have had a torch at home but definitely not one that worked. We had passed the house several times. Rita had been told it was a grey house with red-brick trim. At night they all looked grey and none of them seemed to have any bricks whatsoever.

Anne and I hugged. A woman wearing a face I once knew but now framed with grey hair cut short. Anne is one of the statistically high gay contingent of the Gladys Society. I was glad. Her boyfriend at high school never seemed right for her. Now she has a delightful partner, Barbara, who works as a social worker for women with breast and uterine cancers.

We sat in Anne and Barbara's beautiful house with its hand-painted kitchen and lovely art work. A house of two females and no children. We talked about the past and I reminisced about her mother.

'She was a Southern belle, right?' I said as a statement.

Anne laughed. 'No, she was from Philadelphia.'

'But she had all that stuff about manners and society. She knew how long fingernails should be and when you should wear white gloves and she—'

'She had all that stuff but she was from Philadelphia.'

Anne studied in Ohio, then Texas, then broke up with Cindy and came back to the East Coast.

'How did you pay for all that studying?' Paul wanted to know.

'I got my masters by teaching bowling,' replied Anne.

This silenced everyone in the room. I don't think even Rita could imagine a degree riding on several spares and a strike.

'Now I coordinate a crisis management programme for elementary schools.'

I found we were endlessly rolling down alleyways of conversation that I didn't fully understand. Elementary schools are for little people. What kind of crisis could they have that would need to be managed? There was a short period of time in my junior high school when the National Guard pitched up but that was during the nationwide student protests against the war in Vietnam, when some college kids were shot at Kent State

University. We didn't have that kind of trouble in Mamaroneck. I think mostly the guards hung around and traded baseball cards with the kids.

Rita, bless her heart, was keen to talk about gay rights. None of the gay people in the room was that bothered and Paul would have preferred to chew glass professionally. I like Rita's attitude to the subject: it is commendable, but it had the same effect on me as would being especially nice to any Third World people who might happen to come in for drinks.

'So, Barbara,' she said brightly, while Anne opened some much-needed white wine, 'how long have you two been together?'

'Seven years,' replied Barbara.

'And is it still a romance?' Rita enquired.

'I said seven years,' said Barbara evenly which made me laugh.

'I bet it is,' said Rita, who is kind enough to want it all to be wonderful for homosexuals without really understanding that seven years would be a long time to sustain romance in a pair of astrologically suited love birds. I don't think gay people want gay rights. I think they want equal rights and mostly what they wanted that evening was dinner.

*The arrival of the Irish is a formidable attempt of Satan and his sons to unsettle us.*

Puritan minister, Boston, 1654

We headed for dinner in the heart of Irish Boston. The city's strong Irish connection was quite literally built upon the backs of immigrants from the old country. Before they came to labour in the town and reclaim land from the sea, Boston was no more than three miles long and a mile wide. Then, in the spring of 1654, the ship Goodfellow arrived in Boston harbour. On board were hundreds of Irish men and women. There are now ten times as many people claiming to be Irish outside Ireland as there are in their native land. They were the first large foreign ingredient placed in the famous melting pot of America. They originally came as slaves and later as refugees. During the great Irish Famine of the mid-1800s, one-third of all Irish men, women and children died of starvation and disease, one-third survived and the rest went to America. They went to Boston and New York – natural ports across the Atlantic – and by 1857 almost half the Boston population was Irish. I've always thought it was ironic that the potato came from America and that it was the lack of potato that brought the Irish to these shores.

The Puritans were about as keen on the Irish as they were on Quakers but the pilgrims shipped in as many Irish servants as they could get. Irish girls were often sold into servitude and the kidnapping of Irish boys and girls by English sea captains became fairly common practice. When in the early winter of 1626 a forty-foot vessel heading for Virginia from Ireland was wrecked off Cape Cod, Governor Bradford wrote: 'Most of her passengers were Irish servants'; and apparently a fair number ran off 'to live with the Indians', which seems to have been preferable to living with the English.

If you want a bit of the Emerald Isle in Boston, and it's almost *de rigueur*, then the place to go is Doyle's Pub. It has been serving up baked beans and brew to the Irish on Washington Street in Jamaica Plain since 1882. It claims to be 'The Best Pub in All of America'. Surprisingly, I think this might be quite a hotly contested title.

One of the more notable things about Ground Zero had been how many Irish pubs there were in the area. All of them with shamrock green awnings now covered in dust and all of them closed. I know that much of the money for the IRA has come from America, from Noraid funds collected from Irish-Americans. It was a curious twist of circumstance that the Taliban had such an impact on the Irish troubles. I doubt the bearded men of Islam had given much thought to the Irish Republican movement. The decommissioning of IRA weapons which had taken so long, finally happened close on the heels of 9/11. It can only be that the money dried up; that the American supporters of violence suddenly looked at the World Trade Center on their doorstep and thought, Oh, I see, that's terrorism. Oh, that's not good.

It's a terrible thing to say but perhaps they had to have something happen on their doorstep to get the message. So much of what happens in the world is distant and alien to America.

In Doyle's pub we had arrived in Kennedy heaven. Mention the Kennedys to Bostonian Irish Catholics and they automatically genuflect. You might as well have mentioned His Holiness the Pope. Boston is full of high society and you don't get any higher than the Kennedy clan. At Doyle's you can't help but trip over family paraphernalia. The place is littered with blurry pictures of the murdered President John Fitzgerald and sundry family members. Every wall beams down with photographs of JFK in endless handsome poses like early cigarette or sweater ads.

Doyle's is wonderfully old fashioned. It has a strange tin ceiling, a long oaken bar to meet new friends, wooden booths to meet old friends and mural-covered walls. On the rear wall of the Michael Collins room, an eighteen-foot mural portrays the Irish legacy – the likeness of seven Boston mayors and forty-five other significant politicians, pals and patrons. Here you can eat and drink on a cash-only basis.

We settled at a small booth and the waitress came to take our order.

'Please may I have spaghetti and meatballs?' I enquired.

'What would you have done if she had said no?' laughed Barbara.

I thought about it for a moment. 'I would have ordered something else.'

While we re-read the menus to make sure we had ordered what we really wanted, we all became middle-aged and discussed the need for spectacles. Anne had always worn glasses.

'I'd have that laser surgery but my corneas are too thin,' she explained.

'How fabulous,' I muttered, thinking I would like to have any
part of my body medically declared too thin. We had all put on
weight. We all needed help with our eyesight. God almighty, we
were getting old.

Paul was obsessed with The Big Dig. He wanted to buy a book
on it. Of course he did. My seven-year-old son loves pictures of
dumper trucks and men in hard hats.

'What are they going to do with the bit on top? The big space
where they are digging now?' he asked. It was an area we had
come to know well as the Heritage Trail passes right over it. At the
moment it was occupied solely by several rather down-at-heel
Halal butchers. If the area became smart, I thought they probably
wouldn't stay the course.

'No one knows,' said Anne.

'It's going to be a park,' said Barbara.

'I hadn't heard that,' said Anne.

'It's a pain in the ass,' said Barbara.

I began to talk with pleasure about large engineering projects
which benefit the next generation and not our own. 'I think it's
wonderful,' I enthused. 'The Victorians did it all the time. It shows
vision. Like planting trees for an arboretum which you'll never see
mature in your lifetime.'

Barbara looked at me and nodded approvingly. 'That's very
good, Sandi.'

'What is?'

'You have made a very good, positive reversal and my students
would like that.'

A positive reversal? It's another language. I had no idea what I
had done so I changed the subject. They wanted to know about the
British Prime Minister Tony Blair and how great he was for standing 'shoulder to shoulder' with America.

'Yeah, what do you think he wants?' I asked generally.

There was silence at the table broken only by the delivery of my
spaghetti.

'Wants?' said Rita. 'Why would he want anything?'

'Well, everyone does, don't they? I mean Pakistan is going to get their debts written off and Blair must be going to get something back . . .' I faltered. I looked to Paul for support but an Englishman doesn't discuss politics when he is eating . . . or driving . . . or walking . . . or . . .

'What could Europe want?' asked Anne.

'Well . . . lots of things . . . the . . . Kyoto agreement?'

'Why?' asked Barbara, seemingly genuine in her bafflement.

'Because the world is dying. I mean I see it. You know, if I go skiing in the Alps I can see the destruction on the trees where acid rain . . .'

It sounded like a poor argument. People should be more conscious of the environment; Americans should spend more money on petrol so that I could get a better experience when I went skiing. No one agreed with me about Kyoto. Everyone agreed we should have dessert. Somewhere Tony Blair was no doubt busy doing things just because it was good for America. I think my fear was that they were right.

Rita changed the subject. 'Do you guys remember Steve Immerman?'

I did, only vaguely but I did. He was a young man whose Jewish identity, even at high school, had been hugely important to him. In fact, I think it was the only thing I could remember about him.

'He found out he wasn't Jewish,' announced Rita.

'What?' Anne and I exhaled together.

It seemed Steve's grandfather had died not all that long ago. Steve had gone to his house to go through his papers and made a startling discovery. His grandfather was a tailor. He had arrived in New York via Ellis Island and he had quickly discovered other tailors. These tailors were Jewish but Steve's grandfather was actually an Italian Catholic. He decided it would be better to be a Jewish tailor. So he changed his name. Steve Immerman was not an Immerman at all but something with more of the hint of pasta about it.

This was one of the funniest things I had ever heard. I thought it was a hilarious tale about the human condition. About the ridiculous elements we gather up to create an image of ourselves.

'What if bin Laden suddenly discovers his grandfather has lied and he is actually a Hassidic Jew from Yonkers?' I asked. 'I think that would be great.'

Barbara and Anne laughed but Rita did not think the story was funny.

'The good thing was that his father married a Jew,' she persisted.

'Why?' asked Paul, who didn't know Steve Immerman but liked the topic better than politics or environmental issues.

'Well, if your mother is Jewish then you are Jewish,' Rita explained.

'Yes, but his name isn't Immerman,' I said giggling. 'He's Dagostino or whatever.'

'He's still Jewish. That's the point,' she insisted.

I paid the bill. Anne had been a little reluctant to meet up, I felt. She had been slow to answer my emails and less than enthusiastic to make arrangements. She had been one of the Gladyses I had tried to meet in Arizona when I had my unfortunate equine encounter. Now, as we stood outside Doyle's she said, 'When are you guys leaving town?'

'Day after tomorrow,' I said.

'You wanna have dinner tomorrow night?'

I felt like I was suddenly in a hit show.

The next morning I was out early again. Like Mr Revere himself, I was looking for the great white steeple to guide me into the North End. Here, Barbara had assured me, I would find a Little Italy full of Italian family dining at unsociable hours. I wandered up the Paul Revere Mall, a broad memorial walk where the names of men, many men, of the Revolution and the Civil War are commemorated. The sun was just beginning to shine on a giant statue of Paul on horseback, either delivering his news or the bill for the same. I think I was over-tired.

'Where are the women?' I shouted up at Revere, who sat proud by a twist of poetic fate. 'I don't believe they were all at home wringing their hands!'

Where were the women who farmed, butchered, sewed, cooked, baked, gardened, brought up the kids and probably ran a business on the side? Where was the tribute to Katherine Goodard, the female printer of Baltimore, who published the first signed copy of the Declaration of Independence, and the blacksmith Betsy Hagar, who helped repair weapons and cannon for the colonial army. What about Deborah Sampson who joined the continental army as Timothy Thayer? After her true sex was discovered she left, only to join the 4th Massachusetts Regiment as Infantry Private Robert Shurtleff. I was very conscious when I was a child of the need for feminism. I look at the Gladyses and at the women I know and I can't help but feel anxious that nothing much has changed.

I never found Little Italy but ended up in a place called Theo's Cozy Corner on the corner of Salem and Sheefe and in the shadow of the North End Church. Here everyone spoke Portuguese. Two men sat at the three-stool breakfast bar wearing clothes straight from The Big Dig and baseball caps on backwards. One of them was on a loud walkie-talkie. The reception was bad and he couldn't hear properly so he turned it up – now we could all hear that the reception was bad. Two other men at an adjacent table were discussing a production of *Who's Afraid of Virginia Woolf?*. The place smelled like any other greasy spoon and I didn't have high hopes for my coffee.

A young Portuguese woman slouched over to the men at the table. One of the young men began to order.

'Could I get an egg and cheese sandwich?' She wrote that down. He held up his hand. 'No, could I get the bagel special?' She wrote that down. He held up his hand again. 'Actually I'll get the toast with the bacon.' The short order chef put some bacon on the grill. The woman looked at me.

'Do you want coffee?' she asked.

I did and I didn't want to change my mind. It never came. She took my order and went to sit at the counter without mentioning it to anybody. As she sat the young man called out, 'Did you start cooking yet, 'cos I'll get the French toast instead.'

He got what he wanted and my coffee never came. Shades of the Algonquin. Invisible women.

I met Paul and Rita and we wandered around Quincy Market. There was a stall for the Boston Historical Society. Here two women volunteers were bickering about stall layout.

'I was wondering if you know why baked beans come from Boston?' I asked. They didn't know but the rather keen younger woman went to look it up. It turned out to be a cheap food for Irish immigrants. The town was awash with molasses from the Caribbean trade so they would shove that with some beans in a pot and take it to be cooked at the local bakery while they attended to their souls in church.

The older woman nodded at this information. 'I am always telling my daughter-in-law – why don't you just make baked beans? When I was a kid it was a meal. I say to her, don't do all this other stuff. Baked beans, I'm telling you, it's a meal and my son would love it. She doesn't know what he would like. Only the other day I said to her . . .'

My heart went out to the daughter-in-law.

We couldn't visit the replica boat where the Boston Tea Party had taken place because, like Margaret Mitchell's place, it had burnt down. Apart from maybe preserving some actual antiques, it seemed to me that people interested in American history would do well to invest in a few smoke alarms.

We went for a trolley ride and drifted about for the rest of the day. I had booked a table for the evening at the Union Oyster

House, which is the oldest continuously operating restaurant in the United States. They have been serving since 1826 which must be an annoyance to Durgin Park, the other old restaurant in town, which opened a year later. It's a great place. The building itself is more than two hundred and fifty years old and once housed Hopestill Capen's fancy dress goods business which was called 'At the Sign of the Cornfields'. I don't know if I have ever had a call to buy fancy dress goods but I should like to have seen what Hopestill had on offer.

You can't escape the Revolution in Boston and it was on the upper floors of this house that America's first newspaper the *Massachusetts Spy* was printed, calling citizens to arms. Then, during the 1776 war, it became the place where troops came to get paid. No doubt even Washington popped in for his expenses. But it's the small stuff of history that I like. The tales which make all the grand people a little more human. It was in the Oyster tavern that in 1796 you could have had French lessons from the king of France himself. Louis-Philippe lived in exile on the second floor. He made a living by teaching verb declensions to rich young women before eventually going home to be king. I like this. By appearing on television there is a general presumption made about me that I have riches beyond my wildest dreams, that I need never work again but merely dally with tasks for my own amusement. Entertainment has changed beyond recognition in Britain. It is not the world I first entered. There is less and less work and less and less of it worth doing. I thought about the king. A man reduced to putting a sign out: 'French Lessons Given'. I could end up like that myself, except my ad would be on a sticky label in a phone booth.

Downstairs the large semi-circular bar is made of beaten copper. Here Daniel Webster of *Webster's Dictionary* daily drank his tall tumbler of brandy and water with each half-dozen oysters. He often had six plates after which, I imagine, he started making words up. Good fellow, Dan. Here the toothpick first came into everyday use. Charles Forster of Maine imported the picks from South

America and as a promotion he hired Harvard boys to eat at the restaurant and ask for toothpicks.

Rita, Paul and I were early. I gave the woman at the front desk my name. She ticked it off and said nothing.

'Can we get our table?' I asked politely but using Americanese.

'Not till your party is assembled,' she said, without looking up. There was a rather long pause. 'You can go to the bar if you like.' JFK came here so often he has a booth upstairs dedicated to his memory. I bet he could get his table when he wanted. We looked in the gift shop instead. Here you could buy any lobster thing you may ever have thought of – lobster-shaped ovengloves, lollipops, pens, notepads . . . I wondered what the chances were of having steak for dinner.

Anne and Barbara appeared and we were allowed into the inner sanctum. I had booked early and was anxious that we would get a good table. We were led through a lovely dining room, full of people enjoying themselves at intimate tables. It was quite a big building and we finally came to a halt at a back room full of picnic tables for coach parties.

'Isn't there anywhere in the actual dining room?' I asked Charlene, my waitress for the evening.

'I'm afraid it's full,' she replied, smiling.

What a good thing I had bothered to book. We were not the only ones who had been given the short end of the toothpick. At the next table but one was another group of adults.

Charlene served us. She was very pleasant despite the fact that no one except Paul and me ordered anything the way it appeared on the menu. We two English had the lobster and everyone else had a combination of foods unique to themselves. Meanwhile one of the men at the next table had begun humming.

'UHHHHMMMMMMMM!'

It was very loud and completely toneless. No one at his table said anything. They just carried on as normal.

'UHHHHMMMMMMMM!'

Patently the man was suffering from some kind of syndrome or possibly, syndrone. It was like sitting at an RAF base with incoming Spitfires. Maybe that was why they had been put in the back room where no one wanted to sit. That was understandable. Perhaps the unfortunate man had been droning loud enough to cause vibrations in the crockery cupboard. I wondered what it was about our party that had led the restaurateurs to think we too should be isolated. We were very politically correct and tried to carry on our conversation, but it wasn't easy.

'UHHHHMMMMMMMM!'

The quiet, elegant meal I had imagined was turning into a trial. Everything we said was accompanied by sounds normally generated by a faulty and irritable boiler. The lobster arrived amid a wealth of tool options to crack the life out of the thing. I once read that lobsters, like people, are left- and right-handed, well . . . left- and right-clawed. If you examine the claws, the claw they favoured in life will be larger than the other. I also read (and I begin to think that my choice of literature would not stand up to examination) that when lobsters outgrow their skin they shed it and wander about naked for a while. I eyed my left-handed potential nudist and wondered as to the best mode of attack. Barbara came to the fore.

'UHHHHMMMMMMMM!' went the man.

'This reminds me of that time I was teaching class on racism,' she said, as she cracked the back of my benthic dweller, 'and there was this person at the back with Tourette's syndrome. I'm talking about racism and he's in the back chanting "Fucking nigger, fucking nigger". It wasn't my best day at work.' Barbara took her index finger, shoved it up the arse of my dinner and promptly pushed out in a great lump all the meat the creature had once called its own. It was one way to get to know somebody.

I looked at Anne and then Barbara and we got the giggles. The humming continued, rising and falling in volume, throughout the meal. Finally the poor man and his companions were ready to leave. The man got up just as his large friend next to him struggled to put on a leather jacket. As the friend pushed his arm into the coat, his heavy sleeve swung round and struck the aeroplane impersonator square in the face. Maybe the friend was clumsy but maybe he had been annoyed with all the noise. There was a loud 'thwack' followed by a sharp intake of air and it completely knocked the hum out of the man. Perhaps it was a medical technique. Like the Heimlich manoeuvre.

Barbara, Anne and I got the giggles again and I don't think I stopped for the rest of the evening. Rita persuaded Charlene to give Paul and me our plastic lobster bibs to take home as souvenirs. It was kind but I couldn't think what on earth we would do with them.

We left Boston on route 95. Rita was asleep and I stopped to get petrol at a US Petroleum station advertising gas at $1.19 regular. $1.19. Less than a quarter of European prices. Kyoto, Kyoto . . .

Rita woke up as I was paying and was cross.

'You mustn't put that stuff in the car,' she said.

'What, petrol?' I asked, wishing I was sitting with Webster, bantering words and brandy.

'Only put Mobil gas in the car or it will stop.'

I drove the delicate Japanese car on to the freeway. I had no idea. I wondered if you could develop Tourette's syndrome at will. We stopped en route at some outlet shops. Rita did not think this was a good idea.

'Do you know your prices? You must know your prices in outlet stores.' I probably didn't. She warned me that they often sell off substandard stuff.

'I once bought pants from Liz Claiborne and they were too tight because they were made with less material,' she explained.

I buy trousers which are too tight because someone has overstuffed my body. Anyway, I didn't really want cheap trousers, just something to eat. I asked Rita if she thought the place also had food outlets.

She snorted at me. 'They're not food outlets . . .' she began confidently and then faltered. 'They're . . . food . . . sources.'

Food sources. How stupid of me. I bought a revolting hot dog from a food source. I didn't know my prices but I did know my taste buds and chucked it in the bin.

I had lost the ability to fill up the car, name a fast-food provider, say anything remotely comprehensible and Steve Immerman was Jewish because of his mother so that wasn't funny either.

# CHAPTER 10

# Lisa – Gladys Twelve

Now the thing about the next Gladys is that I didn't particularly want to see her. It sounds terrible but it's true. I know I've gone on about how cosy and lovely it all was with everyone but the fact is with Gladys Twelve that I didn't really know her. She wasn't, to my mind, a proper Gladys. You have to understand that I came back from my first term at English boarding school mutated into an entirely different being. It's what boarding school is for. It's partly because of the nature of the place. Everyone is the same sex, everyone dresses as if they had no sex and sex is the subject in the forefront of everyone's mind and, indeed, in the forefront of other places as well. I remember an English hostage being released from some God-awful foreign jail and when he was asked how he had coped he said anyone who had been to a British boarding school would have been fine.

I went to a school where they were paranoid about sex. Well, they had to be paranoid about something and it wasn't education. We had many rules to stop our bursting hormones from rubbing up against someone else's. Girls were not allowed to walk arm in arm into town, it was forbidden to sit on the beds unless 'actually getting in' and no one was permitted to have a long-handled hairbrush. The last one flummoxed me for some time. I now suspect that the whole concept of educating children in single-sex institutions was conceived by a coven of therapists trying to breed new clients.

The very act of putting on a uniform had begun to straitjacket me. I don't know if I had been funny before but I was funny now. Following my being sent to Coventry as an opening welcome I had made the discovery of humour as a weapon and I made good use of it. It hadn't protected me fully. A seventeen-year-old in my boarding house had appeared to make friends with me. She was the first and I was pathetically grateful. Then she seduced me and I was overwhelmingly perturbed. (Please note, all therapists – I'm over it and can't be bothered to sit in a small room and discuss it.)

My parents, brother and sister were still living in New York. When I returned, after what can only be described as a life-changing three months, what I longed for was my other family – the Gladyses – who had been so overwhelmingly important to me. The first Friday night that I was home for the holidays I went to stay, as usual, at Anne and Sue's. It had been a Gladys custom for any number of us to share the big bed in their spare room on a Friday night. But that Friday, no one else came. Everyone was busy and it was just Sue and me. We played cards till late and then she sent me to bed in the spare room next to hers. I was scared. I had got used to sleeping in a dorm full of others. I went back in to Sue's room.

'Sue, can I sleep with you?'

She rolled over in her bed. 'You can sleep on the floor,' she said gruffly. And I did. Before, she had always let me sleep with her. I hadn't said a word to anybody about what had happened but I determined, in my childish paranoia, that she knew something about me had changed. Something she didn't like. The next morning another girl came over for breakfast.

'Sandi, this is Lisa. She's going to be a Gladys.'

I didn't know Lisa. She couldn't be a Gladys. She hadn't been there. She and Sue gabbed away. Lisa was her new friend. Lisa was a Gladys now and I felt terrible.

So Lisa was a Gladys because Sue had said she was and I had to include her. The only thing I knew about the grown-up twelfth Gladys was that she, like Anne, was gay. That between us, we three had upped the homosexual statistics from a rather random group of women to 25 per cent. My first attempt to contact Lisa was via email. Richard had conceived a notion that it would be terrific if the women-loving women of the group met somewhere with an interesting backdrop. He became determined that we should convene at a women's rodeo event in Arizona. It would look great, it would be full of American icons and he wanted to get a picture of the three of us riding into the proverbial sunset. Richard made the plans and I started to make contact. On reflection it was an insane idea to fly two people, one of whom you don't know at all and the other whom you haven't seen for years, three thousand miles to get together on a horse. For a while, however, everything went splendidly. Anne wanted to bring Barbara. We couldn't afford to pay for her but they had air miles so that was good. Lisa was surprised to hear from me but seemed open to the idea of meeting. Richard booked our flights, which were cheap and unchangeable, and started sending me material from a surprising selection of cowboy websites where some of the best moustaches were on the women. I continued to email Anne and Lisa and now I mentioned the fun idea of the rodeo. Anne was still fine (although the air miles were proving to be the wrong kind for the airline we had selected but Richard would sort it) but Lisa had a problem. Actually, I think it was an understandable problem. It transpired that she was a senior figure in an animal welfare organisation and she didn't include bucking up and down on a wild bull as entertainment. I didn't like to tell her that we had now also discovered an event in gay rodeo called 'goat dressing' which involved putting a pair of Y-fronts on an animal that would rather eat them. I was mortified and had that same sinking feeling I get when I accidentally wear leather shoes to a wildlife charity meeting.

Still, Richard and I felt it could be amusing. I could write something censorious about rodeo and the involvement of animals to please Lisa, and Anne could still come. One Gladys was better than none. Two days before we left and Richard was going demented with air-mile options for Barbara and possible times for flights. A week later Richard and I were in Arizona on our own and I was being forcibly introduced to the American medical system. As I lay, strapped in a CAT scan, I knew that if I wanted to see Lisa, which I didn't really, I would have to go to visit her.

*We could not go anywhere without sending word ahead so that life might be put on parade for us.*

Infanta Eulalia of Spain, 1864–1958

The next part of the trip was an all-round American experience. Within twenty-four hours I had taken part in a parade, tried to find the tune in Cambodian music and purchased a Thai meal from a German bier-keller. As a result Rita was very agitated, Paul somewhat surprised and I was beside myself with delight. We had driven north of Boston, up through a corner of New Hampshire and on through the state which eats up all the remaining East Coast land to the Canadian border. Maine is a bigger place than you might think. They say there are so many deep bays along the Atlantic here that all the navies of the world could find safe harbour together. Sounds like an idea worth trying to me. What else can I tell you? It is the land of the lobster, the home of the blueberry and the producer of 90 per cent of the country's toothpick supply. It is also as far north as I will be going on the Eastern seaboard.

We had driven about fifty miles north of Boston under pleasant New England skies and past an endless array of English place

names. Near our destination of Kittery (Est. 1647 – the oldest town
in Maine), Paul, Rita and I checked into a motel. Paul was thrilled
as the motel was very Norman Bates: long, low buildings with
individual parking spaces in front of each room. The next morning
I was up for my usual early perambulation. I drove across the
Memorial Bridge which straddles the Piscataqua river from Kittery,
and into New Hampshire. Here giant neon lobsters were luring me
to consume at a waterfront restaurant. I think I will forever associate
lobster with loud humming concluded by unexpected violence, so I
headed instead for breakfast in the Friendly Toast café. Portsmouth,
New Hampshire, like the Portsmouth of home but smaller, hums
with the sounds and smells of the sea. The clang of halyards
against aluminium masts echoed in the empty streets. A seagull, the
size of a reasonable Christmas dinner, blocked the road as it stood
defiantly holding an entire slice of abandoned pizza in its beak.

Settled in 1623, the town has the distinction of being America's
third oldest city. It doesn't feel like a city. It is 'quaint' and certainly
at sunrise there aren't enough bodies around to make up a
quorum at bridge. The Friendly Toast was very 1950s which, I
have to remind myself, is the decade in which I was born. Unlike
me, however, this was not the real McCoy but a deliberately
themed eating experience. Not actually old but very like. I sat at a
chrome-edged Formica-topped table under a lamp where a bright
woman in a 1950s swimsuit waved confidently to me from her
water skis. No doubt she would soon come ashore for a menthol
cigarette which she would believe was good for her. The Andrews
Sisters sang brightly about some girl and the band and how great
life would be when she finally heard church bells chime.

Despite the early hour I was not alone. In the next booth a male
student was eating a gargantuan breakfast just with the aid of a
fork. Without further cutlery skills he seemed to bring his mouth
to the food rather than the European system which is the other
way round. The choice thing was upon me again. The menu
offered many options including:

Vegetarian Bacon at $2.25 or

Bacon at $2.00.

I couldn't account for the difference in price and could only presume that vegetarian bacon must be more difficult to make. Certainly it would require a very cooperative and somewhat zen pig. My waiter offered many kinds of bread with which I might enjoy my friendly toast.

'I don't really want toast,' I said, looking at the ring through his nose and still thinking about the pig.

'Everyone has toast,' he mumbled. 'It's the Friendly *Toast*.' He was clearly under strict 'No toast is not an option' instructions. It reminded me of a story, possibly apocryphal, which was circulating the States.

Apparently the crime column in the *Ann Arbor News* in Michigan reported that a man walked into a Burger King in Ypsilanti, Michigan, early in the morning. He produced a gun and said, 'Give me your money.'

The clerk said he couldn't. 'I can't open the cash register without a food order,' he explained.

This stopped the would-be robber for a moment who finally ordered some onion rings. The clerk shook his head. 'Can't do that, sir, they're not available for breakfast.'

The man, frustrated, walked away.

I was enjoying time to myself. Time to think about who and what I had become. After so many years in British broadcasting it is not always easy to be anonymous and I was relaxing into it. Trying to decide who I was beyond the accidental nationality I had inherited. I wanted to look at what I had done with my life so far. Trying, presumably like Steve Immerman, to find a true identity. I wandered out into the waking town. Here there were yet more claims to history. The North Congregational Church where George Washington once worshipped on a November day just like the one I was experiencing but back in 1789. The memorial to the town sons William Whipple and John Langdon, who both signed the Declaration of Independence. The Music Hall Theater, standing on the site where leading black abolitionists once spoke with passion as the anti-slavery movement banged the table for the right to freedom. I was feeling very liberated. Beginning to believe that I had returned to my past in order to free myself of old conceptions and move forward. I liked wandering by myself in a place where I knew no one and where no one knew—

'Excuse me, are you Sandi Toksvig?'

I was walking past the open doors at the back of the theatre when a woman called out to me. She was wearing the obligatory black of a theatre technician. Great chunks of scenery were being moved on to the stage at this early hour. Clearly there was to be a show tonight. I was sure I had never seen this woman before.

'Yes, yes, I am.'

'I thought so. I've seen you on *Whose Line is it Anyway?*. Great show.'

'Thanks.' Small world and all that.

We had arranged to meet Lisa at her house for dinner after she finished work at the 'rescue facility', her partner had come back from teaching and they had collected their daughter Channy. We might be travelling round the world but they had lives to lead. It was dark by the time we pulled out of the motel car park and headed up the main road to Kittery. The area reeks of New England with quiet streets, small attractive bays and neat wooden houses. There were no street lamps and things were already a little tense. There was a large 'rotary' or roundabout that had to be negotiated. I know these are unusual in America but Rita did give me quite a long talk about how to deal with them. I was probably not feeling at my most charitable when I suddenly glimpsed a red light in my rear-view mirror. Then we heard the sound of a siren.

'That's a fire engine,' said Rita from the back.

'Yes,' I said. By now I could see many red lights in the mirror and the noise was getting louder.

'In our country we pull over for a fire engine,' explained Rita.

I pulled over into someone's drive on the narrow, country lane. The red lights were still some way off but by now I could see that it was not one fire engine but about six and, despite the urgency of the flashing lights, they were all driving at no more than ten miles an hour. I could only presume that the local tax office was burning down and no one much fancied lending a hand. The cacophony of sound was increasing as I noticed that the tortoise-like engines were being followed by a large bus, several trucks and about a hundred cars flashing their lights and tooting their horns. I let the engines pass, then the bus and pulled out into the front of the line of cars.

'What are you doing?' yelled Rita from the back of the car.

'It's a parade,' I said. 'No one goes to a fire this slowly, not even at a crematorium.' I put on my hazard lights, started bashing the horn and rolled down my window to yell at passers-by.

'You don't know where you're going!' pleaded Rita.

'I do,' I said, pointing to the bus directly ahead of us, 'I'm following that bus.'

The parade wound through smaller and smaller streets and got louder and louder. Soon I couldn't hear objections in the car at all. At last we pulled into a large car park outside a vast modern building called the Traip Academy which appeared to be some kind of high school. The noise was deafening now as the emergency services let rip with every decibel at their disposal and the car drivers leant on their horns with every calorie-fuelled ounce of their bodies. Lights flashed, sound meters were broken and Englishmen were left open-mouthed. Rita had been speaking in the back but I couldn't hear. Finally I caught the tail end of something.

'. . . and you don't even know why we're here.'

I got out of the car to find out. By now many nubile young girls were descending from the bus to wild adulation. I stopped to speak to a man who had an accent like one of the Kennedys.

'It's the Traip Academy girls' soccer team,' he shouted in my ear. 'They just won the state championships.'

'Fantastic!' I enthused, having no idea who the hell they were but delighted by even the mention of a local triumph.

'It was real close,' screamed the man and proceeded to give me all the scores of the last six games at voice-breaking volume.

'Great school!' he enthused. 'Brought back the Pledge of Allegiance, you know.'

I didn't know and I doubted they had done it on their own. Standing up with your right hand over your heart each morning to pledge allegiance to the flag of the United States of America was something I had done every day of my American school life. It had been done at homeroom each day. The homeroom teacher would tick off the fact that you were there and then the crackling tannoy would spring into action. Inevitably the principal would lead the chant of the pledge which would then be followed by various announcements about cheerleading practice and requests not to leave old gum on the underside of your desk.

'They stopped it because some people didn't want to say "One nation under God".' The man was still yelling in my ear. 'But after 9/11 I think people know we need him now.'

This suggested it had not been a matter of belief for people but God's usefulness which had been in question. Someone started singing what I could only presume was an old Traip classic. Despite my enthusiasm I was unable to join in as I didn't know the words so I got back in the car to share the good news.

'The Traip Academy girls won the state championships!' Maybe it was a serious lack of team sport in their lives but no one else seemed as thrilled as me.

We wound back through Kittery with the parade still ringing in our ears. Soon we left the klaxons and the flashes behind and it went silent and dark but I couldn't stop smiling.

'We need to buy wine,' I said, trying to be cheerful. The atmosphere was a little strained. Clearly, I felt, I was no longer to be trusted as a responsible chauffeur. Certainly, I felt, I needed wine.

Kittery is, thank God, not a town which has fallen to the

hammer of globalisation. There were no Dunkin' Donuts or 7-Elevens on the way but there was a tiny glass-fronted shop called Frisbee Market. This was the kind of cracker-barrel grocery store that Europeans imagine New England is full of. It had maple syrup, fresh pieces of pie and an extensive fridge filled only with Chardonnay. I wanted to buy everything but mostly I wanted a small eight-inch-high cloth doll of Mark Twain. I knew it was Mark Twain because he had a small tag round his neck which said so and announced the fact that in 1902 Mark himself had popped into the Frisbee Market for some beer and a slice of pumpkin pie or whatever. I liked the idea of this. Maybe there could eventually be a small doll of myself or, in keeping with modern marketing methods, twelve 'collectables' of all the Gladyses.

'How much is it?' I asked the shopkeeper.

'Mark Twain is $2.99 plus tax,' she said, reading off a list. The fact that she had to look him up suggested I was not holding a hot item.

I wondered how Mark would feel about being $2.99 plus tax. Mark Twain, the man who once said a cauliflower is nothing but a cabbage with a college education. I also wondered about the whole tax thing. In England the price on any goods is the price you pay. In America the tax is always added on at the till. It varies in every town and every state and you can never be sure how much it is going to be. It's a very disconcerting approach for the shopper. It smacks of Americans continuing to keep their distance from tax which first caused them to throw tea into Boston harbour.

'Why don't they put the tax in the price so you know what you have to pay?' I asked the woman.

'Because the store keeper doesn't get that money,' she replied.

'Really?' I said, knowing I would have been too stupid to work that out for myself.

Kittery was named after a Kittery Court in the English county of Devon. Yet another legacy of people from the past seemingly fresh from English shores and homesick to boot. Unless, of course, they were actually all tailors from Italy who thought being English would be a better bet.

Where you come from and who you perceive yourself to be has been an important part of my journey and it was particularly important in Lisa's house. Lisa and her partner Mandy live in a small house. It is a miniature place much like the English two up, two down. Lisa works for animals and Mandy teaches children with special needs. Neither one is doing the kind of work that makes any money. They are what I think of as classic poor lesbians. Women generally make less money than men. Put two of them together in a couple and you are likely to get caring people with nothing to show for it. I thought about a gay male, millionaire couple I once met who sip champagne on the profit of formatting forgettable television and I wondered who decides the value of things in the world. I decided I was becoming maudlin.

Lisa was framed in the kitchen door at the side of the house. The front door opens straight into the sitting room and would knock over the only armchair. Here, in the small square kitchen, Cambodian music was playing on an old tape recorder. Lisa was warm and welcoming while Mandy was smiling and a little more reserved. None of us, after all, really knew each other. Everyone's attention was drawn to a tiny pixie-like figure who clung to Mandy's leg. Lisa introduced us to the tiny toddler with her shining Oriental face.

'This is Channy.'

Mandy and Lisa's adopted daughter, Channy is from Cambodia. She is tiny, beautiful, talkative and she lives here with her two lesbian mothers. She has many Western names but everyone calls her Channy. Mandy and Lisa play Cambodian music to her to help give her a sense of her cultural identity. I don't know if we have music genes which recognise the tunes of our heritage as something other than atonal. I couldn't understand it myself but then I can't think of a single contribution Denmark has made to the world of composition. (Please don't write. I am fine with my ignorance.)

Channy was mid-potty-training and there were potties every-where. We had arrived in the land of perpetual toilet concern. Both Mandy and Lisa had that haunted, tired look that we had at home for years with the children. They were worried they were doing it wrong. They were worried that they weren't dealing prop-erly with her sleeping. They were, like all new parents, worried. But they were not like all new parents. We sat in their front room surrounded by small toys and plastic lavatories. We tried to play with Bella, their nervous honey-coloured Labrador. Bella was ter-rified of everything and had survived as a rescue project of Lisa's. Bella only liked Paul, who we know is not mad about dogs. I think life is like that. I am scared of cats and never met one that didn't want to sit on my head.

We proceeded with the fast catching-up of history that I have become accustomed to on my journey. How Lisa and Mandy met at a local dance five years before. How Lisa had wanted to do wild life management, but it went wrong. How she ended up going to three colleges because one went bankrupt and then one wouldn't take credits and it took five years and she didn't get what she wanted after all that. For a while she worked at a local entertainment agency, booking weddings, college functions, alcohol-free New Year's Eve parties and such like. Now she runs an animal welfare organisation with twenty staff dealing with the many animals left in cardboard boxes on their doorstep and any other pet rescue problems.

We went through religion. Lisa is Unitarian like Rita. I know this helped make Rita comfortable. To an outsider it is odd. I really like the whole Unitarian approach but fundamentally it is a religion based on letting you believe in anything. It is a dark area for me. Mandy is Catholic. This is a darker area for me but I was interested how the shared Unitarian experience helped to con-nect Lisa and Rita. I realised that I was more immediately relaxed than I had been for some time. I had felt the same in Anne's house and I knew instinctively that I felt a bond because of our shared sexuality. It had nothing to do with the past but everything to do with our present living. I'm not saying all gay people get on but we do have a common experience which transcends all nationalities.

Mandy talked freely about her Catholicism. 'If there is such a thing as a gay or lesbian Catholic,' she laughed. I have so often felt the hatred and oppression of many organised religions that I always marvel at those who continue to stay within the fold. This brought up the story of Steve Immerman again.

'Of course he was really Jewish because his mother was Jewish,' said Rita once more. It is the critical part of the story for her. It was the mother who was important. Rita's kids have her surname and not Ron's. I decided *she* should have been Jewish.

I looked at Channy and wondered about the impact of heritage. Will she end up happily at Traip Academy and cheer for a soccer team her ancestors had never heard of? Mandy and Lisa are delightful people but not perhaps the mostly widely travelled, yet they went to Cambodia to collect a child whom they had never met and bring her home.

'We put in the application at Christmas,' explained Lisa, 'and then we got her in August. It took about nine months.'

This seemed about right.

'Did they check out your relationship?' I asked.

'No,' said Mandy. 'They didn't mention it.' I thought this was marvellous and a sign of the liberal times but it turned out that no one had mentioned it because neither did Lisa and Mandy. Because the law does not allow gay couples to adopt, Mandy decided to go ahead and adopt as a single parent.

'I knew it would be Channy when she was three and a half weeks old and then when she was five and a half months, we went to Phnom Penh to collect her.'

I could not imagine this kind woman from a small seaside town in Maine flying to the East to begin mothering a child already on her way in life. I could not imagine doing anything quite so brave.

I was concerned that Lisa's position seemed vulnerable to me and I talked briefly about my split from the mother of my children. About the plans we had made in case the unthinkable happened and then how we had actually dealt with the reality. Clearly it was not something they could imagine. They asked me what I thought the critical thing was in raising children in 'unusual' circumstances and I, foolishly, said, 'Just one thing – truth. Always be truthful with them and with everyone. It is the secrets that are a cancer on the soul.'

Sounds noble, right? That was when I found out that Mandy isn't 'out' at work and that being in education it was difficult and so on and on. More people, more loving people, being made to live in fear. She teaches eleven-year-olds with special needs. Where the hell is the place for prejudice in that? I felt like an idiot.

We changed the subject and Lisa and I went to collect a takeaway from a Thai restaurant a couple of miles up the road. It was a curious place. It had been built as a sort of German bier-keller with a fake barn-like interior and a vast mural of Hansel and Gretel heading off into the woods. Sadly, it seems the people of Maine did not want to party like *The Student Prince* and now the place was devoted to delicate Oriental fare. Pictures of King Bhumibol and Mrs Bhumibol of Thailand hung gilt-framed, below Gretel's feet. I am particularly fond of King B and indeed named my dog after him. While being guided through Bangkok, I once asked a petite Thai gentleman what the Thai people found funny. He smiled and half bowed. 'We laugh a great deal at many things,' he explained, 'but never at the royal family. It is forbidden to make jokes about the royal family but that is very easy for us for there is nothing funny about them.'

I looked at the unfunny royal couple and realised I had never expected to see them here in an American tavern of *das Vaterland*. Somehow the whole collage of nationalities in the take-away was a symbol of the America I was trying to come to terms with.

Lisa, the person I had not wanted to meet, was a delight. She and I chatted as we drove, the car steaming up with hot noodles and satay sauce. I realised that, under different geographical circumstances, we could have been friends. That she was a fine Gladys.

At home Channy ate stir-fry noodles and listened to music played on some plucked string. At pre-school she has a friend who is also from Cambodia and also has lesbian parents.

By chance, the next morning the *New York Times* had an article about Cambodian adoptions in the US. It made uncomfortable reading. Until recently almost a hundred babies a month had passed through Phnom Penh to a new life in the States. Now the US government had stopped the traffic completely. The concern, apparently, was about corruption. The article was full of stories of Cambodian mothers given tiny amounts of money, perhaps $100, for their healthy children on a promise that the child would grow up in better circumstances and then be returned to help them. The child would have a richer life and a good education which it could bring back to Cambodia. The mothers did not know about the $10,000 to $20,000 being paid by Americans to adoption agencies for the same children who, in fact, they never saw again. I didn't know if Channy was an orphan or if somewhere she had a mother waiting for her to return. What I do know is that Channy may look Cambodian just as I look Danish but that will not necessarily be enough to define her. If there is an advantage to be found in the endless breakdown of barriers across the world, it is that each one of us should be able to settle in the place we can find comfort in calling home. Will Channy have a *better* life than she might have had? I don't know. She will have a good life.

# CHAPTER 11

# Regina – Gladys Seven

*People who are always praising the past*
*And especially the times of faith as best*
*Ought to go and live in the Middle Ages*
*And be burnt at the stake as witches and sages.*

Stevie Smith, English poet

I suppose if the Gladys Society had existed in the infant America of the late seventeenth century we might well have been accused of witchcraft. A secret society of girls getting up to all sorts of no good. We headed south from Maine en route to visit Regina, Gladys Seven, the drama teacher who had first brought us all together. Anxious as I was to see her, I could not in all good conscience allow us to bypass the extraordinary town of Salem. (It is one of the advantages of being the driver. You can ignore instructions and join parades or whatever else you fancy.)

Churches dominated the centre of each town scene we passed through. Always white, stark white. You could find a New England church in the dark. Religion at the very heart of every community – religion but not tolerance. Rita was having troubles. Every phone call home seemed to contain some fresh drama – homework, homesickness, home something. Her family were not used to her absence. Julie, her daughter, emailed me to thank me for helping her to be more independent by taking her mother away but still the calls kept coming. I felt there were perhaps mixed messages being sent and it was hard for Rita. How the world has stood still since my mother and even my grandmother's day. Women should be at home. Women should be more careful.

The story of what happened in Salem, Massachusetts, is one every American schoolchild learns early on. It is a story of religious intolerance and hysteria. In the summer of 1692 a group of young girls, stimulated by voodoo tales told by a West Indian slave called Tituba, claimed they were possessed by the devil. They accused Tituba and two other women of practising witchcraft. Special trials were set up and soon the list of accused grew and grew. In the end nineteen innocent people were hanged, only to have the fanatical court itself finally repent and recognise the injustice of what had occurred. Frankly, I think it could have happened to anyone.

We were heading for the Salem Witch Museum but I felt compelled to take a detour first to 'America's Oldest Living History Museum', Pioneer Village, which lies just outside Salem. Now I think I have made it clear that I have a definite fondness for the American way of presenting the past and this place has to be up near the top of my list. Calling it a Pioneer Village is something of a stretch: it's more of a Pioneer three houses and a blacksmith. The small clearing is surrounded by chain-link fence, on one side of which is the sea and on the other the local baseball field. The place consists of three small two-storey log cabins and a covered forge. Each house has a solid wooden door and tiny windows with very little light bleeding in. To be fair to the living interpreters we did arrive at the very end of the season. No doubt they had all been busy being living interpretations and they were tired. Certainly the blacksmith was almost too exhausted to fan a flame into usefulness. He stood in his leather apron and looked at us. Me, Paul, Rita and a woman from Idaho who was killing time till she met her sister. The blacksmith took a long chug of liquid from a leather tankard and put it down with a bang.

'I only answer questions,' he barked. 'I don't give a long talk. Ask me a question.'

As we knew nothing about him this was a little tricky. The woman from Idaho sidled off to see if perhaps her sister was early. The blacksmith glared at us.

'What are you drinking?' I managed.

'Water. Only water. I need to rehydrate. You think I can do that with beer?' he barked.

That was, in fact, exactly what I thought. I thought I had read that they always drank beer. That the children drank beer. That everyone drank beer because it was water with the impurities brewed out of it. Indeed, I had imagined pilgrim life as being rather a pleasant state of continuous intoxication. I also thought, while we were busy living history, that rehydrate perhaps wasn't a word on every pilgrim's lips. Meanwhile, the handful of other interpreters were occupied trying to make the smallholding look busy. Ample-hipped women in long skirts kept brushing past us, saying 'Excuse me', and then coming back the same way two minutes later. I found it rather irritating. No one in the past seemed to have any sense of body space. Having learned what little we could from the blacksmith we moved on to some of the houses.

Downstairs, in the largest property, a woman dressed in a long skirt and sombre bonnet was sitting beside a giant slab of uncooked raw beef.

'That'll be some time cooking,' I commented.

She looked up as if she had seen a ghost. Then she rose and went over to the small four-poster bed in the corner.

'This was . . . like . . . a bed,' she said, fingering the mattress. It was in fact so like a bed that I thought it could only have been a bed which made me realise why I would never make a living history interpreter. She had lost the will to live and sat down to stare at the large chunk of mad cow on the table. Upstairs two Pilgrims were drinking coffee in cups from Dunkin' Donuts.

They seemed to be deep in conversation so we trooped into the empty room opposite. Unlike the other rooms, this one had no fireplace and was entirely empty save for a large barrel in the corner.

One of the men with hair down to the middle of his jerkin, appeared in the doorway. He had finished his coffee and stood with the incongruous empty container.

'Do you have a question?' he asked.

'Yes,' said Paul and I couldn't have been more delighted that someone did. 'Was this a storeroom?' We all looked at the solitary barrel and thought it was a good question.

'Yes,' replied the man and went downstairs to find a bin. We stood and looked at the room with its single barrel. It was a storeroom. Who would have guessed?

Outside, a concession to the notion of a village needing livestock had been satisfied by the enclosure of two goats behind a handmade wooden fence. The female was butting her head against the fence post while the male rather solemnly licked his balls. I knew just how they felt. If life was like this in the seventeenth century, it's no wonder they turned to a bit of devil worship. The place was getting crowded as two French people had turned up, so we headed into town.

I'd been to Salem before when I did the obligatory bus tour around America in my early twenties. I remembered the Witch Museum as being delightful and about as real as Ben Franklin's place in Philadelphia. I couldn't wait to show it off. The town itself was not as picturesque as I had remembered. It lies on the Massachusetts coast but lacks the charm of the smaller places we had already passed through. Much of the place looks tired now as if everyone has heard the story and can't be bothered with the bloody witches.

The Salem Witch Museum is in an old church which is either appropriate or ironic, I couldn't decide. The woman behind the desk offered us tickets to watch the half-hourly presentation.

'Do we have to watch the show?' I asked, keen to get to the museum bit with the witch stuff in it.

'That's all we are,' said the woman. 'Well . . .' she looked at me as if I might be trusted with a glimpse of a cauldron or two hidden out the back '. . . there is the gift shop.'

The gift shop had everything you could want in witch vending as well as, curiously, Kate Atkinson's novel *Behind the Scenes at the Museum*, and the history of golf in Boston.

For the show we were ushered into a large black room about the size of a real tennis court. Here a series of tableaux told the story of the hysterical girls and the even more hysterical reaction of the religious fathers of the time. The entire thing was a sort of *son et lumière* with many effigies made out of papier mâché lit in sequence, accompanied by a poor recording in which many amateur actors had vainly screamed in the background. It was fantastic. I learned nothing but it was fantastic. One of the worst things I've ever seen. A complete joy.

Spurred on to start my own coven we headed down to the harbour to see if we could find a witchcraft shop. In a small shopping arcade we saw a couple clearly dressed for Beelzebub bonanza. She was all in black with a long sleeveless coat, while he bobbed along in vivid purple knickerbockers and top. Polly and Peter Pagan out for the day. They were emerging from a witchcraft shop where they had obviously spent a fortune. In Boston I had already turned down the opportunity to buy a Jesus action doll, a paper cut-out figure of the Pope and a punching rabbi puppet. I looked around the shop and realised this wasn't the retail opportunity for me. Rita conscientiously took her time to spend $7 on six coloured stones for her children. Each stone was advertised as having particular powers which she went through with enormous care.

'Any kryptonite?' I asked Winnie the Witch behind the counter but she just smiled. I don't know if she was a real witch but she was certainly off with the fairies. There were lots of books about the craft, one of which suggested that many people first became interested after seeing the film *The Witches of Eastwick*. I saw that film and all I thought was that I never wanted to get as jowly as Jack Nicholson. Apparently, it's a good time to join a coven because it 'was much harder to be a witch only a few decades ago'. I was tempted to buy *A Book of Shadows* to keep my notes in but we moved on.

> *Cohasset for beauty,*
> *Hingham for pride,*
> *If not for its herring,*
> *Weymouth had died.*

Late-sixteenth-century saying, but I have no idea by whom

Not a popular verse in Weymouth I would guess. Now, here is one of those serendipitous things. Cohasset, a gorgeous town on the rocky Atlantic coast, is not just stunning to visit and home to the next Gladys, but it is where they shot the film *The Witches of Eastwick* and I didn't know that till we got there. As I've been taking you along the coast of this fine state, I realise that I have quite neglected to go through the 'things' of Massachusetts and, truth be told, I don't know if I can be bothered; the lists are all starting to look the same. All I will tell you is that the state insect is the ladybug, the state beverage is cranberry juice and no state muffin will look you in the eye unless it is made of corn. I know it's someone's job to think of these things, but really.

The history of Cohasset is like the history of the USA in miniature. It is a beautiful place of hills and ponds once carved out by some sweeping glacier. The name, corrupted from the Quonahasit tribe, means long, rocky place and that about covers it. It's a stunning, long, rocky place. Here the Vikings came, the French and then the English. In 1633 King Charles I granted 20,000 acres of New World land to a small band of Puritans who settled the nearby town of Hingham. Then Cohasset was just used as cow pasture and that is what has happened to the world. Today I live in a converted barn in England and Cohasset is a town of rich people living where bovines used to bring their dinner up for another chew. We have all come to rest in the stable. Captain John Smith arrived with instructions to change the name of the town to London but the Puritans forgot. One white man carried either measles or scarlet fever and 2,700 of the 3,000 Native Americans living on the bay died in one year. One hundred and twenty of the 165 men in town fought in the Revolution and the splendid local son, Zealous B. Tower was a brigadier-general in the Civil War. It is quintessential New England.

Rita and I were both excited to see our old drama teacher. In my seventeen years of formal education I only had three teachers to whom I still bend an imaginary knee and she was one of them. She was young and beautiful in 1972, with long, brown hair hanging down over a freckled face with an ever present smile. The sort of teacher you fell in love with in a minute. From the moment I met her she took me under her wing. Even when I had auditioned for the spring musical and had proved to be a double threat to the show – couldn't sing, couldn't dance – she had winked at Mr Aaron, the bandleader, and let me in.

The year I left Mamaroneck High was her last year there as well. She had met a man called Jerry and they were to marry and move to Massachusetts. All the Gladyses and, indeed, all the Henrys went to the wedding. As the couple emerged from the church we all sang 'Another Opening, Another Show' from *Kiss Me, Kate*. Not surprisingly none of us was invited to the reception. Today she is still married to Jerry but I hadn't seen her since.

The drive to Cohasset was fabulous. It is one of the most stunning parts of America. Even though the light was fading as we arrived, we could see that we had entered a land of considerable wealth. We passed some incredible and vast colonial properties. Of all the people I had visited, my drama teacher was the one I felt most nervous about. Why would a teacher want to see you after all these years? Surely she had had many classes and many students and there was nothing to suggest that the year of the Gladyses was any more important to her than some other year. As I've explained, Rita had done all the arranging. She had had several conversations with the teacher but she hadn't told her about my life. No matter how long I live I hate the endless 'coming out' of it all when you meet people. I had liked feeling comfortable, not having to explain myself to Anne and her partner and then Lisa and hers. I always sense people think it is some kind of confession and I hate watching their faces to see the reaction. I became progressively more irritable as we got closer. I wished Rita had been more of a gossip. Our teacher's good opinion was very important to me.

I tried to shut my mind down and turned on the radio. I couldn't find any music. Instead there was a rather serious discussion about whether the US borders should be closed to keep aliens out. Being an alien myself this had an uncomfortable Orson Welles *War of the Worlds* ring to it. A journalist was trying to persuade a Republican senator that sealing off the country might not be a practical idea, that it might not be the best thing just to shut up shop and hide. The senator, who was a bear of little brain, finally backed down a bit and said, 'Well, I suppose people with visas could come.'

This seemed a strange notion of protection. As far as I know all the perpetrators of 9/11 bar one had had visas. I decided that British politicians go into Parliament because they're no good at anything else and American ones do it . . . actually, I may have hit on a similarity here. We didn't discuss it in the car. Politics had become a no-go area.

Rita had been provided with many instructions so that we pulled into the sought-after drive as if the car knew where to go. We parked beside a huge tree between the double garage and the wooden house. It was an old place, a beautiful, big old place. Well, it would need to be as three of us were spending the night there. I was so nervous I couldn't remember how to turn off the lights in the car. Rita couldn't remember how to turn off the lights. I became quite girly and felt sure Paul as a boy must know how to turn off the lights. He had no idea how to turn off the lights and . . .

We were all feeling a little tired. Rita knocked on the back door but there was no reply. It was like being on a quiz show where they keep delaying the moment when they tell you if you've won or not. I quite wanted to leave now. It seemed silly to waste the perfectly good light spilling from the car and, anyway, we had *tried* to see her . . .

Rita led our small band round the front and on to a grey porch. A dog wearing a bandana went mad and there was my old mentor.

'It's all right, Cassie, shhh now,' she said to the little collie. After thirty years I'd have known her anywhere. Shorter hair, but otherwise the same smile and the same welcome. I felt thirteen again. Rita called her Regina. This seemed rather forward and took me some time to get used to. The house was superb: an eighteenth-century gem. A genuine piece of American history with polished floorboards and exquisite furniture that would have made Martha Stewart weep into her tomato cobbler. It was a house of many small sitting rooms, a vast kitchen and bedrooms which led away from corridors with sloping floors.

'They say it's haunted,' said Regina as she led us upstairs. I did hope so. Jerry and Regina have three grown-up children who have flown the nest but the bedrooms they grew up in are still intact. Rita had the spare room, I had the daughter's room in which I could admire many posters of ballet shoes while Paul was in the two sons' quarters in the sprawling attic. Here he could admire pictures of girls not even wearing as much as ballet shoes.

How odd to sleep in the white-canopied single bed of a young girl I had never met. How strange to think of Regina's daughter lying there with her childhood dreams. Everything felt very sur-real. Pieces of her childhood were all around me as I tried to piece back mine. It is quite the fashion to blame every grown-up character defect on your upbringing but this was a nice room. I suspected that Regina's daughter had no need to wander the highways of adult life hugging her inner child.

We had an enjoyable evening. We drank wine and it was all very adult but I still felt thirteen. I remembered the friends of my parents when I was growing up. Watching, it seemed to me, the men stride out in the world while the women led smaller, more confined lives. Marriages were different then. They had a different balance. Jerry was pleasant, Regina was lovely but their relationship was very different from anything I see with my friends now. We looked at their wedding photos. Two happy people about to drive off into wedded bliss in an old Jaguar. The car was Jerry's pride and joy. He still had it in one of the double garages. It was sold to him by a man called Cyril who made him promise that no woman would ever drive it and no woman ever has. Jerry took Paul off for a spin and Regina laughed as if that might be funny.

At supper she prepared the food and set the table while Jerry opened the wine. Jerry and I discussed an American organisation called the DAR or Daughters of the American Revolution. I was interested in the whole notion of snobbery in the States. It's a much trickier subject to access than in England where aristocrats wear their badges of breeding on their tongue. The DAR is an obvious home for inherited snobbery. It is a patriotic society for women whose membership is dependent on proving lineal blood descent from a relative who directly aided America in gaining independence. Eligibility claims must be supported by a genealogical file of births, deaths and marriages. It is not good enough simply to claim that your distant aunt once slept with Paul Revere. While not a DAR den, Cohasset clearly has some class issues. Jerry, who is retired from the world of finance, wished he had put his name down for the golf club earlier in life. It took him sixteen years to get his boat in the water of the small harbour which you can just about see from the front garden. By the time he has a card to let him on the first golf tee he may be making up a four with players from the Gospels. It is not the egalitarian America portrayed in the movies. I was fascinated but the conversation veered away from any discussion on this. Jerry, like Rita's husband Ron, liked to tell jokes. Maybe talking politics with women just wasn't polite.

We went through the past fairly rapidly. Oddly, it too had been an important year for Regina and she remembered it well. We talked of a boy who had had such perfect pitch that the orchestra used to tune to him. I wondered what had happened to him. Was this a useful skill to have been born with? Did he sit now as an adult next to some violinists, humming to keep them in line? We spoke of one of the Henrys, the handsome Ray, who is now Michael O'Keefe, an Oscar-nominated actor, and still talks about Regina's influence.

'Regina was an extra on one of his TV shows,' said Jerry, smiling.

'I called his producer and said I had been his drama teacher in high school. They said I could sit in one of the scenes with a lot of people. So Ray comes in and there's all these people and the first thing he says, in front of everyone, is "Regina!"' So he should, I thought.

Roger, her cousin, who had choreographed for us, had died of Aids. It was a moment, perhaps, to talk about myself and my life but I couldn't. In addition to bringing up her kids it seems our muse of drama has continued to inspire new generations. She worked at the local high school and included sex education in her lessons because no one else did.

'Do you know there were sixteen-year-olds who didn't know how to put on a condom?'

I suspected that the world was packed with them but it had never occurred to me to do anything about it.

'What did you do?' asked Rita, despite the fact that we were eating.

Regina laughed. 'I bought some condoms and a bunch of bananas.'

'Wasn't everyone embarrassed?' I asked, clear that this would be worse than catching something which needed penicillin to cure it.

'Well, we laughed a lot but they learned.'

Jerry sat at the head of the highly polished, dark wood table and talked about their kids, two boys and a girl. Regina explained softly that one of her boys wanted to be an artist. Jerry laughed. The boy had obviously been absurd. Jerry came from the world of stocks and shares.

'I got him a job working a trade floor in the San Francisco stock exchange. He loves the excitement,' he said, convinced that it was true. Jerry did not stop there; he got his daughter her job as well.

'So, you sorted two of your kids' careers out,' I said, because I can't shut up. He looked surprised but I don't know at what. My audacity at pointing it out, perhaps. It seemed only one boy had gone his own path. He had become a ski instructor in Jackson, Wyoming. Good for him, I thought, but there was no escape.

'It's a hard life,' said Jerry, 'so we bought a house out there and in the fall we're going to live there for six months with him.'

Jerry was a devoted father, a watchful father, an ever present father, still paying out for and controlling the kids' expenses. He and his wife bickered about one son's cellphone bill.

'He has to be able to call with the bridges and everything,' worried his mother. A fresh announcement had been made that morning warning that the bridges of San Francisco were under terrorist threat.

'He has to learn to budget,' said his father and, bridges or no bridges, the discussion was over. I looked at my old teacher and was back at the tables of my past where wives sat to the side and were not in charge. Maybe it was the wine but I could see her eyes had faded. I thought the house probably was haunted but that the ghosts were recent.

*The more he looked inside the more Piglet wasn't there.*

A. A. Milne

I was starting to have the strangest sensation of disappearing. I had established for myself that I was as Danish as Channy would grow up to be Cambodian. It was a genetic starting point, not a blueprint for life. Now I was beginning to see that though I had grown up in and loved America, I no longer instinctively understood the place.

The next morning at about six, I was reading when I heard Jerry in the kitchen. He had been out and returned with a cup of coffee in a cardboard cup. This struck me as bizarre, as coffee is so unfailingly terrible in shops and the nice thing about being at home is that you have proper cups. Breakfast was jolly and then we went for a walk to the ancient graveyard which lies between their house and the sea. Regina, ever the teacher, was keen to point out the glacial formations which had sculpted and carved gardens and byways in the town. Roads swooped and dipped and the graves rose and fell on small hillocks. Many of the dead had escaped this life in the 1800s. There was a Celtic cross commemorating some shipwreck which stated that 'about forty-five' men had been lost. This seemed rather vague and you could only wonder if they had come ashore in bits so that no one could be confident of a head count. And all the time I could not talk about myself. I was vague about the children and my life and everything I had said to Mandy and Lisa about truth was made a nonsense. I don't think for a moment Regina would have been anything other than marvellous but I didn't want to take the risk.

We had lunch at the seaside in Hull. Here the properties were cheaper and the place had a down-at-heel Atlantic City feel. Jerry wanted to eat at Jakes in Hull. We drove there and then drove to several other places Regina preferred. There was something wrong with each one and we drove back to Jakes. I don't know why we had pretended to try the places she wanted – it was clear from the outset that Jerry would decide. It was raining. Across the road I could just see through a glass pane to the bright colours of the Great Carousel of Hull. Galloping horses frozen for the season. People ordered fish but everyone had an instruction about how it had to be cooked. I had never heard fish ordered 'well done' before.

'It needs to be dry,' the patient waitress was instructed by Rita.

'It just needs to be dead,' I muttered.

We drove down to the harbour, where a man could grow old waiting to moor his boat. The weather was worse and the waves lashed against the treacherous ledges off the Cohasset coast. In the distance we could just see Governor Island, Bassing Beach and the light from the 150-year-old Minot Lighthouse. It flashes 1–4–3, a romantic 'I love you' signal. I stood there with people from my past and I didn't belong any more and I just wanted to go home.

# CHAPTER 12

# Fran – Gladys Eight

*There is no God and no universe . . . there is only empty space, and in it a lost and homeless and wandering and companionless and indestructible Thought. And I am that thought.*

Mark Twain

As this was not Paul's journey into the past, he was able to return home. Rita had already overstepped the mark in parting from her family and she too returned to her domestic life. I, however, had two more distant calls to make before I was done. Mark Twain and I headed west. Since finding him in that grocery store in Maine I had been carrying him in my pocket. I decided that Twain was good for me. He made me humble because he was such a brilliant writer, but he also made me want to be humble because I knew he had had an ego the size of Bill Gates' bank account. Unlike me, Twain thrived on the limelight and was fond of saying, 'I am not *an* American, I am *the* American,' which probably didn't get him a lot of dinner party invitations.

It's an interesting thing to say about oneself. I once sailed round the whole of Great Britain and realised how odd it was that such a diverse group of people, leading such different lives, could all be grouped together as one. A people who faced their foes united. I remember when Margaret Thatcher invaded the Falklands and we were all supposed to be on side. For the life of me I couldn't bring myself to dislike the Argentinians. I was fairly certain I had never even met one. Now that the forces of the enemy seemed to be gathering round religious flags I wondered for how much longer nationality would be a critical factor.

When you fly to the West Coast of America from Europe, you fly the same distance over the States as you did over the Atlantic. The place is immense and yet you know that below you the people all have a strong sense of being American. The *New Yorker* ran an article at Christmas about the American media's failure to report accurately that Bush actually did not win the election. He was in the White House through error or default or fraud. The singer Cher, who had been fiercely opposed to Bush before his election, was asked this week what she thought about him now. She shrugged and said, 'He's the president.'

There is no doubt that the Afghan war is the best thing that ever happened to him. My travelling has taught me to put to rest the idea that I am at heart American because of my upbringing. I am not. It is a wonderful country but it is not mine any more. Confirming a negative, however, did not help determine who I was.

When I was en route through Los Angeles Airport to Seattle, Washington, a 'Notice to Overseas Travellers' caught my eye. I was an overseas traveller and, finally alone, a nervous one. I read every notice within three miles of an aeroplane. This instruction had a large picture of a whale on it. It said the following:

MARINE MAMMAL PROTECTION ACT OF 1972
It is unlawful, with certain limited exceptions, to take or to import marine mammals or any parts of or products made from marine mammals. Whales, porpoises, seals, sea lions, walruses and polar bears are included in this protected group of animals.

I read this twice and could only hope the seal in my carry-on luggage would be quiet.

It was surprisingly warm. I was glowing in a ladylike manner and wanted a drink. I bought a bottle of water to take on board the plane not just because I was thirsty but because no one in America ever seemed to be far from one. It is the new accessory. This particular brand of water was clearly designed only as an accessory. It was so viciously sealed with plastic that I couldn't undo the lid. I never found out if someone had put something in my water, as Rita warned me all that time ago in Central Park, as I never managed to open the damn thing. The news-stand offered several publications to entertain me on my flight north, including a book about black box information gathered from plane disasters. Finally faced with a selection of books, I decided I wouldn't read at all and merely bought a slim guide to where I was going.

On the plane I was seated beside a five-year-old who practised rhythmic kicking on my thigh. The on-line booking system had worked nearly perfectly and my requested aisle seat was only two away from me as I sat by the window. I had so rarely in the last few months of travel sat next to an adult that I was thinking the only way round this was to demand to sit next to an infant when I next checked in. Given the airlines' delight in never knowingly satisfying a customer I thought this might do the trick. I was flying on Alaskan Airlines, a carrier I had previously been unaware of. The captain announced that 'flight attendants are here primarily for your safety but we're here to serve you as well', which was certainly a switch of emphasis from the old coffee, tea or me era. The safety-conscious flight attendants went on to remind me 'in the unlikely event of landing on water' not to inflate my lifejacket until after I left the aircraft. This seemed odd to me. It suggested checking the thing once you were in the ocean and I wondered how many people would dare wait.

We 'pulled back from the stand', 'doors to cross check' and all that. Out of the window I could see a man walking alongside the plane with an orange stick in his hand so that the pilot could see him. Really, I thought, nothing has changed since men were employed to walk in front of cars waving a red flag.

'Folks, we're on our way to Seattle and Spokane. Crew please be seated.'

Folks? It seemed a casual mode of address but I let it go and decided to presume a captain of this obscure airline knew what he was doing. It was more than I could say for myself. I was travelling as far west and north as a body can go on the main continent of the US. There are other more geographically distant parts in Alaska and Hawaii, but to my mind those states have always been slightly wild cards in the pack. I knew where I was going but I was not sure why. As usual, left to my own devices, my planning had been poor. I had managed to make vague email contact with Fran after Lori found her for me on the internet. I had also made a last-minute booking on the phone at LA airport for a Seattle hotel, selected only because it was the first one in my book. Fran was not definitely expecting me. The hotel was, but it could be terrible.

Of all the Gladyses, Fran had moved the furthest from home and from her old life. She had been the stage manager at school, a serious girl with long dark hair which hung down over her owl-like glasses. She was very organised and I don't recall ever seeing her without a clipboard covering her chest. Fran had been particular friends with Joyce and Rita and not really with me. We had got to know each other better when, for reasons I can't fathom, Rita, Fran and I had joined the French club trip and gone to Montreal for a few days. Certainly Rita and I weren't members of the club. Fran might have been but she kept it very quiet. We'd had a great time staying in dorms at the university and doing a small show for the local club. Presumably they were an English club as they already spoke French but I don't remember.

'I can't sing! Are you crazy?' protested Fran, when Rita and I had asked her to perform with us. 'I do stage management. I'm a techie, backstage only.'

Rita and I were determined. We had a whole routine which we mimed to a recording of 'You Could Drive A Person Crazy' from the musical *Company*. It needed three people. Normally Cathy was in the group but she definitely wasn't in the French club so she wasn't coming. Patiently we had spent hours in Rita's parents' sitting room teaching Fran her part and it had been a triumph. I don't recall speaking a word of French but it had been splendid till I tried to cross the American border in a pair of Red Chinese jeans. I had bought them in Canada and the others had been aghast.

'You can't wear Red Chinese jeans in America!' Rita had said in her emphatic way.

'Why not? I bought them in Canada.'

'Yes . . . but Canadians are . . . different.'

There had been a great hoo-ha on the bus home as we crossed the border, with Fran and Rita refusing to let me stand up in case customs saw the label on my arse. I did get over. No official stripped me of my illegal garb but I never wore them again. Much too nerve-racking.

Now on the plane to Seattle I realised what a terribly anxious and hopeless traveller I was – really a very bad quality in a travel writer. At the start of the runway an enormous sign instructed the air crew: 'After take off – no turn before coastline.'

This worried me. It suggested pilots could take off without a sufficiently clear idea of either the rules or where they were going. It seemed like an interesting metaphor for my entire journey. Flying blind into the past without proper preparation.

I had nearly finished the journey I set out on some time ago. I had travelled thousands of miles across land and sea and journeyed far into the past. I think many people travel without really seeing. Oddly, I felt I had seen too much and I didn't know if I could absorb any more. I'm not sure it's a good thing that so much of the world can be covered so quickly. Bring back steamer trunks and the hours wasted at sea.

A vast strip of narrow sunshine-coloured beach appeared below us almost as soon as we took off. I couldn't see where anyone could have made a turn any sooner. The mountainous coastline of

California spread out along the endless seas of the Pacific . . . in the unlikely event of landing on water . . .

For some reason the plane was full of small orthodox Jewish boys, all wearing dangling strings from their waist and round black cloth circles on the back of their heads. One of them was about four. His identity had been chosen for him. Poor old Steve Immerman.

Once we were aloft I calmed a little. The sky was that brilliant blue which threw the American painter Georgia O'Keefe into a creative frenzy when she first flew above the land. I never see that light through a plane porthole without thinking of her. There are no clouds over Los Angeles and if you ever do see one it is disc-shaped and isolated like a UFO checking for signs of intelligent life. It was not long before we saw snow below and an endless wilderness of trees. The air began to turn grey. A dark green landscape under a carpet of low cloud. As we neared Seattle, I could see a range of snow-covered mountains in the distance. The Olympics, I think. Below there were endless inlets of water where it seemed as though the ocean had been clumsily spilled on to the land by a shaky giant hand. Here you could see the islands and lakes left behind when the Vashon glacier buggered off so many thousands of years ago, from the Puget Sound basin. Small parcels of earth which were uninhabited till humans decided to cross the bridge of land that once linked Asia and Alaska, and then drifted south to what is now Washington State.

The waters of the Sound were incredibly still. A single boat trailed a white line across a small bay. I thought I could see a glacier in the distance but I didn't know if that was possible. I had never been to this part of the world. Twenty-five other states in my time but not this one. A ferry crossed from one of the many islands, but I couldn't see where it had come from or where it was going. Snap. I was exhausted and I couldn't remember why I began what I was trying to finish.

I think you can guess that I wasn't feeling great. It wasn't terrible. I wasn't rushing home to check into a clinic or anything but I was feeling depressed. Before I left New York I had taken the time to stop in at the old high school. I know that reunion is quite the thing at the moment but be careful of confronting your child-hood dreams in case you don't like what you find. My dreams weren't big but I was still clinging on to some. One in particular was that I still really wanted to wear a high school graduation ring. You can sweep the board at an English institute of education but no one gives you anything to commemorate the event. I wanted what American high school graduates get – a great ruby-infested piece of gold with illegible Latin on it. A grotesque display of academic achievement. The English have nothing like it. Nothing so ostenta-tious. We don't even like Ph.D.s who call themselves doctor. We know the truth. Ph.D. doctors may be able to quote Chaucer but that won't save you at the scene of a major accident.

I had pulled into the high school car park, suddenly feeling very grown up. The ubiquitous American yellow school-buses stood waiting outside. The exterior of the school looked as impos-ing as I remembered – vast buildings with huge pillars screaming of academic respectability. Inside, things were less impressive. The halls were deserted and everything seemed much grubbier than I recalled. Times had clearly changed. Posters advertising a gay help group were prominently displayed as were advice lines to help with bullying related to sexuality. A computer-generated sheet had been stuck up on the walls:

> The average high
> school student
> hears an anti-gay
> slur 25 times
> per day.
> Help change this statistic
> Join the Gay-Straight
> Alliance

I had never even heard of gay people when I was at high school. Some of the advertised activities seemed less than gripping. The Students Against Drink-Driving Lunch was probably not a barrel of laughs. Long tiled corridors led on to other long corridors lined with steel grey lockers. Past the coke machines, past the gymnasium (now renamed the rather trendy Sports Hub) where I stumbled across the principal, Dr Mark P. Orfinger. A trim man with a neat grey moustache, he made me slightly nervous. There was a hint of the Ichabod Crane about him. For once I had planned ahead and he was expecting me. We went into New York speak straight away.

'Are you coming to see me, Sandi?'

'Sure. When's good for you?'

'Now's good.'

'Good.'

'Good.'

We went and sat in his office feeling very good. I'd never been in the principal's office before because I was never in that much trouble. The truancy thing had been dealt with by my guidance counselor and my rather irritated parents. The principal and I sat and talked about old times. I felt quite nostalgic and even began to believe if I had but stayed I would have received an actual education. I was still thinking about the ring so I asked the good doctor, 'I never graduated from high school. Is there any kind of test I can take to graduate?'

He smiled at me. 'Did you go to college?'

'Yes.'

'There's no test that you can take. You could probably get some kind of honorary diploma, given the fact that you went on to college. You'd have to write me a letter and we could look into it. What college did you go to?'

'Cambridge.'

There was a pause. Finally he nodded. 'I think that would do.'

It was quite satisfying. I felt it put the old Alma Mater neatly in its place. Having realised how ridiculous I had been I decided to stop in and see the old school theatre. Now named the Maclean Auditorium, it was here that I had made my first entrance through the house as Gladys Antrobus. I had waited in the corridor till my mother (played by Ginger – Gladys Four) had yelled from the stage, 'Henry! Put down that rock! Gladys! Put down your dress.'

Then I had run down the red carpeted aisles, past the blue velveteen seats and on to the stage with its huge red tabs and wooden floor. I thought things were supposed to look smaller when you grew up but the place still looked enormous. How bizarre it was to stand at the very spot my career had begun, the very spot from which I knew what I wanted to do. I mean, if you were a surgeon would you remember the precise moment someone first let you have a sharp knife and something to cut into? Probably.

'Theater', as the Americans call all performing arts, was taken very seriously at MHS. Backstage there had been a small room where I had spent more time than anyone on the school staff had thought sensible. During my absences from class I had sat in that back room wishing I were more grown up than I was. Sitting and watching a boy called Coad draw on the walls in black and red felt tip. Coad wanted to be an artist and he took the room as his canvas. I climbed on to the stage and into the small room. I flicked on the light and stepped back in time. There, still swirling across the white paint in a psychedelic pattern, was Coad's masterpiece. No one had had the gall to paint over it. The only thing missing was the slogan which Lori had scrawled above the mirrors, 'Welcome to the theater. You fool, you'll love it so.'

And I did love it so back then. A passion which had sidelined almost everything else. Suddenly I was confronted with a rather heart-lurching realisation. Something had been niggling at me for some time, and there, in the room where my career had effectively begun, I knew what it was. I'd had enough. What had been niggling at me was that if I could, I felt I would give up my career. I wouldn't mind at all no longer doing the thing that had driven me for so many years. Ever since Ginger called out 'Gladys put down your dress' I had been prancing about in public showing my knickers. Maybe this journey was about growing up. About realising that I didn't need to do it any more. Certainly in that moment I had lost the thirst for it.

I went to the loo. In the bright lights of the many cubicled facility I noticed, for the first time, three or four grey hairs on the top of my head. I am blonde so they were hard to spot but there they were. I looked at my face. I had recently been told by a senior BBC producer that the corporation needed only new talent now; that no one wanted to work with people over thirty who were, in her words, 'tainted with experience'. I looked at my face. Twenty-one years of broadcasting. Not so much tainted as vigorously deformed.

It would be fair to say that I headed into Seattle feeling less than cheerful. I was busy putting my past behind me with no idea of what lay ahead.

*I know the human being and the fish can coexist peacefully.*
George W. Bush, 29 September 2000

Seattle – home of the dot.com, the sit-com *Frasier* and the big con Microsoft. It is also, bizarrely, where the American coffee revolution began. It was here that someone started Starbucks and soon the myth spread across the world that everyone must have a 'daily cup' but it must be so thin that you could see the bottom of the cup. I can't think why it happened here – you couldn't be further from the home of a Java bean if you tried. This is, of course, salmon country. Indeed, the first thing you see as you leave the airport is a billboard which reads:

Greetings From What Used To Be Salmon Country.
Save the Salmon While We Still Can.

I don't know if the last word is an unintentional pun but I entered the city in a fever about fish. The papers were full of the fact that the actor Kelsey Grammar had just signed for $1 million an episode of the next series of *Frasier*. It was only because of that sitcom that I recognised the skyline with its legendary 'Space Needle' which spread before me. When the first settlers arrived here they were faced with great cliffs which made up the seven hills of Seattle. They promptly set about levelling the place and it is an interesting thought that 40,000 tons of Seattle cliff lie beneath Telegraph Hill in San Francisco. They called the place New York-Alki, which sounds like a description of several people I know rather than a town name. Alki was a Chinook word so the whole thing meant New York By and By, but soon a founding father named the place in honour of Chief Seattle of the Duwamish tribe. The chief wasn't keen on the idea. He lacked the ego. The Christians then baptised him 'Noah'. How sad is that?

The *Seattle Times* made rather good reading as I rode in. The property section was full of tiny classified ads offering me wilderness property for no money at all. I could get a '39+ acres Mountain Hideaway' for just $37,000. There was a 'Mountain cabin on 20 treed acres' for $39,500. Immediately, I skated off into one of those fantasies in which I sold everything I owned, moved somewhere mortgage-free abroad and spent my time writing slightly bawdy novels that no one wanted to read. Two things niggled at me, however. One was the word 'treed' and the other was the thought that the sort of people who usually buy those properties are *folks* making plans to bomb government buildings. I'd move in and there would go the neighbourhood.

There was also a rather chilling news story that morning about cheerleading, that quintessential element of American sporting life. It is actually much more dangerous than anyone had previously supposed. Apparently, last year alone 22,000 cheerleaders were admitted to hospital emergency rooms with 'cheerleading related injuries'. I arrived at the hotel determined never again to be lured into doing the splits when holding a baton.

I think I do well with taking much of life at face value. The unknown Edgewater hotel turned out, as I had imagined, to be a romantic hotel on the edge of the water. It is a faux hunting lodge with red and green tartan carpeting, floor to ceiling windows looking straight over to the waters of Elliott Bay and metal pillars in the lounge, covered in tree bark. It sounds ghastly but it did actually work. Sixteen television screens in one wall of the bar were showing splendid footage of the whale I failed to get in my hand luggage. My room was intimate and cosy. It had a small fireplace and a balcony hanging above the sea. I stepped out to say hello to the gulls. It was cold and I had a true sense of having moved nearer the Arctic. I read somewhere that all seagulls are born in California. I can't believe it's true. If it is, I could only think they were here for the winter sports.

Each room had its own small pitched roof and the gulls seemed to have selected one each to oversee. Although the night was clear there was a blast from the horn of a large ship. In the distance, a lighthouse blinked at me. It was not the 'I love you' signal of Cohasset but enough to make me lonely. There is no point in staying in romantic hotels on your own.

I turned on the TV and, thank God, my old friend Maury was there. People were revealing shocking secrets which, pleasingly, make my life look rather tame. Tony was here to confess to her mother, Carol, that she had a brain tumour. They hugged and cried, the audience cried, Maury managed to stay dry-eyed. Shannon, aged fifteen, revealed to her husband Chris (Husband? Fifteen? Are you following this?) that she had 'prostituted my body between fifty and seventy-five times' and not surprisingly, she wasn't sure who the father of her eight-month-old baby was. Maury offered to pay for a paternity test at which point Chris got up to leave.

Maury: 'Wait, Chris, where are you going? What's your problem?'

Chris didn't say a word, probably because he didn't know where to begin. Anyway, it turned out that he *was* the father, which is good and, even better, I learned that if I do have 'acid reflux disease' (apparently it's likely) then I can do something about it. I have worked in television all my adult life but this stuff, the broadcasting of today, is nothing to do with me. I fell asleep while outside my window my personal gull turned a worm into mincemeat.

*Ah! the clock is always slow;*
*It is later than you think.*

Robert Service, Poet Laureate of the Yukon

Fran and I were due to meet after breakfast and, as had been the case with every other encounter, I was nervous. It hadn't happened yet but I felt sure I was due at least one person spitting in my eye. I had been awake since five, watching ferries come in across the bay with their lights on. Seattle is a long way north and the sun took for ever to decide to turn up. I was hoping it would snow. They say the lift in the Space Needle goes up so fast that when it snows, from inside the flakes seem to be falling up.

Fran was waiting for me in the lobby. I recognised her although she looked older, with a different hair style and much trendier glasses than the spectacles of her youth. We hugged, although I am sure that was something we had never done in our lives. I think we were *both* nervous.

'What do you want to see?' she asked.

'Everything,' I said unhelpfully and we headed out. We walked along the harbour front trying to get to know each other.

'Have you been to Seattle before?' she began.

'No,' I said, suddenly horribly English, 'but I recognise the skyline from *Frasier*.'

Fran nodded. 'Yeah, that's actually not what it looks like. They moved the Space Needle somewhere else for the shot.'

I couldn't think why but I knew she didn't mean literally. It was just another in the long line of real things the entertainment industry changed to suit itself. We wandered past the Imax theatre which claimed to be showing both Mount St Helens and Michael Jordan. I presumed not on the same bill and that he was taking time off from being a franchise.

Fran has recently left work after twenty years in the criminal justice system as a social worker. We talked about her career. About how hard it was to maintain liberal views after you have children. How you are so desperate to protect them that suddenly 'care in the community' seems harder to commit to. I could see immediately that she was an honest and bright person and that this would be a good day.

We looked across at the Olympic mountains and the San Juan islands. The air was crisp and clean and I thought about the cheap parcels of land available in the distant wooded hills.

'I could live here,' I declared as we stood on the deck of a ferry taking us out to the quiet isolation and beauty of Bainbridge Island.

'It's nice but I miss New York,' smiled Fran. 'I miss the culture and the energy. I think people have odd ideas about Seattle. They think we're practically in the Arctic.'

It felt like the Arctic. Fran moved here partly because of the Gladys Society. Sue was living here for a while and Fran felt safe moving this far from home. She settled, Sue moved away and now Fran is bringing up her family here. Her husband is a prosecutor for the District Attorney's office and they have two daughters.

Seattle seemed a world away from the other places I had visited. We quickly left the city behind on the chugging ferry and headed out towards a simpler, more rural life on one of the islands. When Fran first came she said you could see cowboys walking the streets. Once gateway to the Alaskan gold rush as well as fortunes in timber, Seattle still has a slight frontier feel about it. This was the very edge of America.

I liked it. I could imagine living out on Bainbridge Island, where many a writer has settled, in the exquisite wooden houses lining the harbour with gardens that run right down to the water's edge. The Suquamish people used to call the place home but now the place is open house to the tourist. You can buy a heck of a cute quilt or a scrap of art and still have one foot on the ferry.

Fran's children were beautiful. After our wander out to Bainbridge, we returned and met them off the school bus. Little girls with dark ringlets tucked into colourful bandanas and full of chatter. They live in the Queen Anne district, a place as steep and impossible to cycle in as San Francisco. Here the original trams had needed a counter-balance system of pulleys and ropes just to get them up the hill. Fran's husband Marc was delightful – a squat little man with the body of a clown. Before donning the cloak of the law he had been a street performer, a mime. It must have suited him. He looked as though he had just stepped out of the Le Coq School in Paris.

'Do you ever use your clowning skills in court?' I asked him.

'I did once start a closing statement with some mime,' he said, 'but the judge stopped me.'

'Why?' I said, thinking the judge was narrow-minded.

Marc laughed. 'Everything has to be entered in the record and they couldn't write it down.'

Marc was a clown who thought he should get a proper job. I had done the reverse. I had trained as a lawyer and become a clown. I have no idea which is the better way round but the two professions have a lot in common. I asked him if he ever wanted to be a judge and he looked at me seriously but with a twinkle in his eye.

'You have to understand that Seattle is a very politically correct city. Being made a judge is a political decision. The only way I could make it is if I were a handicapped Native American lesbian.'

'How about just a limp, a tan and a slight lisp?' I asked.

'That might do it.'

Seattle is a strange, liberal metropolis in an otherwise some-what conservative state. It is an unexpected place of art and culture in an endless wilderness. Unlike the neighbouring state of Oregon, Washington never banned the residency of African Americans. That doesn't mean it is all forward thinking and at peace.

Outside the windows of the fish restaurant we chose for dinner, there were signs of a harbour in dispute. Above a memorial to dead fishermen, fresh with new photos of lost young men, was a placard reading 'Yachts don't feed people'. The fishermen were battling for their harbour and on the doorstep was the death dance of a traditional industry which John McCarthy and I had watched disintegrating as we sailed around Britain.

Fran had not changed her name and we talked about that. Her daughters, Loren and Siri, have Marc's name but then she has her father's. I have been travelling to discover my identity for myself and have decided that I like the Native American idea of the descriptive name – 'She who must have big cup of tea in morning', 'she who lives by the joke' – something which makes you unique. My great-aunt Signe belonged to a society of women in the 1920s who campaigned not to change their names. From the outside I liked Fran and Marc's relationship. He seemed to be a good friend to her, but I wondered if men and women would ever settle down to understand each other completely. A small gift shop by the restaurant offered T-shirts with the sentiment, 'Women want me, fish fear me.' I stopped wondering.

When I got back to the hotel and phoned home, I found my youngest daughter had won her netball match, the other had been to soccer and my son had lost his sweater at karate club. I was the same age as my eldest child is now when I had a magical year which has stayed with me ever since, but this was the important stuff. With a sudden lurch I realised that I had not had the best time in my life as a member of the Gladys Society, but was actually having it now, and it was important to put the past in perspective or I would spend the rest of my life feeling nothing had ever really matched up to that experience.

The next morning I set out to explore the city on my own. I took the trolley car which runs along the front to the old quarter. I thought it was exciting. I wanted the conductor to think it was exciting. I wanted to have one of those friendly American chats. She wanted to read her paper. I was travelling the world but she was at work. Undaunted I decided that I needed somewhere 'different' to have breakfast. I got off at Pioneer Square. The area is a mix of rather fine bookstores, gift shops and people sleeping rough. It used to be the red-light district but now it is 'artistic' and designed for the rich. No one had told the men asleep on the park benches covered in newspaper. It was too early for the rich. In the centre of the square stood a magnificent and towering totem pole. The generally peaceful people of the Suquamish, Duwamish, Nisqually, Snoqualmie and Muckleshoot tribes had once lived here. They spoke mostly Lushootseed or Whulshootseed dialects. No doubt great languages, but hopeless if you suffered with a sibilant S. Stupid they were not. The totem pole in the square had been stolen from a local tribe and set up by some white settlers. Then the darned thing was cut down so the city fathers sent the elders of the tribe a cheque and asked for another one. They cashed the cheque and wrote back, 'Thanks for the money. That will pay for the first pole you stole. If you want another one, you'd better send a cheque.'

And they did.

I wandered past the Last Supper Club. A fine name for a restaurant. As good as the Toronto bar I once got hammered in called the Betty Ford Center. Down Yesler's Way, the original skid row where lumber had once skidded down to the docks and men had hung around looking for work and prostitutes in equal measure. I had meant to find somewhere elegant but I found myself outside

Seattle's oldest saloon on First Avenue S. Next door at Larry's Blues Café, Home of the Blues, breakfast of sorts was being served. It was 9 a.m. but not too early for the bar to be already filling up with men drinking beer. The place was lined with posters for rhythm and blues records. A large clock over the serving hatch was ringed in red neon, advertising breakfast burgers, while purple light spelled out the words 'Rhythm and Blues'. Apparently I had just missed Dr Funk playing live the night before. In fact, I think I could still sense a certain Funk smell in the air. A few old wooden tables with a rough covering of light green Formica and wooden chairs had been set up on the tiny ten-foot-square black stage which smelled of beer.

'If you hate globalisation as much as you do then this is the place to eat,' I said sternly to myself and went and sat on stage, by the window. The waitress was a very blowsy blonde with several previous meals spilled down the front of her black T-shirt. I thought you could probably guess the menu by analysing her top. She brought me a Hangtown Fry which I ordered because I had no idea what it was. It came and I still had no idea. It was omelette style but there its similarity with other food parted company. It seemed to have eggs, certainly, but also contained every other known food group. There was bacon, oysters, spinach, hash browns, cheese, sour cream and an inexplicable slice of orange, presumably for Vitamin C. I can't say whether I liked it or not; I just know that I'll never have the same again anywhere else in the world.

The Klondike Gold Rush Museum was just opening for business. It tempted me to go in and trace the Chilkoot Trail where bearded and rough-hewn men had once tramped looking for gold. I saw fresh fish for sale as I walked the red cobblestones in front of Pike Place Market, I drank terrible coffee in the oldest Starbucks in Seattle and a man in the street tried to sell me a 'work of art'. He was a black Rastafarian and his collection of art appeared to be any old piece of wood dipped in purple paint. On one a childlike scribble of a man's face had been scratched.

'I call that the milkman,' he said to me. 'It's $18!' he called to a passer-by, who wasn't the least bit interested. Why $18, I wondered? How did he fix his prices?

Across the slightly choppy waters of Elliott Bay I could see that the grey clouds had broken over the snow tops of the mountains. The light was hitting the snow in great shafts like torch beams from above and I thought again of Georgia O'Keefe and her art. I, who had been tired of travel, wanted to stay. I wanted to see the dormant volcano at Mount Rainier, visit the isolation of the San Juan islands and one day hike the Chilkoot Trail but I wanted to do it with the people I love. My partner and my children. The air was fresh and clean and I felt as though I was beginning to wake up again.

# CHAPTER 13

# Ginger – Gladys Four

*Here Lies*
*Jonathan Blake*
*Stepped on the gas*
*Instead of the brake.*

Epitaph in Ripley's Believe It or Not Odditorium,
Hollywood, California

It was nearly the end of my journey. I was off to Hollywood to seek, along with everyone else, fame, fortune and spiritual well-being. Actually, none of those things pitched up for me but I did find a tobacco enema kit for restoring the dead. It's in a glass case in the Ripley's Believe It or Not Odditorium on Hollywood Boulevard. The device looks for all the world like a brass bicycle pump. From what I can gather from the rather scant instructions you put one end of the hosing up the arse of a drowned victim and blow tobacco smoke in the other end. This was intended to stimulate the deceased back to life and probably gave the smoker a bit of a turn as well. It's a substantial item that would make anyone sit up straight on a beach. It was something I felt I could do with. On the very last leg of a several thousand mile journey, I now needed to make sense of it. It may be that I had not chosen the ideal venue for contemplative thought.

Ripley was a legend when I was a child. My brother and I used to devour his *Believe It or Not* books in which the curios of life were paraded before an aghast audience. In his Hollywood museum many of these oddities are on display. There is, for example, the wreath made from human hair which was designed to hang as a morbid memento of past love. Apparently it was not uncommon in Victorian times to make such a souvenir from the hair of a loved one who had presumably failed to respond to a final rectal smoke or whatever. The wreath was first placed on the coffin of the now bald departed person, and then displayed over the mantelpiece in the sitting room.

I drifted past photos of the Ubangi tribe, the world's tallest man, looked at a bikini also made of human hair, and the two-headed skeleton of a human baby. I passed a sign which told me that according to Dr Jelle Atema, a biologist at some lab in Woods Hole, Massachusetts, the lobster has a taste system a million times more sensitive than a human's. I thought about Barbara in Maine performing high colonic lavage on my lobster. Of myself, cracking and sucking on creatures who ironically have a palate ideally suited to selecting the accompanying wine.

Oddities from the past, but I was aware of ones from the present. The *New York Times* was running a story about a woman called Sharon who lives on a mountain in Idaho. She had decided that because of terrorist threats she would not fly again. Of course she hadn't flown for twenty-two years but that, it seemed, was not the point.

Outside, on the boulevard at Grauman's Chinese Theater, a big crowd had gathered to watch some filming. Muhammad Ali was receiving a star in the Hollywood Walk of Fame. There were many cameras watching the great boxing hero, now shaky with Parkinson's. I couldn't think of a single film he had made. Ali's sign was not to be placed on the ground but rather to hang on a wall. Apparently he didn't want anyone walking over him. Oh, to have the power to stop that happening.

On the other side of the road, the entire height of a large office building was bordered by a large sign which read Scientology. Many men were busy white-washing the front wall of the building.

I am not a scientology fan and thought it rather an apt metaphor for what was no doubt happening inside the building. Throughout the town religion was on offer. The place was awash with self-realisation fellowships and even the magazine in my hotel room described LA as 'The single best destination for searchers the world over to come discover their dreams. Often these dreams have involved movies themselves, with people aspiring to become successful actors, writers, directors. However, other dreams abound, as people seek spiritual answers and inner fulfilment.'

Great writers drawn to the movie money, like Christopher Isherwood and Aldous Huxley, stayed to seek a more peaceful inner life with the likes of Swami Prabhavananda from India and Manly P. Hall, a handsome fellow who dressed somewhere between a mystic and a big-band leader. Everywhere, the separation between the celluloid, the temporal and the spiritual dream was hard to spot. Even the Christian Science Reading Room advertised that it had 'movie reviews' in the window as if that might draw someone in.

They say Los Angeles is 'the city with the greatest religious diversity worldwide' and I think it is all connected to the weather. Even nearing winter the skies were blue and the sun beat down pleasantly on my back. Perfect for D. W. Griffith and the like to roll cameras, but warm enough for the out-of-work actor to think about spiritual needs. In New York they'd be too busy thinking they might freeze to death.

I didn't feel I had the energy to search for eternal truth. I was tired and, anyway, I had decided truth was a slippery devil. There was a story in the local paper about the actress Gwyneth Paltrow. The item claimed that Miss Paltrow is keen to cleanse her body and this purge includes coffee. It was the sort of story you expect in California where health 'issues' rule, cheese is considered a lethal weapon and you don't drink water with bubbles because it gives you cellulite. Anyway, this cleansing had apparently made Miss Paltrow hypersensitive and she now can't drink out of a cup which has even just once had coffee in it. She was at some event and her assistant was reportedly running about the place looking for a virginal cup. Was it true? I hope not. I hope as I write this Gwyneth is laughing her head off and chugging caffeine out of one of those mugs with rings of coffee stain inside them which the rest of us have at home.

*Tears are the safety valve of the heart when too much pressure is applied.*

Ginger, 1972 Yearbook, Mamaroneck High School

I had actually managed not only to speak to Ginger but arrange to meet her. My last Gladys, and finally I was contriving to organise things on my own. Ginger had moved to Los Angeles after graduating from Yale University in drama. She had always wanted to be an actress but then things had taken a detour and she had spent some time in Midwest married bliss. Now she was back in Tinseltown and Sue had managed to get her address. Ginger was the oldest of the Gladys students. The mark of a senior, a graduating high school student, in the Mamaroneck yearbook was that they had an individual photo printed with a quote of their own choosing. The one about tears being the safety valve of the heart was Ginger's. I never gave it much thought but I realise now that it wasn't exactly cheerful. Apart from our drama teacher, Ginger had without a doubt been everyone's favourite. She lived alone in an apartment with her mother. We rarely went there as, looking back, it was not a place Ginger felt comfortable taking her friends to. Ginger was pretty, she was talented and she was smart. She was the star of the show, she was my hero and an absolute role model.

After high school she headed off to the blue-chip confines of Yale University to be a doctor. Within a year she had changed her mind and gone back to studying drama. I think we all believed if there was success to be had in the group then Ginger would be the one to have it. If I am honest Ginger was probably, although not in a sexual way, my first love outside my family. Well, there was my kindergarten teacher, Miss MacDonald, when I was five but I don't think I would recognise her today.

Just because I was in town didn't mean Ginger didn't have a life to lead. Like many another struggling thespian she had found an alternative career in the restaurant business so I had a couple of days to kill before we could get together. You'd think Hollywood would be a Holy Grail for someone like me who has spent her professional life in the entertainment industry but I wasn't sure. Everything about Hollywood sounds romantic. The very name Sunset Boulevard suggests a life shot through gauze and accompanied by swelling strings. Sadly, it isn't like that at all and as for Hollywood Boulevard . . . well, if I'd come looking for glamour I would have sobbed aloud on the sidewalk.

It is a filthy place, lined with large bronze stars which have been embedded in the sidewalk on both sides and for some distance. As I checked out the names, Superman and Crocodile Dundee sauntered past me followed by a small parade of young cheerleaders who in turn were shadowed by a man with scarves wrapped around his feet for shoes. It was impossible to tell who was in town for entertainment purposes and who was on the loose from some restraining authority. I kept my head down and followed the parade of granite stars. Their location was not always felicitous. I found Dean Martin outside Fore Play – a bondage wear shop; Otto Preminger outside a wig shop; Fatty Arbuckle, rather pleasingly, outside a deli; and the debonair Spencer Tracey beside a particularly evil-smelling fast food place. The sort of place you only think smells good if you are pissed. A magic shop offered me 'Instant Pussy' while Fredericks of Hollywood Lingerie beckoned me into the Museum of Underwear where you can stare at the underpants of the famous, the gussets of Mary Tyler Moore, Shirley MacLaine, Robert Redford and the like. Here you can stand and think about the information that Alfred Hitchcock had no belly button. Time, in fact, to contemplate someone else's navel. Fame indeed.

I did wonder what it would be like to stay in town as a big star. I had started out quite successfully in the Lux Hotel on Rodeo Drive in Beverly Hills. The normal price of $325 per night had been slashed to $119 on-line. There are no shops in the area with anything that might sustain everyday life but it is fantastically convenient if you suddenly need a $3,000 handbag. I had rarely been so neatly placed to pop into Van Cleef & Arpels or Cartier. I had never been in those places in my life but I was neatly placed. Up and down the drive, shops were laid out like art galleries with individual handbags displayed like sculptures. Many down-lighters, much marble and stone shelving, but little anyone would actually want to purchase. Up the road, the entrance to Ralph Lauren was narrow and lined with many conifers. Indeed it was something of an arboreal fight to get in. I only went because they claimed to be having a sale but there were no price tags visible anywhere. I think one wasn't supposed to look for the price and scrabbling around inside the garments to look for a ballpark figure was clearly frowned on by the staff. I wandered into the women's section and immediately felt totally out of place. These were clothes for people who never intend to move very far or very fast. There was little cloth given over to covering the midriff and, unlike Mr Hitchcock, it is an area of my body I wish to draw a veil over.

People, however, patently live near Rodeo Drive. If you wander just two minutes from credit card alley you find pinched women scooping dog mess into plastic bags and eyeing you with suspicion as they slip back into their apartments. These residents must buy milk and bread and indeed haemorrhoid preparations somewhere. All the same, it seemed like a veneer of life rather than life itself. A woman drove past in a vast smart car putting on lip-liner as she steered. Half an eye on herself and half on the road. It is the modus operandi for Beverly Hills. Far from the treed acres of

Seattle, the local property pages were offering a different league of
real estate. How about 4.16 acres of land in Bel-Air for a mere
$13,900,000? Here I could apparently 'create my own world'. This
suggested to me that even at that price the place wanted work. I
decided against.

I had only booked in for one night at the Lux as I had no idea
what the hotel would be like. It had a strange boutique chic but it
would do.

'Do you have any rooms for tomorrow?' I asked Christian, the
somewhat camp man at reception who probably would have been
happier talking about permanent eyelash tinting.

He eyed my trainers and the rather tired BBC fleece I was wearing. 'No,' he said firmly.

'Can you recommend anywhere?' I asked.

'At the price you paid?' he sneered loud enough for a woman
nonchalantly bouncing her platinum Amex card at the end of the
counter to hear. Patently Christian could not. I was to depart. It's
funny how staff in expensive places sometimes become bigger
snobs than their customers. I didn't want to waste time searching
for accommodation so I picked a place out of the *Yellow Pages*. My
mistake was that I chose the Holiday Inn in Hollywood. These
two place names sounded identical to my Armenian cab driver
and neither he nor I had any idea where he was heading. In addition to being foreign my chauffeur, sadly, was also deaf. It's a killer
combination for a man whose living involves taking instruction.
He had few words of English and the few he had he couldn't hear.
Frankly, I had been lucky to get a cab at all. This is not a city where
anyone ever steps into a street to hail a cab. They all get into their
own cars and I had made a mistake in not hiring one. I had
thought long and hard about changing my career on this trip and
I realised I had all the qualifications needed to become a cab driver
in the city of angels.

Arnold Armenia and I wandered about Los Angeles seeking
anywhere that would take me in. We drove past an enormous

eatery entirely made of tin, a diner made from a train carriage painted yellow and any number of other places, all of which looked like movie sets rather than actual venues. I realised that no restaurant on the strip had ever taken over an old building and thought, This is charming – it just needs a little work. They had bought a property and then torn it down and built a themed building which represented their chosen cuisine. It is an attitude the British don't really understand.

They say my great comic hero Lucille Ball haunts her old house in Hollywood. She loved it so much she continued to live there after her divorce from her husband Desi Arnaz. When she died in 1989 (I can't bear it. It's not that long ago and I could have met her), the new owners immediately set about what the Americans call 'a complete remodelling' which means the house was never the same again. Now she is said to wander the property disconsolately. I'm not surprised. Lucille Ball was a television and comedy pioneer, the very sort of person whose history this town needs to preserve. Where is its sense of the past?

Los Angeles may be the land of dreams but they exist cheek by jowl with great poverty. Just that day the *LA Times* was running a story about evictions in the city being on the increase. They compared it to New York where more than 29,000 people now live on the streets, half of them children. It is not the American Dream of the movies. Outside my window we passed a parade of incomprehensible things. A '16-minute Smog Station'; IN and OUT Burgers, which I hoped referred to the drive-in facility they offered, rather than the quality of the food; We the People Legal Document Services, currently offering divorce for $189; Zone Perfect offering to keep you on your diet by delivering three meals and two snacks to you daily and Starbucks advertising a Banana Bran Muffin the size of one of Mae West's breasts.

Everywhere billboards advertised movies, stomach remedies and 'gated communities' such as Belmont Village Senior Living where pensioners could live in safety. I had only recently heard

about the first lesbian one in New Mexico. It was hard to imagine.
A whole community of sensibly dressed women who were good
with power tools. All part of the endless specialisation of the
world. Somewhere between Mae's mammaries and the La Brea Tar
Pits we got more lost and the cabbie had time to tell me about
Armenia and how much he missed home because everyone he
loved, his mother, his father and so on, was there. I was feeling
quite tearful when at last the Holiday Inn hove into view. Soon I
would know real pain.

We had come a million miles from Beverly Hills. Here everything looked seedy and down at heel and no dog owner stooped
to gather up doggie mess. We had gone from the land of haute
couture to haute manure in a heartbeat. Next door to the depress-
ing and less than pristine Holiday Inn the Hollywood Hills Beauty
Center and Spa was offering a European spa pedicure with either
paraffin wax or mud from the Dead Sea. I didn't want to check
into the hotel and stopped to look at this. Where would such a
place get mud from the Dead Sea? A Dead Sea mud importer presumably. What an odd business to be in – mud importer. I
wondered how it worked? Was it a large business or just a man
with a bucket and spade and a large stock of watertight envelopes.

In the lobby, all human life was there. A woman dressed neatly
in a suit from a catalogue was talking to the porter about Canada.

'I've been there,' she said. 'I started a church there.' Words I
would love to drop into conversation. 'I'm a church planner,' she
explained.

Church planner, LA cab driver, mud importer . . . there had to
be something out there I could do. At reception the sort of woman
I now know Maury favours on his chat show was standing, holding court. She was dressed somewhere between an ordinary
member of the public and a hooker and was no doubt what the
Americans call 'white trailer trash'. It seems she had been flown in
to appear on the real-life television court drama presided over by
Judge Judy. Here members of the public air their disputes and

allow Judge Judy to judge and make snide remarks as a side bar. The people at the desk seemed as reluctant as me to go through the checking-in charade so I had time to gather that the woman had lost her case. It seems she had been claiming $2,000 because a tyre had come off her car when it was being driven by a friend. I don't know what the money was for – new tyres, damage to the car or possibly driving lessons.

None of this was the Hollywood experience I had thought I would find. I fled from the hotel to seek the land of make-believe at Universal Studios up the road. As soon as you arrive at the studios a sign directs you to 'Enjoy Yourself. You're in Hollywood now'.

Indeed, from the moment you are within earshot of the place until you leave there is never an instant when someone isn't telling you what to do. I was very much out of season and the place was not busy. A red carpet buffered by giant Oscars leads to the main gates but I was nobody and was directed round the side. Here I pretty much had the sole attention of a smooth-looking grey-haired man who wandered about making many deep-voiced announcements on a hand-held mike. He looked as if he had stepped off the set of a soap opera where he had been busy giving his 'older rake' performance. I wondered if he was disappointed with his life or thrilled at living on the fringes of the big movie business.

'If you need a map in another language—' he began,

'—then you probably won't understand when I tell you where you can get it,' I concluded out loud, but no one was listening. Everyone – announcer, ticket-seller and the three other tourists – was taking this very seriously. I was supposed to be in awe. The world's largest studio and movie theme park advertises with the slogan 'You can't get any closer to the real Hollywood'. Which implies that you, you poor schmuck, are never going to be a star.

A Pinkerton private security guard checked my plebeian bag of belongings. He wore a black straw Canadian Mountie style hat which is a difficult look for a thick-set man to carry off. The announcements continued against a backdrop of endless, exhausting, sweeping John Williams-type music on a loop. The music had an urgency that suggested we were all about to head off on a Luke Skywalker kind of adventure. Retail opportunities presented themselves the moment I entered the car park. I went to buy sunglasses because I was in Hollywood now. There was a gentleman from Russia ahead of me who had clearly been provided for my benefit as entertainment. He had the sort of cod accent which can only have been provided by central casting. I stood waiting to purchase my *Thelma and Louise* glasses while he went through the American coin system with a member of staff recently arrived from Guatemala.

'Dis is ten cents?' boomed the Russian.

'Let me look,' replied the Guatemalan who also turned out to be myopic. They went through every coin in the realm. All life was there.

At last, my eyes concealed behind black plastic, I stood on a great walkway in the heart of the park and looked out over the Hollywood hills. In the distance I could see what looked like the Warner Brothers studios. They had once threatened to sue Groucho Marx for using the word 'Casablanca' in a film title and he had threatened to counter-sue over their use of the word 'brothers'. There was acres of space and hours of sunlight. Movie-making heaven. I decided to start with the tour on a trolley. The assault on my senses got worse.

I can only assume that no one connected with the park has ever stood in the queue for the tour or they would be checking into the Betty Ford Clinic in a breath. To combat the danger of anyone getting bored the queuing area is lined with displays of stills from famous movies, while at least four different soundtracks can be heard simultaneously. It was an astonishing barrage of babble. No visitor was allowed to stop and think independently for a minute. I'm afraid I did think if a Muslim extremist turned up at Universal they would probably decide they had been right about America. It was an exhausting place of excess.

A still from *Schindler's List* reminded me of my great friend the writer Alan Coren and how he loved to point out each time we got in the lift at work that it had been made by the Schindler company and was therefore Schindler's lift. I stood and stared at the images of the movie stars. I suppose I should long to be enshrined on the displays of such a place but I didn't. On a board of Leading Ladies there was a picture of a woman I had been at university with. We had been close in those days and when I had run into her years later, I had been delighted. She had unexpectedly treated me with a strange and deliberate distancing. A coolness which suggested I wanted something from her. It was horrible and hurtful but she was a very big star now and she had got used to a different kind of behaviour. I have seen it before and I don't know who fame makes more of a mess of – the people who don't have it or the people who do.

The tour set off down Bob Marley Avenue. I realised that, along with Muhammad Ali, there were a whole host of people I don't associate with being captured on celluloid whom Hollywood claims as its own. Larry 'I'll be your guide' had patently done the tour before. He had learned his patter and, by gum, he was going to steam us through it if it killed him. We galloped through the fact of Universal City having its own mayor, fire station and post office and the exciting news that they were currently shooting the pre-quel to *Silence of the Lambs* with Anthony Hopkins.

I won't spoil the tour in case you decide to go. I thought it was worth it. We met King Kong, experienced an earthquake in a tube station, where a truck fell through the road above and would have crushed us if it weren't for that fire which would have annihilated us if it weren't for that flood . . .

Having Jaws come at you on Amity Island was okay but I did nearly shit myself with the scarab beetles on the *Mummy* set. The main thing was how busy it all was. The studio is a working place and everywhere people were building, painting, preparing for some new extravaganza. The thing that grabbed my attention were the bungalows on the lot where writers under contract sit and churn out ideas. People living by their imagination, the very thing that had failed to happen on 9/11. Some of the greatest writers have sat in there: Dorothy Parker, F. Scott Fitzgerald, and scores of others. Being looked after so they could sit and think and create. We have nothing like it in the UK and I was overwhelmed with jealousy. Now that I would like. That I would like a lot. Not that the studios truly appreciate the writer. The tour had begun with a small video clip that posed the question, 'How do movies begin?' and had answered it by showing a producer behind his desk saying they began there. Of course they don't. They begin in someone's head, in the bath, shopping or walking in the garden. I don't mind if no one recognises that. I just would love to be looked after to enable me to write. I thought of my great-aunt Signe and her financial supporters. I have a million ideas for books and movies but endlessly find myself at some corporate event for drainage engineers or whatever in order to make a living. Interesting to reach a stage in life when you realise that all you want is to be patronised.

I went to have a meal at one of the many fast food outlets. On the way announcements warned me not to sit on the escalator (a thought which had never crossed my mind), to hold on to the hand rail, to be careful – to be endlessly instructed in what I might or might not do, presumably so that I wouldn't end up in court before Judge Judy. At the food counter my meal options quite literally dripped with grease. A family so fat that three of them were sitting at a table for eight, were silently eating under a barrage of music and instructions. I realised that it is not anthrax that will kill the nation but cholesterol. Perhaps the Taliban have actually gone into catering.

Not knowing which hotel I would end up in I had arranged to meet Ginger back at the Lux Hotel on Rodeo Drive. As I stood in the street waiting, a tanned woman in hot pants went past on the amorous arm of an extremely old man. How odd for a woman to be satisfied with a dissatisfying life if someone bought her clothes and jewellery. A young woman with long brown hair drove past on the other side of the road in a black Mercedes. I thought it was Ginger. I knew she had got divorced and had remarried. Maybe she had some older man who now spoiled her and cared for her and maybe that wasn't so bad after all. I was in fantasy land when a small, Japanese car which would have failed its MOT test in the UK pulled up and Ginger got out. She looked the same, smiled the same and hugged me the same, but her long, brown hair was now long and completely grey. I realised I had been looking for someone from thirty years ago.

'Sandra! I'd know you anywhere,' she beamed.

Sandra? I don't know if I'd know me anywhere.

I got in and we headed for her home. She kicked off her shoes and drove in bare feet. It was something I remembered she had always done. I looked at her feet and for a moment nothing had changed. It is the minutiae of the past which will suddenly send us back. We drove north through the deep canyons of Los Angeles where even modern technology cannot provide a decent signal for a mobile phone. The sun was setting and it was beautiful. Ginger was chatting and she too was still beautiful. A filing cabinet rattled in the back of the car.

'Sorry,' she said. 'I've been helping a friend.' Of course she had. She was always helping out. Over the years her voice had deepened. It no longer held that girlish uncertainty.

Ginger and her husband Eric live in a small suburb of LA called Sherman Oaks. Here they rent a cramped upstairs apartment with a lovely quiet courtyard below. I was excited to meet Eric. Ginger had told me he was a screenwriter. Perhaps one of those very people I had idealised, living in a protected bungalow. Eric, as it happened, wasn't excited to meet me. The apartment consisted of several small rooms none of which was designed for more than two people. In their sitting room there was one comfortable arm-chair, a chair for a person with chronic back trouble, and a television the size of a small seaside cinema. Squeezed in a corner was a bicycling machine and a mat for sit-ups. Whatever else Eric and Ginger did, they did not sit together to watch TV.

Eric was younger than Ginger and immensely thin with large glasses. Eric did not want to share tips about screenwriting techniques or even software. He had had a bad day. He had been over to see a friend to watch the game and the friend had gone for a massage in the middle and it had all gone wrong. Ginger brought in a chair from their computer so I could sit down.

'I don't think we've ever done this.' She giggled as Eric, with his bad back, watched her move the furniture. Entertaining was clearly not a priority pastime. Ginger showed me an alumni book for the high school where I was listed along with the address I had only recently moved from. I could only think Sue must have put it in. How strange. I was an alumna of an American high school. I had never felt more distant from a thought in my life. I met Ginger's cat who was very old and about as pleased at having company as Eric was. Eric, who wants to write action movies, had had enough actual conversation and decided he wanted to go out.

'Where shall we eat?' asked Ginger. Patently neither one of them cooked. They were both rake thin. Still, not cooking was what all the Gladyses did. Apart from Regina everyone else either went out or got their mother to do it.

Eric laughed. 'You can take Sandra anywhere. She'll be glad to eat anything. She's from England. They don't have anything worth eating.'

Union Jack bunting fluttered out in my head as mentally I rushed to the barricades to defend English cuisine. It was not a battle position I had ever imagined I would take up.

'Have you been to England?' I asked. Eric nodded. It seems when he is not writing he earns a living selling film rights. This work had taken him to Europe, which was a shame as there appeared to be nothing about the place that he liked. Venice smelled and, at a pinch, you could 'eat that Plough Mans' in England. That was just about okay. I tried to think of the last time I'd had a ploughman's. Our local pub does Thai food. Eric went to the movies, presumably to see something with no words in it, and Ginger and I walked out into downtown Sherman Oaks. The town was full of dining possibilities. It was wall-to-wall neon signs offering fast foods. Clearly the idea that it might sometimes be good for food preparation to take time was alien. We stopped in at a diner called Solleys. Here Clyde was pleased to serve us. He handed out menus which were much too big to deal with and then proceeded to give us a verbal list of specials. Ginger offered to order something we could share. I was delighted, partly because I didn't have to wade through the choices and partly because, not that I would tell Eric this, I knew that no matter what I ordered it would taste the same. Ginger is a vegetarian now. A non-smoking, non-drinking, non-acting vegetarian.

I had been so sure that of all the twelve theatrical Gladyses Ginger would never give up the cause of theatre, that she would be fighting to the bitter end for fame and fortune. It had been in her blood. She told me her grandfather had been in show business. It seems he was quite the dandy and wore spats when he did his act on the Jewish theatre circuit. All this was news to me. I didn't even know Ginger was Jewish but then she wasn't really Jewish because her mother was Italian Catholic and everyone knows that the Jewish thing passes through the mother and Steve Immerman's mother . . .

I asked her about the quote in the yearbook and she said she had felt defensive about crying all the time when she was growing up. I don't remember her crying once. Same past, different picture. I caught up on her life. How her mother had died of a brain tumour. How she had struggled to find acting work in LA and then met her first husband John. After both trying to make a go of show business they had moved to his small hometown in

Wyoming. Here they had been 'Mr and Mrs Theater' to the town where he worked in real estate and she taught aerobics. Then he had wanted to come back to the big city and soon it had all fallen apart. How she had to help get her sister deprogrammed from some cult.

'I found a deprogrammer in San Francisco,' she explained and I longed to ask what section in the phone book you look under for that.

Now her sister lives near by on disability. Ginger works in a smart restaurant in Beverly Hills and spends her free time studying to be a marriage and family therapist.

'What about the acting?' I asked.

'Oh, I don't do that any more.' She shrugged and smiled.

It was incomprehensible. Of course she did that. That was what Ginger did, but apparently not. At forty-seven, she told me, the only singing she does is in the car. She was always the sympathetic one and felt she had a natural talent for therapy. Already it supplements her income.

'Some friends of mine said they get more out of talking to me than to their therapists. Could they pay me?'

And I think that is what has happened to the world. We grow up and move away from our homes and in the end need to pay people to listen to us.

I had a small album with about a dozen pictures of my children. Ginger had an album of her cat. She showed me the cat on the sofa, cat on the bed, cat in a hat . . . She had never had children and never wanted to. It was not what I would have predicted for either of us. She was lovely, she was kind, but I was a grown-up now and everything was different.

Back at the flat Eric had returned from his movie. I still wanted to know about his screenwriting or at least his ambitions for writing. Over dinner I had learned that he has not had the success he wished for and it has been hard. I was keen to talk about the whole film-making process but Eric was not.

'There is no European film industry,' he said after I fired an opening gambit. I wondered if Harry Potter and its English writer were also dismissed but I got no chance for debate.

'You two will want to talk, so I'll watch TV,' he announced and clamped on headphones like leather Mickey Mouse ears. On a nearby shelf sat a book entitled *Writing Screenplays That Sell*.

'I had a crack at screenwriting,' said Ginger, 'but it's hard. You know, the woman who wrote *ET* never wrote anything again.' I didn't know that but I bet she at least had some conversation.

Eric sat watching sport, which unfolded silently on the large screen. It was almost impossible to associate my old friend, who interacted so well, with a man wearing headphones watching TV. How curious to be a writer who seemed so uncurious about some-one who had travelled thousands of miles to visit, who also wanted to write and who lived in a place he had been to. Eric's writing friends who had succeeded had done so with scripts for series like *Star Trek*. Perhaps they don't require interaction. A hockey puck flew across the screen. Perhaps he lived in a world of action. Maybe but I was disappointed.

'I'm eight years older than Eric,' Ginger explained. I decided that with a woman's maturity and everything that adds up to about twenty years. I didn't know if I could wait for Eric to grow up. We arranged to meet again but it was complicated. Ginger's life was busy and although she was pleased to see me I was no longer a part of it. When I looked at her as we said goodbye I realised more ghosts had been laid to rest. Ginger said she had finally 'found her niche in life' and I believed her. It wasn't what I had imagined but she would make a good therapist. Everyone would want to unburden to her. Everyone, of course, except Eric.

On my last day I did what I should have done at the beginning and hired a car. I drove out to the coast and here, at last, I got my brush with fame. On Santa Monica pier, sticking out over the rolling waves of the Pacific, faded metal signs declared 'No over-head casting'. This was rather appropriate as a film unit were busy on the pier casting extras to ride the frankly rickety-looking roller-coaster above my head. A large crowd of diverse folk had gathered in front of an officious woman with a clipboard. The director's chair had the single word '*Angel*' stencilled on the back which I took to be the name of the programme and not a comment on his demeanour. The gathering of lights, cameras and other technical equipment was much bigger than any UK TV show I had ever seen, but one of the main security guards explained it was a production of the television show *Angel* which I had never heard of.

'Background people, let's go!' called Mrs Clipboard. A woman next to me grabbed a pushchair containing a baby doll which seemed to be in urgent need of medical attention. If poorly plastic could get a part then surely I could. For a moment everything went deathly quiet. Suddenly someone called 'action' and the place roared into life. Above and around me all the rides took off as the extras pretended to have a good time by squealing. Near me a woman took off her sweater to reveal a bikini top and began to walk across the pier, swinging her hips. I wandered casually after her. I don't know what the plot was but in years to come I believe *Angel* aficionados may read something into the enigmatic English woman on the pier.

Confident that I had given my all, I moved on down the pier. I have always loved these seaside structures. The worn wide planks stretching over the sea are the same the world over as indeed are the fishermen. They stood in tight little groups, all men, all set up for the day, some solitary, some chatting, some playing cards. Here they were all Spanish. Gulls squawked overhead. The sound is the same on any pier, anywhere. They say that whales in different oceans have different accents. I couldn't hear it with the gulls myself.

On the beach a man was digging a hole almost as deep as he was tall. He wore ill-fitting orange boxer shorts and nothing else. All morning the weather reports had kept threatening rain but it was just a bit cloudy. Many women wearing very little passed me by, running their hearts out.

At the end of the pier there was a board with a rather curious history of the world. I had the place to myself as no one else was that interested. The lay-out of the history gave pause for thought.

1907 Picasso paints *Les Demoiselles d'Avignon*.

Financial panic hits the US.

I was sure the two incidents were not related just as I was sure Michael Jordan was not a franchise. It had been the same year that surfing had come to California from Hawaii. Then in 1911 someone had learned that faults in the earth caused earthquakes and in 1943 smog had been named. It took a while for me to get on to things I could actually remember. The 1969 Apollo 11 moon landing, which I had watched from inside Mission Control in Houston; Woodstock; Kent State; US troops invading Cambodia; Watergate; Bobby Kennedy and Martin Luther King assassinated; the My Lai massacre occurring while the US watched *Laugh-In* on TV . . . world events which I had been hyper aware of.

I walked back. *Angel* was saving the world and the man on the beach was still digging but now two large phallic shapes stuck straight up from the top of his sand pile. It bespoke hidden 'issues' in his life and I wondered if I should give him Ginger's number.

I was not done with fame for the day. I drove on, a few miles south, to Venice Beach. I think I was being pursued for my talent for here Universal Trucks were out in force. I strolled past the Venice Beach sidewalk market – 'A spliff a day keeps the doctor away' – and on a piazza facing the beach I found more cameras whirring away. This was yet another piece of television and I knew instantly that it was something altogether grimmer. As I arrived, a monster with a double-headed executioner's axe was about to chop off someone's head. It was clearly going to be gruesome as there were many quarts of blood on stand-by. A small group of extras dressed in jeans and white robes appeared unconcerned, despite the fact that they were holding posters declaring that the end of the world was nigh. The monster kept practising his axe-swinging, for even a ghoul wants to look good for the cameras. It was hot and the monster was beginning to sweat. He lifted his rubber face up for some air and showed the actor underneath. He looked a cheerful enough fellow with a small moustache like an escaped caterpillar. Not natural casting, I thought. More the musical comedy type.

'Could we have the zombie over here?' called the assistant to the director's assistant. How ignorant I was. A zombie. Not a monster at all. The people in charge of blood began to remove sheets of plastic from the dummy who was to be decapitated. Now I could see that it too was dressed in jeans and a white robe. No wonder the other extras looked so cheerful. At least they didn't get that part.

A man got out a small set of steps. Carefully he removed the dummy's head, put a funnel in its neck and began to pour in blood. It looked very fake under the sky which was now a brilliant blue and held no threat of rain whatsoever. More blood poured from the funnel. It was all taking rather a long time. Two policemen on bicycles cycled past. There was a fluid mix of the real and the unreal on the beach and I couldn't tell if they were actually policemen or men who yearned to do *Hamlet*. One of the extras had tired of his task and sat down on a low wall beside me.

'What's the show?' I asked him.

He couldn't remember the name of the piece or, more importantly, why the end was nigh and had to ask around.

'*Providence*, I think,' was the final answer from a girl on her mobile. The extras sat in small knots discussing who had heard what about the possibilities of other work. My new friend was called Carrido. He was about thirty. He had a neat, trimmed beard and was fairly newly arrived from Mexico.

'Aye cham chan chactor. Aye chwant to bay in dey moooovies,' he explained and spat in my eye. I thought this seemed an unlikely career and that he was quite lucky anyone had understood he wanted a job at all.

'Everything ready? Background people!' came the urgent call as some of the extras started roller-blading, police looked busy about their persons and I wandered around trying to look concerned about the end being so nigh.

'Action!'

Now the adrenaline pumped into the zombie, he swiped the practised swipe and cut the dummy clean in half.

Applause, laughter.

'He's dead for sure,' called the extra with the mobile.

'Good job!' said props.

Now the dummy needed surgery, redressing, more blood. The whole thing was turning into *ER* and I didn't have the time to give any more. Still, enigmatic in the back of *Angel* and a glimpse of me looking concerned in *Providence* was enough Hollywood fame for one day. What a ridiculous business. What was I doing even on the fringes?

One more port of call before I took the plane home – the Queen Mary ocean liner at Long Beach.

*It is better to travel than to arrive.*

Irritating Chinese proverb

My family and I first arrived in the United States on one of the great ocean liners. Each summer we would take the slow boat back to Europe and return on another to our adopted home. Of all those journeys, my favourite had been on the old *Queen Elizabeth*. Not the *QE2* with its steel door handles and high-tech lines. No, the old Queen. A stately ambassador for Cunard with gleaming wooden staircases and a history of glamour and excitement. The *Queen Mary* was her sister ship and sits as a permanent attraction and hotel at Long Beach, a few miles south of LA airport.

I like the alleged story behind the *Queen Mary*. It seems Cunard went to see the king, George V, and said, 'Sir, we'd like your permission to name our new ocean liner for the greatest queen England has ever known.'

'Great,' said the king. 'The wife'll be thrilled.'

And so the vessel became the *Queen Mary*. Cunard had to go back to the ship and take out all the things that said Queen Victoria on them.

As I walked out on the gangway I had the boat to myself. Swing music was playing over the tannoy and I remembered how they had broadcast *Anchors Aweigh* and thrown coloured streamers, each time we left port. A poster of a 1930s couple encouraged me to visit America. I entered on the promenade deck where we had often taken a morning stroll. The wide wooden floor was protected from the ocean wind by large plate-glass windows. We had walked to make room for the three enormous meals a day plus morning bouillon soup and afternoon tea on the sports deck.

I wanted lunch now but the only food option was provided by a hideous place called California Shakes. A Latino girl was alone behind the counter. She made me a chocolate malted milk and completed the entire transaction while talking on the phone. I remembered the caviar served in the back of a carved ice swan, the applause for flames of baked Alaska and I knew that Cunard was turning in his grave.

I stood at the stern of the great old lady and felt overwhelmed with the loss of my father. How often we had stood in just such a spot, our hands beside each other on the gleaming wooden railings as the mighty engines chugged water out in a regular and rhythmic wake. We had travelled to America the right way in those days. As I stood there, a dirigible flew above Long Beach – the Goodyear Blimp – an image of a different kind of travel. Special clothes, special trunks. A journey which took a long time and you had cause to stop and think.

It was on a ship, a smaller one but still at stern, watching the water rush beneath us, that my father had once and only once talked about me being gay.

'Before I knew,' he said, 'I thought you were living your life without passion. I couldn't bear it if you didn't have passion.' We never mentioned it again.

Mixed with my grief was a knowledge that the sun felt good on my back and that only older people ever appreciate that. Then, on the farthest railing I saw a one-legged gull standing watching me. What could happen, I wondered, to a gull that might cause it to lose a foot? Did it affect take-offs and landings? What did the other gulls think? Was the one-legged fellow an object of gull ridicule? Did all gulls really come from California? And that was it. I suddenly felt better. I realised I did not want to retire from the world entirely.

Standing on the deck of the *Queen Mary* I knew I had come full circle. I stood as an adult facing the child who had travelled on such similar decks. In the harbour a salvage tug had placed a large inflatable yellow ring in the water. They were trying to gather something in the middle and it was difficult. It seemed to me that it was precisely what I had been doing on this trip. In the distance, in Long Beach itself, I could see a barrage of cranes hard at work on some construction project.

There was much discussion in the papers about what would happen to Ground Zero after the 9/11 tragedy has been cleared. Some people want a park, others want more office space on this prime piece of Manhattan real estate. Richard Anderson, President of the New York Building Congress, an amalgam of developers, contractors and realtors, said, 'The people who died here weren't sitting in a park on September 11. They were sitting at desks in an office building, and that has to be part of any final developments we approve.'

This was a curious take on what happened. It suggested that if those poor people who were killed could have predicted and chosen their place of death then sitting earning the corporate dollar would have come first.

At least I didn't do that. I may be in a profession which now only admires youth, which does not want people 'tainted with experience', but there are other things to do. Going back had allowed me to close one chapter and look ahead to the next. I was not defined by a country. I think you can live in any country where you understand the nuances of daily life. I no longer have that in America. There is much I don't understand. I could not live there now. I still love the mad, add-the-tax-at-the-till, bright-orange-cheese-melt country, but I do not belong.

It is good to look back but it should not be a preoccupation in life. My mother refers to herself as 'middle-aged' which means she will live to be about 150. I like that attitude. She believes she is only halfway. I hope the best is yet to come. Georgia O'Keefe horrified her family when at over ninety years old she took a lover in his twenties. Everyone said he was trying to steal her fortune, but in the photographs she's just smiling.

It was good to know that the Gladyses were all right. Eleven feisty women spread out over thousands of miles. No one had passed away. No one was really sick or destitute. Some had found their niche and others, like me, were still looking. The serious papers were full of international news. Everywhere young men filled and caused trouble spots with guns and grim determination. Yet another former congressman, senator, member of world politics, or whatever, was pictured turning up on the world stage to bring peace to some God-forsaken territory. Inevitably the peace broker was a man in a casual bomber jacket; it is always men in casual bomber jackets. They wear them to prove that they are good guys who plan to roll up their sleeves and get the job done. Personally, I'd like to send a task force of the Gladyses. Put the dozen of us in a trouble spot and I think we'd have it cleared up and fresh flowers out on the tables in a minute. But that would be my desire and not theirs. Among the women, with one or two exceptions, I found reflected an American preoccupation with the domestic. A worrying disregard for the big picture as the country plunges headlong into greater and greater isolationism.

I still know that if any one of them came to my door I'd be there for them. For all the self-absorption that Americans display they do make good friends. Loyal and kind. I believe each and every one of them would help me if I asked. Would I seek them out? Not all of them. I have laid that part of my life to rest. It happened and I can't go back.

Next? I promised my younger daughter we would eat Chinese food in the shadow of the Great Wall, the elder one wants to go riding in the Grand Canyon and really I should take my boy camping on the San Juan islands. For myself? I don't know. I am a grown-up now. Maybe I won't show my knickers any more, except there is the offer of this play and . . .

# Conclusion on a Plane

*I don't believe in survival of the fittest. I think it should be survival of the wittiest. That way at least those that die go laughing.*

Jane Wagner

12 November 2001 – John F. Kennedy Airport, New York – 12.40 p.m. Almost exactly two months since the World Trade Center tragedy. It was Veterans Day, an American public holiday, and I was trying to go home. I had checked in early and suffered the new and often pointless security measures. I was made to walk through the metal detector with my boots off, an unhappy Englishwoman showing my socks in public. My boot laces proved to be harmless but the two Swiss army knives I had forgotten about in my bum bag went through unnoticed. I was exhausted. It had been many miles and many impressions and I no longer knew what I thought about anything. I pulled my laptop out of its bag to place it on the plastic tray as requested when a young woman behind me shoved her coat and bag in front and pushed past, her need clearly greater than mine, her reawakened humanity from 9/11 already forgotten. Everything went according to routine. I found my aisle seat and sat down. No child sat beside me. Finally I was getting the hang of this.

We taxied out to the runway as the plane ahead took off and then there was silence. I looked past the vast American man sitting at the window and saw that the airport had become eerily still. Not so much as a baggage cart was moving. At last the tannoy cracked into life.

'Uh, ladies and gentlemen . . .' The British pilot cleared his throat. 'There has been an . . . incident at the end of the runway . . . we're going to be . . . delayed . . . I will bring you further information when I have it.'

I didn't know then but the poor captain had seen the plane directly in front of us, an air bus heading for the Dominican Republic, rise up from the runway and plunge down vertically into the busy neighbourhood of Queens. Slowly, a kind of contained panic spread through the plane. People began calling on their mobile phones. You could hear the beep of text messages arriving throughout the cabin. Far from displaying the restrained calm I would have expected, the crew seemed to be running everywhere. A stewardess ran past me, yelling and pointing to someone on their phone, 'Turn that off now! Unless you want to end up like those people over there.'

How a plane could have been brought down by a mobile phone was a mystery. It was not a comforting response in the face of a crisis. The young Asian girl across the aisle from me began to shake with barely controlled hysteria. Her boyfriend worked at La Guardia Airport in Queens. Maybe something had happened to him, maybe it was a bomb, maybe we were next. We sat there for an hour and a half with almost no information. Word spread row to row of the crash. We had been the next plane to take off. It could have been us. No one knew what had happened. Was it like the Twin Towers? Would we be next? Through the window, seemingly at the end of the runway, the sky was filling with strangely white smoke. It didn't look horrible. It was rather pure – as though a cloud had landed and was now expanding and expanding to fill the sky and the earth in equal measure. Rumours began to circulate of something having been placed in the aviation fuel. The tiniest spark could bring a new meaning to the words 'airline terminal'. Were we sitting on a bomb? The crew were now silent. Perhaps they knew nothing but even the nothing they knew would have been a comfort to share.

At last we were returned to the departure lounge. Here, if possible, there was even less information. As we 'de-planed', an expression I had never heard before, the airport authority was making an announcement:

'Ladies and gentlemen, Manhattan has been closed, Manhattan has been closed.'

This was news I didn't feel we needed. It caused more and unnecessary distress. The daughter of a journalist, I did what I thought my father would have done. I went straight to the duty free shop and bought a radio. The girl behind the counter was the calmest person in New York. Nothing swayed her from her undivided attention to her nails. She might be about to blow up but she would go with a fine manicure.

The radio was not a great piece of technology and there was only one station which beamed in with any clarity. I don't know what *The Don and Mike Show* deals with on a regular basis but I suspect it is not investigative journalism. Certainly, if I had hoped to find the American equivalent of Radio 4 this was not it. Either Don or Mike was explaining as I joined them that '. . . there's not a lot of information around right now, so we thought why not do a show where people can call in and say what they know so we're all in the same boat.'

This opened the floodgates for every unbalanced person in the metropolitan area to call in with their two cents' worth.

Caller: 'I heard they have dirty bombs.'

Don or Mike: 'So, more of a radiation threat than an annihilation threat?'

Caller: 'That's right.'

Where did the person hear this? Who were 'they'? Don and Mike moved on to the next nutter with phone access.

Caller: 'You know, this is almost the exact time those planes went into the towers.'

Must be terrorism then. They do like to run everything by clockwork. Don and Mike argued with no one. It was an appalling piece of broadcasting. At no point was anything intelligent said by anybody.

Caller: 'All those people Bush is killing in Afghanistan I mean their kids are going to grow up and come get us. We need to get them too.'

Don or Mike: 'The way we live right now – it . . . it . . . sucks.'

Caller: 'When people don't speak English it freaks me out to travel. The security people seem to me to be inadequate individuals.'

Caller: 'The Taliban hate everything we stand for – democracy, freedom of religion – so you can't even talk to them. There's no point.'

Caller : 'If you look at world problems they all come from the Middle East. I mean we just need to get rid of it.'

I couldn't listen any more. I had managed to get through to my children who had already heard about the disaster on the news. The local English radio had merely reported that there had been a plane crash at JFK but had given no details of the type of plane, the airline and so on. It is the great danger of instant news that they had already suffered huge anxiety.

In the departure lounge bar, the television had been turned up full and there was panic and mild hysteria on Channel 7 news.

'They said there would be another incident before Ramadan which starts 17 November so this falls within that period.'

This was followed by the comforting news that 'Terrorism will not stop *Strip Pyramid* being shown on Friday'. The hysteria went on and on. It continued even as news began to filter through that this had simply been a terrible accident. I spoke to my brother in London who works for Sky News. Everyone there was being much calmer.

'Looks like a freaky coincidence,' he said.

The Channel 7 team were becoming more desperate. 'I still think this is terrorism,' a man in a suit went on, despite everything which now seemed to indicate the contrary.

Beyond the windows of the departure lounge nothing moved. In the distance we could see the tremendous plumes of smoke continuing to pour into the sky from suburban Queens. The airport staff were becoming agitated as passengers tried to glean some information.

'Why don't you people just go home?' lamented a ground hostess to me.

'That,' I said, 'is what I am trying to do.'

Twelve hours later, when we finally boarded our flight home, the plane was nowhere near as full as it had been first thing in the morning. Everyone looked white and anxious. We buckled up and gave a collective sigh. There had been an article the day before in the *New York Times* about humour. It had suggested that, two months after 9/11, so-called 'foxhole humour' was not helping anyone to deal with the tragedy. It declared that 'Humour soothes the soul, yet it also trivialises', and went on to make laughing something of a no-go area. I was thinking about that when the captain came on the tannoy. He was a new man as I presume the previous fellow had gone off duty.

'Good evening, ladies and gentlemen and welcome aboard delayed flight X. My name is Captain English and I'm incredibly competent (or words to that effect) and I do hope you have a good flight.' He paused slightly and continued, 'I know many of you are seasoned international travellers and you don't often watch the safety demonstration but perhaps *today* . . .'

And a curious thing happened. Throughout the great airliner you could suddenly spot the British because they laughed and laughed. And in that moment I knew one thing for sure: I was going home.

*

On 18 June 2002, with much enjoyment, I opened in a new play
at the Palace Theatre, Watford.

On 28 August 2002, after much soul-searching, I finally applied
for my British passport.